ENERGY RESOURCES AND POLICIES OF THE
MIDDLE EAST AND NORTH AFRICA

THE OTHER FACE OF OPEC

FINANCIAL ASSISTANCE
TO THE THIRD WORLD

IBRAHIM F. I. SHIHATA

LONGMAN
LONDON AND NEW YORK

Longman Group Limited,
Longman House,
Burnt Mill,
Harlow, Essex CM20 2JE

First published 1982

British Library Cataloguing in Publication Data

Shihata, Ibrahim F.I.
The other face of OPEC: financial assistance to
the Third World. – (Energy resources and policies
of the Middle East and North Africa)
1. Economic assistance   2. Organisation
of the Petroleum Exporting Countries
I. Title   II. Series
338.91'172'4   HC60

ISBN 0-582-78336-4

Printed in Great Britain by Spottiswoode Ballantyne Ltd.,
Colchester and London

PREFACE

The name of OPEC is generally associated in the public mind with one phenomenon: ever increasing oil prices.

Inaccurately depicted in the media as a powerful cartel which controls the supply and pricing of this vital commodity, OPEC has been repeatedly blamed, especially by Western politicians, for the world's present economic ills. Under the same faulty assumption, OPEC has been often looked upon as a pool of excessive funds and is called upon, particularly by Third World politicians, to provide financial remedies for the world's ailing economy.

In their preoccupation with the negative effects of higher oil prices, many analysts found comfort in attributing the whole state of affairs to the existence of OPEC. By so doing they have simply ignored the fact that the price of oil was bound to rise with the growing scarcity of this commodity and with the diminishing control of Western companies over the natural resources of other nations. The fact that the oil prices were bound to increase and that the oil producers of the Third World used the proceeds of their oil in a highly responsible manner was ignored. The efforts of these countries to assist both the major oil consumers in the Western World and the poorer countries of the South have seldom been cited in the repeated discussions concerning OPEC and the impact it has. On the whole, the image of OPEC, as conceived by the Western mind, is one of indifference to the world's ills. Indeed, they are alleged to be caused by none other than OPEC itself.

Among the predominant "images" in today's world, this one is particularly false. The major oil exporting countries of the Third World, acting individually and collectively, are in fact playing a major role in assisting other developing nations, especially the poorest. As developing countries themselves, with a recent past of dire financial need and of hard experiences in finding expedient and dignified ways of meeting such needs, the OPEC member countries began their aid efforts with different objectives from those of traditional world donors. While the latter have readily used their financial assistance to create and expand markets for their products or to maintain their political spheres of influence, no such aims were pursued or could, in fact, have been pursued by the OPEC donors. Those among them which initiated the aid efforts in the early sixties were basically motivated by moral commitments toward their neighbours. Their sense of regional community and their awareness of the social requirements of regional stability and security led them to act as donors almost at the same time as they began accumulating surplus funds. This trend was certainly influenced by the traditions of Islam, which gives the deprived an "acknowledged right" to the wealth of the rich and ordains that those who have wealth extend 2.5 per cent of its value annually to those in need.

The current aid efforts of OPEC countries have far reaching economic and political implications. Together they may be said to present the shining face of OPEC. For such efforts represent a form of assistance in which a group of countries, themselves developing, voluntarily share their wealth, and not merely their income, with other countries in need. The donors realize that they may not necessarily be richer than the recipients. But they feel that some of the liquidity currently available to them should be used to meet the financial needs of other developing nations for the benefit of the Third World as a whole and as a voluntary expression of solidarity which is deeply felt. By channelling financial assistance at the present impressive level the OPEC donors play an important role in the international redistribution of income to the benefit of the developing countries. The full implications of this role are yet to be ascertained.

This book consists of sixteen essays on different aspects of the aid efforts of OPEC member countries, and especially of the aid extended by the Arab States of the Gulf region to other developing nations. Most of these essays are based on lectures by the author. They represent the facts and views prevalent at the time of their writing. The first two essays, as well as those published in Chapters 7 and 8, have been recently completed and the essay on "The Working Relationship between the OPEC Fund and other International Development Finance Institutions" has been updated. All the other essays are published here as they first appeared. They should therefore be read with the date of their writing in mind. As the earliest of these essays was first published in 1972, they constitute a recent account of the phenomenon under discussion and there may be some overlapping. By having them assembled together for the first time, however, it is intended that the reader will have a convenient reference on the subject of OPEC aid and investments, a subject which has been the main preoccupation of the author for the last fifteen years.

Vienna, 20 December 1981   Ibrahim Shihata

ACKNOWLEDGEMENTS

The author wishes to thank many friends and colleagues for their help in the preparation of this book. In particular he would like to mention: Mr A. Benbrahim; Mr A. Benamara; Dr M. Ali; Mr D. Ordoobadi who provided valuable assistance in the preparation of some of the more recent material included in this book. His thanks are due, especially to Mr Robert Mabro who co-authored Chapter 3. He is also grateful for the editorial preparation done by Miss K. Eldin and by the staff of Longman Group, especially Miss Janice Paveley.

The views expressed in this book are naturally those of the author, and do not necessarily represent the official views of the OPEC Fund for International Development or of its member countries.

CONTENTS

TABLES AND GRAPHS

PART I

OPEC AID

CHAPTER 1

OPEC AS A DONOR GROUP

Based on a lecture to the German Society for Foreign Policy, Bonn, Germany, 11 December 1980. First published as an OPEC Fund Publication, Vienna, Austria, December 1980.

INTRODUCTION

OPEC is an organization of thirteen countries. Although depicted in the media as the new rich countries, all of them are at an early stage of development if judged by the relevant social and economic indicators and not by false appearances of wealth[1]. As in the rest of the developing world, the success of their development efforts is to a great extent dependent on the good will of the industrialized countries. They are all food-deficit countries, some depending almost entirely on food imports. Not one of them has a powerful industrial base. With the possible exception of Indonesia, none of them has major exports other than oil. At least five of them are debtors in the international financial market.

The image of OPEC countries as excessively rich is based on two facts: (i) the high per capita income of four of them, due to their small populations, and (ii) the liquid assets accumulated by five of them, due to their production of oil at levels well beyond their financial needs. The first fact may mean that individuals in the four countries are getting richer for the time being. It does not necessarily put these countries in the rank of the truly rich countries, whose wealth is based on recurrent production from an established industrial and/or agricultural base. The second fact should not lead us to mistake liquidity for wealth. The transformation of a depletable natural resource into cash, which cannot be absorbed immediately in real new investments, may in fact make the country poorer rather than richer in the long run.

These facts make the study of the impressive record of external aid of the OPEC countries of particular interest, where the lessons to be drawn may differ sharply from those reflected in current opinion.

MEASURING OPEC AID

OECD is still the main source for the monitoring of the flow of finance to developing countries. UNCTAD has also started a reporting system which is limited, however, to the flow of finance among developing countries. Both sources attempt to measure the record of aid of each donor against its GNP. As a matter of course they compare the record of aid of the two major donor groups: OECD and OPEC. Invariably, they conclude that, although OECD is channelling greater amounts in absolute terms, OPEC's record is by far superior[2] if measured against this group's limited GNP. The conclusion is certainly correct. The figures used, however, are questionable and the comparison itself may not be called for.

If GNP is taken as the measure of the ability of the donor to contribute, a major difference should be noticed between the GNP of a typical industrialized country and that of a typical OPEC donor. In the first case, the GNP results basically from renewable productive resources, while it relies heavily in the second case on the extraction of a depletable asset. As oil revenues essentially represent the monetary realization of oil in the ground, they cannot be readily considered as income or at any rate as a net added value to the economy that necessarily enhances the country's ability to contribute to others. A significant "depletion factor" has thus been suggested for calculating the GNP of the major oil-exporting countries[3]. If this factor were applied, as it should be, the GNP of OPEC countries could be reduced significantly, which in turn would make their ODA[4] disbursements to GNP ratio much higher than has ever been announced.

More importantly, OPEC countries are not developed countries. Their oil wealth is not an added infusion to already prosperous and healthy economies but the financial base for building more balanced economies, literally from scratch in many cases. This important fact warrants greater care in the use of OPEC funds than those of a truly rich country, as the whole future of the OPEC countries depends on the manner in which their current assets, which are not lasting, are allocated. This truism is not always reflected in the expenditure behaviour of many individuals in the OPEC countries themselves. Their vision, like that of some observers, is sometimes blurred by the impressive, but temporary, monetary liquidity available at present.

Because oil is their main or only export item, OPEC countries do not, and indeed cannot, use their aid as a mechanism for export promotion in the way that it has traditionally been used by industrialized countries. The aid of the latter countries, when it does not take on the explicit form of export credit and even when it is completely free from specific ties, is still used, in most cases, to pay for goods and services from industrialized countries. The tying of aid is, therefore, almost inevitable in the case of assistance from OECD countries, taken as a group. This is not the case with OPEC aid. In fact, OPEC aid is also used to finance goods and services from the industrialized countries. Both forms of assistance, therefore, benefit the economies of developed countries, in addition to those of the recipients. Only OPEC donors stand to gain no financial return from their assistance. This is particularly interesting in view of the often quoted fact that every dollar of tied aid from an industrialized country is likely to result in a $2-$3 increase in the GNP of that same country.

The above conceptual differences should suffice to show that the comparison between the two donor groups on the basis of absolute figures or of disbursement to GNP ratios is not called for. Other important details make the OECD reporting and comparisons even less favourable to OPEC donors than they should be:

(i) Assistance to countries which cannot be categorized as developing countries (e.g. Israel, Greece, Spain, Portugal and other Southern European countries) is included in the OECD aid figures. When such assistance is omitted and the comparison is limited to aid to the developing countries proper, the OECD aid figures are sharply reduced. The reduction is significant for some OECD donors, especially the US, a large part of whose ODA assistance goes to Israel.

(ii) In computing the aid to GNP ratios of OPEC donors, both OECD and UNCTAD lump together ten donor countries, including countries like Algeria, Iran and Nigeria which, due to their large populations, have a large GNP but due to the needs of their economies have low aid records. If the base were limited to the typical donors (the so-called surplus countries), the ratio would be much higher. Limiting the base is indeed essential as it is not membership of OPEC as such that puts a country in a position to assist. Many developing countries outside OPEC are in a better economic and even financial position than some OPEC members.

(iii) In calculating the non-concessional flows from OPEC countries to other developing nations, OECD does not include sizeable OPEC contributions to the IMF's oil and supplementary facilities. This ignores the fact that such contributions were sought and made to enable the IMF to assist developing countries. The amounts received by the latter countries from the IMF through such facilities have characteristics similar to the other non-concessional transfers included in the OECD figures. In contrast UNCTAD has correctly included OPEC's contribution to the IMF oil facility as part of OPEC's non-concessional flows to developing countries.

(iv) In reporting non-concessional flows, the OECD publications include OECD flows which are mainly of a private character, while only official OPEC flows are reported in respect of non-concessional flows[5]. For instance, the 1978 non-concessional flows of OECD countries were reported as over $49 billion as against $1.6 billion in official flows from OPEC countries. About 65 per cent of the OECD figures, however, covered private flows. The compilation of data on OPEC's expanding private flows to other developing countries is admittedly difficult. A proper comparison should nevertheless be limited to funds of the same type. This is particularly relevant as part of the OECD private flows emanate from agencies located in OECD countries which are partly owned by OPEC sources. Also, the bond issues managed by such agencies for the benefit of developing countries are normally covered in part by OPEC investors. The difficulties involved in identifying the OPEC element in such flows should not result in assigning them an exclusively OECD character[6].

(v) The components of ODA flows from OECD sources include items which are not readily included in OPEC flows. Examples of these include the loans provided by some OECD countries to their own nationals for investment in developing countries and the equity capital invested by their official agencies in developing countries.

OPEC AID FIGURES

While bearing in mind the above remarks, we shall nevertheless rely on OECD publications in explaining the magnitude of OPEC aid. The OECD remains the most comprehensive source of information on flows of aid, as its statistics cover the period up to the end of 1979, whereas UNCTAD's only reach 1976. They also include data on financial flows from all sources, whereas UNCTAD's are limited to OPEC flows. Furthermore the OECD cannot be accused of any favouritism towards OPEC donors or any bias against the OECD countries. From an OPEC viewpoint it in fact portrays a rather conservative picture of OPEC aid, which is presented here as the undisputed minimum.

The OECD data discussed below covers the period from 1973 to 1979, a time in which OPEC financial flows became an important source of development capital for other developing countries.

The overall magnitude of total official net disbursements from OPEC members to other developing countries stood at $1.75 billion in 1973; reached a peak of $8.17 billion in 1975, and in 1978, the last year for which data on total official disbursements are available, amounted to $5.78 billion. Concessional disbursements have consistently formed a high percentage of total official OPEC disbursements. ODA disbursements from OPEC to other developing countries amounted to $1.31 billion in 1973, reached a peak of $5.86 billion by 1977 and in 1979 stood at $5.2 billion. Much of these concessional flows took the form of outright grants. To use the most striking example, in 1973 90 per cent of total OPEC concessional assistance was extended in the form of bilateral grants. This high proportion of grants in total OPEC concessional assistance became moderated somewhat over the rest of the reporting period as OPEC assistance was increasingly channelled through multilateral institutions. The average proportion of grants over the entire 1973–1979 period was 58 per cent. A sizeable grant element (over 76 per cent on average from 1973–1978) is to be noticed, however, in the concessional loans extended throughout this period.

Although OPEC concessional disbursements are lower in absolute terms than those of the OECD, OPEC's ODA to GNP ratio has consistently far exceeded that of the industrialized group. Indeed, OPEC member countries in the aggregate have, in each year of the 1973–1979 period, greatly exceeded the 0.7 per cent ODA to GNP ratio set by the UN over a decade ago, while the industrialized countries have yet to reach half this target[7].

The OPEC ODA to GNP ratio, as applied to ten OPEC donor countries, stood at 1.42 per cent in 1973; reached its highest point, 2.71 per cent in 1975; and, according to the latest available figures, became 1.48 per cent in 1979. The average OPEC ODA to GNP ratio for the entire 1973-1979 period was, therefore, 1.88 per cent.

Thus far we have approached OPEC and OECD as two donor groups. If, however, we separate individual countries from their respective groups, we find that some OPEC member countries have, even in absolute terms, been among the world's largest donors of concessional assistance. In 1976 and 1977, for example, Saudi Arabia, with a GNP of approximately $63 billion, was second only to the US (GNP $2,118 billion) in the amount of concessional assistance disbursed. In the years from 1975 to 1979, three of the world's ten largest providers of concessional assistance were OPEC member countries. For some of the years in this period, the combined ODA of countries such as Kuwait and the United Arab Emirates exceeded in absolute terms the aid of France or Germany. This fact takes on its full significance when one bears in mind that Germany's GNP is approximately twenty times greater than the combined GNP of Kuwait and the United Arab Emirates, while France's GNP is fifteen times greater.

If one were to rank the donors of the world in terms of concessional assistance as a percentage of GNP, OPEC's standing among world donors would be particularly high. In 1975, for example, the seven countries which disbursed the highest percentage of GNP in concessional assistance were OPEC member countries[8]. For each year of the period 1975-1979, at least six of the world's top ten donors in terms of ODA to GNP were OPEC countries.

Ironically, the OPEC members which are singled out for attack in the Western media are the six capital surplus OPEC countries[9]. These countries are at times blamed, even by responsible statesmen in the developed nations, for the world's economic ills and are believed by many to possess a remedy for all such afflictions. It is therefore important to put the role of these countries in its proper perspective.

The populations of most of the surplus countries are very small. Four of the six countries have a total population of less than 3 million people. This fact has a direct bearing on the per capita ODA disbursements of these countries. In 1977, for example, the per capita ODA disbursements of the United Arab Emirates and Kuwait to other developing countries reached an impressive $1,500, or more than 10 per cent of the per capita GNP of each country.

In addition, the *combined* GNP of the six "surplus countries" is but a minute fraction of those of OECD member states. It is one half that of the UK, one third that of France, one fourth that of Germany, one sixth that of Japan, and one fifteenth (or 6 per cent) that of the US alone. Despite the small size of their economies as compared with individual members of the OECD, the total concessional assistance disbursed in 1979 of the six surplus countries exceeded the 1979 ODA disbursements of each of the above-mentioned OECD countries. The concessional assistance of the six OPEC surplus countries was approximately twice that of the United Kingdom and Japan, one and a half times that of France and Germany, and 19 per cent greater than that of the US.

Most OPEC aid has also been given in quick disbursing loans for general balance of payments support. OPEC member countries have, as a result, achieved unusually high disbursement to commitment ratios, exceeding 90 per cent in some years[10].

TWO RELATED ISSUES: RECIPIENTS AND ADEQUACY

The above figures are merely meant to put the OPEC aid record in a proper perspective according to the most conservative estimates of OPEC aid. They are certainly not quoted in an attempt to add to the ongoing debate as to who is doing more for the developing countries, OPEC or OECD. Such a debate may in fact be meaningless. As emphasized earlier, the OPEC countries are themselves developing countries, with only a minority of them accumulating surplus net assets by a process that is not necessarily beneficial to them. A debate of this type may be interesting to those concerned with public relations and the media, but it does not address the challenges of the escalating problems of the developing world, nor does it, in itself, advance the search for a solution to the acute financial dilemmas which many developing countries are facing at present. The point to be made here is simply that the industrialized countries have no moral basis for continually pointing their finger at OPEC while they themselves are lagging far behind in their provision of aid. And, more importantly, the time has come for all those in a position to do so, to expand their assistance to the developing countries in the most urgent and flexible manner. Co-operation among all donors in this direction should replace the endless arguments which ignore the basic issue.

Two points should be addressed, however, in the hope of closing this debate. The first is the widely publicized Western claim that OPEC aid, though generous, is mainly directed to a few countries with close ties to the donor group. A good part of the bilateral aid of OPEC member countries has, it is true, been concentrated on neighbouring countries. This is in fact an almost inherent characteristic of all bilateral aid, which goes to recipients who have special ties to the donors, be they cultural, political or economic. Most French bilateral aid goes to French-speaking countries and most British aid goes to Commonwealth countries, to name only two examples. The same does not apply, however, to the OPEC aid extended through multilateral channels, which accounted for some 30 per cent of total OPEC financial flows in the period 1977-1979. In the case of the OPEC Fund for International Development, for instance, 79 countries in Africa, Asia and Latin America have already benefited from its direct loans, which have practically reached all but the relatively high-income developing countries. What is particular about OPEC's bilateral aid is that it has reached far beyond the neighbouring countries, contrary to the belief which is more often expressed. Since 1974, the charters of the Kuwait Fund, the Abu Dhabi Fund, the Saudi Fund and the Iraqi Fund explicitly provide for the eligibility, in principle, of all the developing countries to benefit from the loans and grants of these Funds. Concessional loans have been extended by the Kuwait Fund to countries as far away from Kuwait as Papua New Guinea; while the Saudi Fund and Iraqi Fund have extended assistance to countries in Latin America. Charity naturally begins at home, but OPEC aid has gone far beyond the countries with direct links to the OPEC donors, even when extended in the form of bilateral assistance. It is this, rather than the concentration on neighbouring countries, which should be pointed out as a distinctive feature of OPEC aid. If there is a concentration in OPEC financial assistance, it is on the poorest countries, an emphasis which is not discernable in OECD aid as a whole.

Another basic point is the question of the adequacy of OPEC aid, as it is often said that the generosity of OPEC donors should not conceal the inadequacy of their aid provision. This is, of course, a relative matter, proper evaluation of which depends on the basis on which the sufficiency of the aid is assessed.

If OPEC aid is to be judged by the standard target optimistically proclaimed by the UN more than a decade ago and recently recommended by the Brandt Commission as the level to be reached by 1985 (i.e. 0.7 per cent of the GNP of the donor country) then the major OPEC donors have by far exceeded that level since 1974. In fact, the target was exceeded in 1975 by more than twenty-two times by Qatar, twenty times by the UAE, eleven times by Kuwait and six times by Saudi Arabia, and is still being greatly exceeded by the four of them and more recently by Iraq as well. In such a context, OPEC aid cannot, therefore, be described as inadequate.

Nor can inadequacy be the proper description if the record of aid of other donors is taken as the basis of measurement. Suffice it to recall, at the risk of repetition, that, relative to GNP, in 1979 the aid of the ten OPEC donors surpassed by more than four times that of the seventeen OECD donors and by thirty-six times that of the Eastern Block donors (according to OECD sources). If the comparison were limited, as it should be, to the four or five typical OPEC donors, the record would of course be much more strikingly in favour of OPEC.

The volume of OPEC aid is still far below the financial needs of the developing countries. No one can reasonably argue, however, that it is the responsibility of OPEC countries to meet these needs or to take them as the measure of the adequacy of their efforts to provide aid. Membership of OPEC cannot in itself, by any stretch of the imagination, entail such a responsibility, which is not admitted even by the truly rich and industrialized countries.

The flow of aid from OPEC countries did not, it is true, match the increased costs of oil imports by the developing countries in the two exceptional years which saw high rises in oil prices (1973/74 and 1978/79). This was not the case, however, for some of the poorest recipients, which received more OPEC aid than their incremental oil bills, or in certain cases than the extent to which their total oil bills amounted[11]. OPEC aid also continued in the years when no significant increase in oil prices took place. As mentioned earlier, this aid reached a high level in 1975, a year which actually witnessed a decline in oil prices. The point to emphasize here is that OPEC aid was not given as a compensation to those who import oil, according to the volume of their oil imports. As a phenomenon, it started in the early sixties, when oil was cheap. Most of it went to the poorer countries, which account for a small volume of oil imports; a good part of it went to other oil-exporting countries, which were nevertheless in dire financial need; and very little of it reached the high-income developing countries, which account for most of the oil imports of the Third World. Any attempt to establish a link between OPEC aid and the cost of oil imports would thus be out of context and, if applied, would work to the disadvantage of the poorest countries[12].

OPEC'S NEW AID INITIATIVES

The above clarification, though necessary, should not suggest that OPEC countries have done all there is to do and that nothing additional should be expected. Fortunately, this is not how the OPEC countries themselves consider the matter. They judge their performance by the standards expected from them in the context of Third World solidarity. Although they are deeply convinced that the developed countries, both Western and Eastern, have failed to play a role commensurate with their relative wealth and capabilities, OPEC countries have not taken this as an excuse to lower or freeze the level of their own assistance. They are at present seriously considering a number of initiatives which aim at enhancing their efforts to provide aid, in terms of both quantity and quality.

Early this year, the OPEC countries substantially modified the *Agreement Establishing the OPEC Fund*, converting it from an international account of temporary character to an ongoing international agency with a wide mandate to assist other developing countries and with open-ended resources which so far exceed $4 billion.

Some members (Algeria and Venezuela) are now calling for a further substantial increase of the Fund's resources (up to $20 billion) and a restructuring of its capital base to enable it to resort to borrowing and to act as an international development bank.

OPEC's Long Term Strategy Committee, on the other hand, has already adopted another proposal, originally advanced by Iraq, for the establishment of a new global Fund for Energy and Development. This Fund is proposed as a joint effort between OPEC and other countries, and not as a substitute for the OPEC Fund. The new Joint Fund would receive its resources from the industrialized and OPEC countries through annual contributions from both. The amount contributed by the industrialized countries would depend on "the annual rate of world inflation as reflected in the price increases of manufactured goods, food and services exported by the donor countries to the developing countries". And the amount contributed annually by OPEC countries would reflect "the adjustment of oil prices on account of inflation on oil exports to other developing countries". These latter countries are not called upon to participate in the financing of the proposed Fund but would be full members of it. Voting is to follow the pattern adopted in IFAD, with one third of the voting power going to each of the three categories. It is interesting to note in this respect that the proposed OPEC contribution to the new Fund, which is based on the increase in oil prices, does not replace the efforts of several existing OPEC-financed institutions. This suggests once again that the OPEC aid effort is not conceived in its totality as a process of compensation, even though some new initiatives would tie part of OPEC aid to developments related to oil prices. Oil revenues are no doubt the enabling factor, though not the *raison d'être*, of OPEC aid provision.

The functions of the proposed Joint Fund are envisaged as combining the financing of energy projects with the extension of loans and grants to developing countries to meet their oil import bills. The financing of other essential projects is not, however, ruled out in the proposed flexible framework. It remains to be seen how the industrialized countries react to this proposal when it is fully endorsed by OPEC and whether ways could be found to reconcile this ingenious proposal with the "Energy Affiliate" which is currently being considered by the World Bank.

More recently, Iran has also proposed an aid plan, to reimburse developing countries on a grant basis for the financial burden resulting from OPEC oil price increases through a new OPEC Fund, to which member countries would pay 10 per cent of their total additional revenues resulting from the increases in oil prices (on the assumption that the oil imports of the developing countries account for about 10 per cent of total OPEC oil exports). This new Fund would be managed by a joint committee of OPEC countries and oil-importing developing countries.

Although it may be premature to predict the outcome of these different proposals, they stand as evidence of the continuing concern of OPEC countries for the financial problems of other developing nations. They should result in greater flows of aid from all sources and, it is to be hoped, in new international institutional arrangements more responsive to the aspirations of the Third World.

In addition to these new collective initiatives on the part of OPEC countries, some individual OPEC members have developed new formulæ for "oil aid", which were initiated on an *ad hoc* basis but have already been institutionalized in some cases. Examples of such institutionalized "oil aid" include Iraq's sale of oil to a growing number of developing countries whereby part of the price, representing the increment after a certain cut-off date, takes the form of concessional long term credit. Venezuela now has an even more complex arrangement in association with Mexico, a non-OPEC oil-exporting developing country which is acting as a co-donor for the first time. In this joint Venezuelan-Mexican arrangement the two countries guarantee certain quantities of oil to nine Central American and Caribbean countries at current prices while allowing for partially deferred payment on soft terms. These terms become even more concessional when the beneficiary country decides to use the amounts involved to finance the development of its own energy resources. More recently, the four African members of OPEC have decided to underwrite oil supplies to African oil-consuming countries at official OPEC prices. It is interesting to note that these initiatives complement, and are not substitutes for, the other bilateral and multilateral OPEC aid activities.

FUTURE AREAS OF CO-OPERATION

In view of the inherent characteristics of the economies of OPEC donor countries, their prodigious and expanding aid provision should not conceal the fact that concessional flows cannot, in the long term, represent a balanced relationship among developing countries. The large liquid assets which enabled this relationship to grow can hardly be conceived of as a lasting phenomenon which will persist on the same impressive scale as is experienced at present. A more balanced, mutually beneficial pattern of co-operation should eventually prevail. The areas with a great potential for expanded co-operation include: concessional flows; direct investment; trade expansion; labour migration and technical co-operation.

(i) The above mentioned *concessional flows* should continue as long as the OPEC donors are in a position to extend them. Ideally, these flows may be encouraged as a mechanism for the international redistribution of income to the benefit of developing countries. As voluntary mechanisms have so far failed to generate the minimum flows required from the industrialized countries to the underprivileged areas of the world, OPEC countries may well use their unique position to ensure that such flows continue at a reasonable level. One possible device which could be jointly considered as a last resort in this context is the imposition of a surcharge, to be added to the price of every barrel of oil exported, and the transfer of its proceeds, through appropriate mechanisms, to developing countries according to their relative need. Although the idea is not new, it has not been discussed in official OPEC circles[13]. It would best be implemented if it resulted from a mutual understanding among all the countries concerned.

Another possible form of assistance could be the provision of oil to the needier developing countries as grants in kind, or under very concessional credit terms, within the framework of a collective pledging mechanism similar to that applied by the major grain-producing countries under the Food Aid Convention. Although this has not been collectively considered by OPEC, it is being partially implemented on a bilateral basis by some OPEC members, as already mentioned. Such oil aid could even be tied to the provision of greater food aid from the major grain-exporting countries.

(ii) Along with concessional flows, there is a great but hardly utilized opportunity for *direct OPEC commercial investments* in other developing countries. Such investments in fact represent the major challenge for lasting economic co-operation among developing countries. The potential for investment opportunities which would preserve and enhance the value of OPEC assets while benefiting the host recipient countries is hampered, however, by great constraints. The physical and institutional structures in developing countries have to be strengthened prior to or concurrently with such commercial investments. Measures also have to be taken by the host countries to improve their investment climate and minimize non-commercial risks. This is an area where action has lagged behind aspirations as attention has generally been focussed on concessional flows. Yet, it is this area in particular which should be prominent in any serious discussions on the utilization of OPEC surpluses, as we shall soon elaborate.

(iii) The third area for expanded co-operation is the *trade relationship* between OPEC and other developing countries. This relationship has witnessed significant growth since 1973, at an average annual rate of 40 per cent in both imports and exports[14]. The full potential of expanded trade among developing countries is, nevertheless, far from being exploited. New mechanisms, including export credit arrangements, should be developed to ensure greater exchange among these countries as they continue the development process.

(iv) *Labour migration* to the labour-importing OPEC countries is already an important phenomenon which accounts for remittances to neighbouring countries of at least $10 billion a year (according to the World Bank, in 1977 ten developing countries received some $6.5 billion as remittances from their workers in seven Arab countries, members of OPEC)[15]. Such manpower movements have their social costs as well, in both the exporting and host countries. Improved planning and management of the flow of manpower is badly needed to minimize such costs and to ensure optimum benefits to the economies of all the countries concerned.

(v) Finally, there seems to exist scope for much greater *technical co-operation*, far beyond the isolated cases of such co-operation at present. OPEC countries could well contribute to the development of energy resources in other developing countries on the strength of their acquired experience in the oil sector. Other sectors may also benefit from this kind of co-operation, given the disparate technical capabilities and experiences of various developing countries and the recent technical achievements in some of them.

THE RECYCLING ISSUE

Expanded co-operation in such areas as those enumerated above is all the more necessary in view of the fact that both OPEC countries and other developing countries stand to gain from it. The accumulation of net liquid assets by some OPEC members has generally been seen as a "problem" facing the World community. The proposed solution to this "problem", as reflected in current literature, has been the transfer of these assets, or their "recycling", to deficit countries in the form of loans and grants. While this "logic" was not applied with the same vigour to the former surpluses of industrialized countries, it is coupled now with the assertion that oil prices and the resultant OPEC revenues have been the main cause of the worsening debt situation of other developing nations.

The resort to borrowing by developing countries on the present large scale has certainly been eased by the availability of OPEC surpluses. This is not to say, however, that the increased costs of oil imports was the main reason for the great expansion in Third World indebtedness. This latter phenomenon was caused by many factors, including the higher cost of oil imports. But oil imports hardly accounted for one fifth of the increase in value of the imports of non-OPEC developing countries from industrialized countries in recent years[16]. One of the less noticed factors was the unprecedented expansion in the external borrowing of some of the oil-exporting countries themselves, due to their ambitious development plans and their improved credit standings. The ten countries which account for 90 per cent of the total accumulated private external debt of developing countries include five OPEC members. The developing country with the largest volume of debt reaching maturity in 1980 was Venezuela, a member of OPEC. The second largest debtor in the Third World today, Mexico, is a major oil-exporter. And the country which has until recently had the highest ratio of external debt to GNP, Egypt, is another oil exporter.

The net liquid assets or "surpluses" of OPEC countries could have been avoided, and could still be eliminated, under more restrictive oil production policies. But such policies would have resulted in higher oil prices and worse still, in serious supply problems. In this perspective, the OPEC financial surplus, strange as this may seem, could be seen as the inevitable result of responsible policies which gave due regard to the interests of the oil consumers, at times at the expense of the interests of the oil producers.

It seems, therefore, that a "problem" as such only exists to the extent that the assets to be recycled happen not to be in the hands of the traditional capital exporters. Until recent years industrialized countries enjoyed the surpluses which constituted deficits in other regions, particularly in the Third World. In other words, they have traditionally appropriated the additional world savings which were

translated into new real investments. Trade stability was well served
by this system. Equity in the distribution of wealth between rich and
poor nations was not served equally well, however. The Third
World may have gained under that system in absolute but not in
relative terms, as its share of new investments and therefore income,
continued to lag behind. A new situation has emerged with the
steady increase in oil prices. The increments to world savings are still
being realized, but their ownership has been geographically diversified in favour of a group of developing countries, namely some
OPEC members. From the perspective of the OPEC countries, this
creates a dilemma that should ideally be resolved through oil conservation on the part of both producers and consumers and through the
development of alternative energy resources. The rewards to the
producers of conserving oil in their own ground are obvious, unlike
the offsetting incentives to these same producers to maintain the
current high levels of oil output. Their continued accommodation of
the ever rising demand for oil, even when it is for the purpose of
stockpiling and not merely consumption, has led OPEC countries to
maintain a certain level of oil production which in turn has resulted
in the accumulation of the paper claims known as the surpluses.

The emergence of surpluses in a new part of the world has created
an institutional vacuum that existing international financial mechanisms have had to adjust to. The private sector has been able to fill a
good part of this vacuum and successfully handle the recycling
process while reaping enormous gains. However, doubts have
recently been expressed about the ability of commercial banks to
continue this role, mainly because of the risks associated with lending to low income countries and over-exposure in middle income
countries on the part of the banks. A growing role is being played at
present in this respect by the increasing number of banks and
investment companies owned mainly or exclusively by OPEC sources[17]. This role aside, the real problem lies in bringing about a
conversion of financial instruments or paper claims into real
resources under present conditions. This problem is further complicated by the need ultimately to translate this conversion into a
geographic rearrangement of real wealth in favour of developing
countries. This process must also take into account the transient
nature of the surpluses held by some OPEC members and the need
to invest them for the benefit of their future generations. The other
alternative of increasing the financial assets through placements and

the like is bound to lead to the gradual erosion of the value of these assets. Inflationary pressures will inevitably follow, especially when the OPEC savings do not result in dissavings in other parts of the world (which cannot be advocated as a solution, for developing countries at least)[18].

It is not only wiser and more profitable to diversify the geographic locations of new real OPEC investments, but it may also be morally imperative that a good part of such investments be concentrated in the other developing countries. Neither group of developing countries, capital exporters and importers, can bring this about, however, without taking major steps to create an appropriate investment climate for the development of available opportunities. The main obstacles in this regard are often represented in the host countries by inadequate infrastructure, shortage of skilled manpower, frequent political changes and other institutional and structural weaknesses. Such weaknesses are further reflected in the lack of adequate mechanisms for capital formation, the lack of a secondary market for the ready disposal of financial instruments, as well as the lack of well defined legal norms and acceptable methods for the quick settlement of disputes. Equally important bottlenecks exist in the capital-exporting developing countries as well, where the need for well equipped financial institutions and mechanisms is yet to be fully met. Financial mechanisms for the protection of OPEC investments against non-commercial risks in other developing countries are also lacking, with the exception of a modest mechanism for inter-Arab investments (the Arab Investment Guarantee Corporation).

Both types of developing countries are now taking major steps to encourage commercial flows among them for direct investment purposes, both through the issue of new regulations and the formulation of new ventures. The success of this trend will depend in great part on the co-operation of the developed countries and their institutions. Their know-how and financial participation could encourage the implementation of new investments and assure their success. This form of recycling would certainly be more beneficial to all parties concerned than a mere expansion in direct lending operations. From a broader perspective, this trend will add to the global reallocation of surpluses an even more significant step: a new distribution of production locations to the benefit of developing countries.

(Annex of Tables to Chapter 1 may be found on p. 248)

CHAPTER 2

SOME PREREQUISITES FOR THE
NORTH-SOUTH DIALOGUE

Based on a paper presented to the Workshop entitled "Energy and Development: Increasing Third World Collective Self-Reliance" co-sponsored by the OPEC Fund, OPEC Secretariat and UNCTAD and held in Vienna, Austria on 7-9 July 1980, of which a summary was published in South Magazine, No. 1, October 1980, pp. 14-17; and on a keynote address to the SEACEN Governors' Meeting, Colombo, Sri Lanka, 14 January, 1981 of which an abstract was published in IFDA Dossier 24, July/August 1981, pp. 63 - 76.

INTRODUCTION

It is widely observed that the developing countries of the South lack a technical secretariat to analyze carefully their collective needs and provide them with the input necessary to conduct successful collective negotiations with the North. It is not as widely recognized, however, that discussions related to economic issues concerning the developing countries, much like their external trade, are mainly conducted with the industrialized world, with little prior exchange among the countries of the South. There is a strong case, therefore, for co-ordination of the South's attitudes, for a thorough examination of ideas among its constituent countries before they are put forward for open discussion with the North. Above all, developing countries should be fully aware of the areas where they share common interests, and better able to find ways of minimizing the friction involved in meeting their divergent, and at times conflicting, interests. Through such conscious efforts, developing countries may rightly aspire to a true solidarity and may eventually attain the often talked of, but hardly achieved, collective self-reliance.

ELEMENTS ABSENT IN INTER-SOUTH
DISCUSSIONS

South-South discussions should also reflect a sense of realism that has often been absent in the formal fora in which the South's demands have been debated. Some important preliminary points are worth emphasizing in this context:

The first is that part of the dilemma which developing countries are presently facing is of their own making. There is no denying that external factors have turned the situation from bad to worse, and that there is little or nothing that a developing country can do to curb the rising rate of international inflation, to restore stability to the international monetary system or to counteract the negative effects of these factors on its economy. But this may present only half the truth. For it is also true that most developing countries are doing little or nothing to check the menacing growth rates of their populations, or to rationalize their consumption. Meanwhile, efforts abound for increasing their military expenditures and multiplying their prestige projects. Whatever has been achieved in the way of co-ordination or collective action among developing countries in the economic and financial fields, especially at the regional level, has seldom been followed by serious, uninterrupted implementation. While we address the external factors affecting our developing countries and try to find realistic solutions to their economic problems, we should not ignore the need for hard corrective domestic measures. Each country is called upon to take, within its boundaries and in co-operation with others, the steps required to ensure a more proper allocation and a more disciplined and efficient management of the limited resources at its disposal.

The second is that promoting easy solutions based on inaccurate data or false hopes can only be counter-productive. Specifically, it would be a mistake if developing countries continue to exaggerate what some of them, e.g. the members of OPEC, can do to assist the others. It is true, as I shall explain later, that OPEC members have done a great deal in the way of helping other developing countries and that they are reasonably expected to continue these efforts as long as they are able to do so. To extend this to saying, as many have already done, that the solution to the present financial predicament lies in the hands of OPEC, or that OPEC is the only qualified midwife for the birth of the New International Economic Order

(NIEO), cannot, in my view, provide a serious contribution to the discussions.

A few statistics will place the capacities of OPEC member countries in their true perspective. The aggregate GNP of all OPEC countries reached $379 billion (US) in 1978, according to the World Bank Atlas. This represents barely 4 per cent of the global GNP in the same year, and 7 per cent of the GNP of the OECD countries. It is less than half of the GNP of Japan, and a mere 18 per cent of that of the United States. The comparison is much more striking when confined to the GNP of the few OPEC countries in possession of significant net liquid assets. In fact, the combined GNP of all the seven Arab members of OPEC, including Algeria and Iraq, stood at a mere 19 per cent of the GNP of Japan in 1978.

Furthermore, the savings of these countries, their so-called "surpluses", are in no way comparable to the surpluses of other countries, as they do not result from the intrinsic strength of a national production machinery. Rather, they are the outcome of oil extraction far beyond the financial needs of the domestic economies of some of the producing countries. In fact, they maintain such high levels of oil production simply out of their concern for the stability and welfare of the world economy. Being the monetary realization of a depletable national resource, these savings should naturally be invested with great prudence. In the absence of such prudent investment, the future generations of these countries would find themselves without oil and without savings and would again be dependent on the little income derived from their other meagre resources. Any helpful proposal on how to ensure future economic security while benefiting other developing countries, would naturally be welcomed. Conversely, ideas which would lead to the loss of this fragile form of wealth can hardly be construed as serious proposals in a constructive South-South dialogue.

Finally, the financial problems of developing countries differ from one country to another in their origin and magnitude. In particular, there is a marked difference between the financial problems of the low-income and those of the high-income and semi-industrialized countries. The generally advocated solutions to the problems of the latter countries, such as greater access to capital markets and elimination of the trade barriers to their exports of manufactured goods, may be of little relevance to the low-income countries. There is an obvious need, therefore, to devise different detailed solutions for the different problems of the various categories of countries and to avoid prescribing panaceas which may provide attractive slogans but not real remedies.

Having said that, I shall be the first to recognize the need for dramatic action and for flexible policies to correct the severe financial imbalances presently faced by developing countries. In the face of these imbalances there is no choice but to adopt policies of readjustment on both the international and domestic levels, in order to enable these countries, over the reasonable time span of five years or so, to reduce their deficits to a level which can be financed by ordinary capital flows. This adjustment process will require a great shift in the strategies of the developing countries concerned and their external sources of finances. It will also necessitate, I must hasten to add, a volume of external financing much larger than that available at present.

ECONOMIC PROSPECTS FOR THE SOUTH

Almost every recent study on the economic prospects of developing countries in the 1980's concludes with gloomy predictions. These predictions may prove to be accurate if no conscious efforts are made to avoid them. Opportunities in developing countries are still considerable, however. With a strong political will and with the adoption of appropriate and timely policies and their serious implementation, the countries of the South could, if they maintain their solidarity, overcome most of the difficulties which lie ahead. A great deal of improvement in the prospects of the South in the 1980's rests with policy and institutional changes which, I believe, could be realistically achieved.

The ability of the developing countries to adjust to changes in the international economic environment must not be underestimated. The experience of most developing countries in the 1974-78 period has proven this beyond doubt. As the *World Development Report 1980* of the World Bank states, the growth rates of developing countries did not fall in 1974 and 1975 to the same levels experienced by industrialized countries during that period. In fact, the countries of East Asia, Latin America and the Caribbean, achieved during 1970-80 growth rates in their GNP and their GNP per capita higher than in the previous decade. Several of the developing countries which improved their economic policies and did well during the six difficult years had previous records of slow growth. For them, improved domestic efficiency went a long way towards off-setting the effects of the deterioration in the world economy. They are now much better placed to weather the current slow-down and recover in the 1980s[1].

The present financial problems should not, therefore, pre-determine the abilities of the developing countries to cope with future difficulties. The South has great human resources, part of which are currently contributing to the prosperity of the North. It has considerable potential for industrial and agricultural growth and, unlike the industrialized North, it is a net exporter of energy. Even the developing countries which are net importers of energy have great unexploited energy resources. Non-OPEC developing countries have huge potential for hydro-electricity of which only 4 per cent is said to have been exploited. These countries account for 9 per cent of the world's present crude oil reserves and 50 per cent of the total prospective petroleum areas in the world. They also account for at least 7 per cent of the world's total gas reserves. Furthermore, the non-OPEC South accounts for 8 per cent of the economically recoverable coal deposits, with India alone accounting for 65 per cent of it.

It is not my intention here to go into detail regarding the problems facing the development process of the developing countries in the 1980s. They have been adequately reflected in the various annual reports and studies of the IMF, the World Bank, and other international and national development and financial institutions. I merely want to touch upon some of these issues as they bear relevance to the points I would like to address later on.

The developing countries will have to deal with an inhospitable international environment in the 1980s. The world economy, which is crucial for their development progress, is characterized by an uncertain outlook: faltering growth rates, high rates of inflation, a growing scarcity of energy and increasingly protective measures by the developed countries against the exports of other nations. This inhospitable international climate has compounded an already difficult development environment at home, where population is growing at alarming rates, cities are becoming overcrowded, per capita food production is dwindling, unemployment is rising, and spending on armaments continues to claim a large portion of available resources.

The combined effect of such domestic and international factors is producing increasing social tension and political instability. The following factors may be of particular importance in their effect on the economic prospects of the developing countries in the 1980s, although they are not necessarily listed in the order of importance:

First, the rapid population growth and the unprecedented shift in population to urban areas are continuously creating problems the magnitude of which seems beyond the capacity of the Governments concerned to cope. By the year 2000, the total population of the developing countries is projected to increase to at least 4.9 billion[2]. Current and projected declines in fertility rates in some developing countries offer some hopeful signs of a slowdown in the growth of the world population, but this decline in fertility is not expected to stabilize population levels sufficiently during this century. Hence, the increase in population will continue to make a major claim on the scarce resources of the developing countries.

Second, developing countries continue to spend a considerable share of their meagre resources on arms and weapons. Spending on arms has reached phenomenal proportions in contrast to the trivial amounts spent on social programmes. For example, the Brandt Commission estimates current global military spending at $450 billion (US) a year[3], of which about $14 billion in foreign exchange was spent by developing countries. (Incidentally, the WHO programme for wiping out malaria requires the equivalent of only two hours of these global arms expenditures.) Also, between 1960 and 1973, the military expenditures of developing countries increased from 3.4 per cent to 4.4 per cent of total GNP, and since then there has been a rapid rise in both absolute and relative terms[4].

Third, the already precarious food situation of developing countries could worsen. According to FAO more than 450 million people, half of them children, suffer from malnutrition. WHO also estimates that about 30 million people die each year from illnesses connected with malnutrition. To meet the rising food demand, the developing countries are resorting to imports which are resulting in additional severe pressure on their balance of payments.

Although world food production has more than doubled over the past twenty-five years, the three developing regions of the world have moved from the food-surplus position, which they held prior to World War II, to one of serious deficit. Imports of cereals by developing countries have increased from relatively low levels in the 1950s to 20 million tons in 1960/61 and to nearly 80 million tons in the year 1978/79. The situation is particularly threatening in Africa, which has the highest population growth rate in the world and a stagnant level of aggregate food production. As a result, this continent is now facing a decline in per capita food production and a sharp increase in the volume and cost of grain imports, whose price has more than quintupled since 1970. Although the available estimates of the total annual gross investment required for agriculture (including support services) in the developing countries vary considerably, they all lead to the same conclusion: the financing required to attain an agricultural base that would eventually eliminate all food deficits involves massive new investments. The FAO[5] estimated that $52 billion would be required in 1980 and up to $107 billion by the year 2000. For the low-income countries alone, estimates of the external assistance needed for the agricultural sector range from $6 billion to $20 billion annually. The International Food Policy Research Institute (IFPRI)[6] estimates the annual external financing required for thirty-six low-income countries at $13 billion (at 1980 prices), assuming that half of the capital costs and most of the recurrent expenditures will be provided by the countries themselves. Such a level of external assistance is far above the approximate $3.5 billion per year currently available to the low-income countries. Additional financing on this scale cannot be assumed to be readily forthcoming. In fact, the increase in OECD bilateral aid to this particular sector has been negligible. There are also no clear signs that the other preconditions for global food security and greatly increased food production in the developing countries are about to be satisfied. The security of food supply can still be threatened by adverse weather conditions in the major grain-producing countries of North America, or a fall in food production in the other industrialized countries.

Fourth, the growing scarcity of energy is seriously clouding the growth prospects of the developing countries. Despite the potential for new energy discoveries, energy supply is expected to remain tight during the 1980s. Oil-importing developing countries are expected to continue to import the bulk of their energy needs in the 1980s, and their energy gap could even widen, from 5.6 million barrels per day (mb/d) in 1980 to 7.5 mb/d in 1990, according to the World Bank[7]. This is expected again to exert severe pressure on their balance of payments.

Most developing countries have to face the problem of meeting the increasing costs of imported oil at the same time as they are trying to develop their domestic alternative energy resources. Consumption of commercial energy, i.e., oil, gas, coal and electricity, in the developing countries continues to rise as a result of economic growth and the absence of effective rationalization of consumption. Total oil demand in developing countries is projected by the World Bank to increase from 9.2 mb/d in 1980 to about 15.4 mb/d in 1990. The incremental demand might be met by the exploitation of the developing countries' own potential alternative sources of energy provided that adequate financing is forthcoming. However, the financial requirements to meet the energy import bill and to develop indigenous resources are, as in the case of food, far larger than what is readily available currently from domestic and external sources. The annual capital required to satisfy the incremental energy demand for oil, gas, solid fuels and hydro-electricity on the part of the non-OPEC developing countries over the decade is roughly estimated by the OPEC Secretariat to be about $12 billion. The World Bank projects the financial requirements of the energy sector in oil-importing developing countries in the same period at $45 billion per year or $20 billion more than the estimated annual investment requirements for commercial energy in 1980[8].

Fifth, the world economy, which is a crucial factor in the growth prospects of the developing countries, is expected to remain sluggish, as it has been since 1979. According to the IMF, the growth rates of the economies of the developed countries, which constitute the centre of the present world economy, is estimated at one per cent in 1980, and may not exceed that rate in 1981[9]. The outlook may improve in later years but growth rates in developed countries are likely to remain below those achieved during the 1960s and 1970s. The World Bank projects an annual growth rate of 3.3 per cent during 1980-85[10].

In addition to slow growth rates in the developed countries, the world economy is currently characterized by an exceptionally high rate of inflation. The developed countries have been blaming the oil price rises for the current international inflation, although a number of studies have firmly established that this assertion is not only exaggerated but simplistic. In fact, there is now considerable evidence that the increase in oil prices has often been the result, not the cause, of world inflation. For example, while world export prices increased at less than one per cent during the 1960s, they increased at 30 per cent per annum during the twelve months preceding the first

major increase in oil prices in 1973/74. One of the reasons for this was
the sharp increase in world monetary reserves, which doubled
within a period of only three years (end of 1969 to end of 1972)[11]. The
huge deficits recorded by developing countries in 1975 were largely
attributable to the industrial recession in that year rather than to the
increased cost of their oil imports, which amounted to only 1.6 per
cent of their total GDP, according to Western sources[12]. Moreover,
the rate of inflation in developed countries averaged about 7 per cent
per annum despite the freezing of the price of oil during that period
and its fall in real terms. The IMF reported that the increase in the rate
of inflation in these countries in 1979 began well before the impact of
that year's increase in oil prices could be felt[13].

According to GATT, the major causes of inflation in the industrialized countries are their monetary and fiscal policies rather than
the increased costs of their oil imports, the total of which constitute
only 2 per cent of the combined GNP of the OECD countries[14].
Strong evidence of the crucial role of such policies in fuelling inflation in these countries is the reduced inflation rate achieved by
Germany and Switzerland, despite heavy oil imports; for the rate
between 1973 and 1978 decreased from 6.9 per cent to 2.5 per cent
and from 8.8 per cent to 1.1 per cent, respectively. A recent detailed
study by the OPEC Secretariat on the inflation in a number of
OECD countries concluded that the contribution of oil price rises to
their inflation was only 0.4 per cent in 1973, 1.6 per cent in 1974, 2.5
per cent in 1975 and less than 1 per cent in 1976 (ranging from 0.5 per
cent in France to 0.7 per cent in Italy)[15].

Inflation imported from the developed countries has been a major
problem for most developing countries since the early 1970s. The
IMF expects inflation rates in the 1980s not only to be highly pro-
nounced but widely spread among the major developed countries[16].
On the other hand, persistent international inflation is seriously
eroding the value of the current account surpluses accruing to the
oil-exporting developing countries. This is posing a serious dilemma
for these countries with respect to their decisions whether to keep the
oil in the ground, or to continue to deplete their limited oil wealth by
turning it into financial holdings whose value erodes over time.
According to OAPEC, the oil revenues of ten Arab oil producers
increased by 56 per cent in nominal terms in 1979 but international
inflation and currency fluctuations depressed their real value to
below 1974 levels. And according to the IMF, the estimated $115

billion 1980 current account surplus of the oil exporters is broadly equivalent, in real terms, to the $58 billion surplus they recorded in 1974[17].

Slow growth and continued inflation are also expected to have their adverse effects on the developing countries' exports to the developed countries. Exports of primary commodities (excluding fuels), which account for some 55 per cent of the merchandise exports of the developing countries, are expected to grow by only 3.3 per cent per annum during 1980-85. Exports from developing countries to the developed countries are facing additional difficulties resulting from the rise in protectionism since 1970, particularly against their manufactured goods. Although such goods account for only 24 per cent of the developing countries' total exports, they are the fastest growing category among all exports. Recent counter-measures, such as the GATT-sponsored Multilateral Trade Negotiations (MTN) completed in April 1979, are of little effect compared to the increasing protectionist sentiment, the recent consolidation of trade restrictions, and the adoption of non-tariff and other trade restrictions by some countries. These constitute a serious cause for concern, especially for the few semi-industrialized developing countries[18]. The increase in the volume of exports of developing countries to the developed countries has not, on the other hand, been accompanied by an increase in the unit price of these exports (with the exception of oil). Developing countries, particularly those in the low-income group, have not been experiencing a satisfactory improvement in their terms of trade. For example, during 1967-72 the annual growth rate in the terms of trade of the developing countries which do not export oil was –1.1 per cent. With the exception of some improvement in 1973 and later during 1976 and 1977, the annual growth rate in their terms of trade has remained negative since 1978[19]. Moreover, the IMF estimates a larger deterioration in their terms of trade in 1980 than was previously predicted.

CONSTRAINTS ON FINANCIAL FLOWS

The situation we have just described clearly points to the difficulties facing the developing countries in generating sufficient resources to reduce their growing current account deficits and to carry out their long-term adjustment programmes. As a result, most of these countries must either have access to sufficiently large amounts of external resources on reasonable terms, or must face serious financial difficulties.

There seems to be little prospect, however, of a massive increase in the volume of concessional aid to the developing countries. The volume of external financing required by developing countries for their food and energy sectors alone is far above the volume of total official flows these countries receive at present from all sources. It is also a regrettable fact that industrialized countries are not likely to increase substantially their ODA flows in the immediate future. Nor are they realistically expected to reach the target ODA of 0.7 per cent of GNP by 1985. Not even half of this ratio was reached in 1979 and the World Bank projects a mere 0.36 per cent of GNP by 1985[20].

It should be noted, however, that most of the required funds are needed by only a few middle-income developing countries. Ten countries, including five OPEC members, account for 90 per cent of the total accumulated external private debt of the developing countries. In fact, the developing country with the largest volume of debt reaching maturity in 1980 ($12.66 billion) is Venezuela, a member of OPEC. The largest Third World borrower in the same year was Mexico, which is also a net oil-exporter. And the country with the highest external debt to GNP ratio in 1978 was Egypt, another oil-exporter. This underlines the fact that debt is not necessarily correlated with the importation of oil or severe under-development.

Over the last decade the developing countries, including OPEC members, have had little difficulty in securing additional funds from international private sources. Between 1971-79, such borrowing increased nine-fold, and by 27 per cent in 1979 alone. However, doubts are now being expressed as to whether their recourse to the international capital markets can continue to grow indefinitely. Many of the major commercial banks are arguing that they have already reached an excessive ratio of foreign to total loans along with a low ratio of capital to total assets. They are also getting dangerously close to what they consider individual country risk limits. Some major banks have actually been directed by their boards or central banks to limit their exposure in the developing countries.

There are, therefore, supply constraints in many commercial banks and private lending institutions, a sharp rise in the debt service ratios of some developing countries and a worsening of their debt servicing capacity. In addition the developing countries will be facing new competition in private borrowing in the 1980s. Such competition stems from the developed countries which are planning massive investment programmes in the energy field, the European centrally-planned economies, which are planning to increase their borrowing, and China, which is entering the financial market in order to finance huge modernization programmes.

PROPOSED SOLUTIONS – THE ROLE OF OPEC COUNTRIES

All the previously mentioned factors lead to the often-expressed conclusion that developing countries will soon have to face lower economic growth, and therefore devastating socio-economic consequences. We should not accept this conclusion, however. The developing countries must face the challenge and look for realistic and effective solutions. It would be presumptuous on my part to prescribe such solutions, but in my view, a good part of the answer to the problems of developing countries in the 1980s and beyond depends on their achieving three major objectives:

  (i) effective socio-economic reforms at home which would enable them to develop efficient management, a disciplined work-force, a fair distribution of economic gains, and consumption patterns consistent with their limited resources;

  (ii) massive flows of resources from the North and between themselves to complement their domestic savings;

  (iii) a more equitable international economic and financial system which would provide the basis for a more acceptable international division of labour and for fair international relationships of production and exchange.

The role of OPEC member countries in co-operation with other developing nations through the difficult years to come may best be seen in the context of the above objectives. Since some OPEC members initiated their aid programmes in the 1960s, their role has generally been seen as providers of funds on concessional terms. This is certainly a role which some of them will continue to play as long as they are in a position to do so. However, it cannot, and should not be envisaged as the only role to be expected from these countries in a lasting and balanced framework of co-operation.

I shall not attempt to dwell here in detail on the aid record of OPEC member countries. The target ratio of 0.7 per cent of ODA to GNP was exceeded four-fold by OPEC donors as a group, as early as

1975. In the more relevant case of the so-called surplus Arab countries, the target was exceeded in that year by more than twenty-two times by Qatar, twenty times by the United Arab Emirates, eleven times by Kuwait and six times by Saudi Arabia. In 1979, Qatar, Kuwait, Saudi Arabia and Iraq ranked at the top of the list of world donors, in terms of ODA as a percentage of GNP. In fact, six OPEC countries have consistently been on the list of the ten main world donors in terms of the proportion of net disbursement to GNP since 1975. Two of these countries (Saudi Arabia and Kuwait) are among the top seven donors on the basis of *absolute* amounts of concessional aid. No need to recall here that not one OPEC country is sufficiently developed or industrialized to use its aid to secure external markets for its products or to ensure control over the sources of the primary commodities needed for its industries. Nor do we have to point out that the figures used to measure OPEC aid and to compare it with OECD assistance are greatly deflated in favour of the OECD group, for many technical reasons which we have elaborated in chapters 1 and 3 of this publication.

It should be stressed that the high level of OPEC aid has been provided out of deep concern for the welfare of the South and the need for fostering self-reliance among its countries. OPEC countries are continuing their efforts to foster solidarity and enhance efforts towards aid through new initiatives. In early 1980, these countries substantially modified the Agreement Establishing the OPEC Fund, converting it from an international account of temporary character to an on-going international agency for development finance with open-ended resources which to date exceed $4 billion.

Some OPEC members (Algeria and Venezuela) are now calling for a substantial increase in the Fund's resources (up to $20 billion) and for the restructuring of its capital base to enable it to borrow from the capital market.

Furthermore, OPEC's Long-Term Strategy Committee has already adopted a proposal advanced by Iraq for the establishment of a new global fund for energy and development to be financed by both the industrialized and OPEC countries. The amount contributed by the industrialized countries to that Fund would depend on the annual rate of inflation as reflected in the price increases of manufactured goods, food and services exported by them to the developing countries. The amount to be contributed by OPEC countries would, on the other hand, reflect the total oil price increase, due to inflation, of the cost of oil exported to other developing countries. Other developing countries will not be required to participate in the financing but will be full members of the proposed Fund.

More recently, Iran also proposed an aid plan to reimburse immediately developing countries on a grant basis for the financial burden resulting from OPEC oil price increases, through a new OPEC Fund to which member countries would pay 10 per cent of the increase in their oil revenues (on the assumption that the oil imports of the developing countries account for about 10 per cent of total OPEC oil exports). This Fund would be managed by a joint committee of OPEC countries and oil-importing developing countries.

Although it may be premature to predict the outcome of these different proposals, they stand as evidence of the continuing concern of OPEC countries for the financial problems of other developing nations. They should result in greater flows of aid from all sources and should lead to new international arrangements more responsive to the aspirations of the Third World.

In addition to concessional flows, the so-called "surpluses" of some OPEC countries have been successfully recycled to both developed and developing countries through private commercial banks and international financial institutions. Despite the earlier outcry about the possible difficulties involved, lending by commercial banks has been especially important in meeting the needs of the developing countries. In fact, in 1974-75 the recycling of these surpluses through the financial markets and the IMF's oil facility enabled many developing countries to maintain a relatively strong economic growth. For example, among the oil-importing developing countries, the largest borrowers from the private banks are reported to have recorded real growth in GDP of 5.3 per cent in 1975[21]. In 1979, concern was again expressed about the inability of the commercial banks to recycle the OPEC surpluses, but the process was in fact relatively smooth and bank lending expanded by about 24 per cent, nearly as high as the 26 per cent increase recorded in 1978[22]. According to the Bank for International Settlements, in 1979 a great part of the OPEC countries' deposits with Western Banks (estimated at 80 per cent) were recycled to developing countries.

As we have pointed out, the worsening external debt situation of the developing countries and the increasing exposure of commercial banks in these countries may slow down private bank lending to them in the 1980s, though not to the exaggerated extent reflected in general reports earlier this year. This situation calls for new initiatives to encourage the private banks to sustain their important role, and to enable international institutions to shoulder a greater responsibility in the recycling process. Unfortunately, instead of searching for new initiatives, it has been suggested in certain circles that the time has come for OPEC countries alone to lend their funds directly to other developing countries. In simple terms the argument suggests that lending to the developing countries has become too risky for Western banks, but should nevertheless be good enough for OPEC lenders. It remains to be seen how responsible investors on the OPEC side can see anything in this argument but an attempt to ensure the continued servicing of the debts previously incurred with the private Western banks.

Banks and investment companies owned or controlled by OPEC countries have in fact mushroomed in recent years (their number is now at least ten times larger than in 1974), and they are becoming increasingly involved in operations in the developing countries[23]. Therefore, a more constructive approach would be to study the ways in which these institutions could expand their exposure in the developing countries without running greater risks than they would normally accept for their investment in the rest of the world. Realistically speaking, however, the recycling problem cannot be solved through direct OPEC loans alone. There is a great need for both private banks and public international institutions to continue to expand their activities in developing countries through new mechanisms which take all interests into account.

Two years ago, during a seminar organized by Chase Bank, I suggested that private banks should consider establishing a collective insurance scheme to protect themselves against the remote possibility of default by developing countries[24]. (I say "remote" because, as far as I know, of all Euromarket loans in the form of bonds there have been only nineteen cases of default, of which eighteen are accounted for by private US borrowers and one by a Japanese company).

The idea is simply to replace the self-insurance sought individually by banks through the higher spreads they impose on developing countries, by a collective insurance pool whereby risks would be uniformly shared by the participating banks, at a lower cost to each participant. A proposal for an international safety net arrangement was subsequently made by the Chairman of the Deutsche Bank to enable banks to share liquidity, when required as a result of delays in payment. The Governor of the Bank of Greece has also advocated the creation of an international loan insurance fund which would be financed by governmental and certain inter-governmental financial institutions. It is hoped that practical measures of this type will soon be taken to lessen the risk of exposure to banks in the developing countries.

Another idea which may be considered is the creation by the developing countries of collective mechanisms for guaranteeing their foreign debts. These mechanisms could take the form of joint loan guarantee corporations or even of institutionalized regional exchange arrangements by which liquid assets would be made available to each participating bank when needed to meet obligations towards third parties. Details could be worked out to ensure that the implementation of such schemes would benefit all participating countries.

We must stress that providing loan financing should not be the sole purpose of recycling. Recycled funds must be put to optimum use to meet the needs of development as well as the structural adjustments needed over the coming decade to reduce the balance of payments deficits. They are needed to increase investment, especially in indigenous energy resources and food production, and reduce the menacing population growth rates. These goals cannot be left to the private lending institutions; the official bilateral and multilateral lending institutions must shoulder a good part of the responsibility.

The World Bank has responded to the long-standing request for programme financing and has redirected part of its activities towards its new "structural adjustment loans" and towards larger involvement in the energy sector. However, the initiative in these new areas should not be carried out at the expense of the other sectors. Therefore, these efforts must be matched by the availability of additional resources through a wider use of the World Bank's capital base and additional substantial replenishment of IDA resources. One may note here that the management of the World Bank has already proposed a substantial increase in the level of the bank's operations in the immediate future.

It must also be noted that the IMF has now authorized lending of up to 600 per cent of a nation's quota over the next three years, which amounts to virtually tripling past borrowing rates and raising its total lending to about $7-10 billion annually. Yet, to play an effective role in meeting the needs of the developing countries, the IMF will surely have to accelerate the process it has already started by adapting its conditionality to the special circumstances prevailing in the developing countries, and by easing the supply constraints in the economies of these countries. The current efforts to bring about greater IMF involvement in lending to the developing countries on acceptable terms should perhaps take priority over the continuous demands for the creation of new funding agencies, especially those which do not provide additional services or necessarily result in an additional transfer of resources.

To allow for a more balanced, mutually beneficial pattern of co-operation among OPEC and the rest of the developing countries, four other areas of future co-operation seem particularly promising. Although some progress has been made in these areas, they will have to be studied in detail to remove existing obstacles and pave the way for a significant expansion. They are (a) Direct investment; (b) Trade; (c) Labour migration; and (d) Technical co-operation.

(a) Direct Investment

There is wide scope for the direct investment of OPEC funds in other developing countries on a commercial basis, especially in the form of joint ventures and similar arrangements. Several Arab member countries of OPEC have already set up joint ventures for projects in the Arab world. Similar schemes have recently been organized in other developing countries, and there exists great potential for a significant expansion of such activities. Some economists in OPEC countries are tending toward the view that the investment of OPEC funds in developing countries may provide a brake against world inflation and therefore against the erosion of the real value of OPEC savings. They strongly argue that the mere placements (deposits and purchases of financial instruments) of OPEC funds in developed countries, which do not represent new real investments, could easily lead to a net loss in the real value of these assets. Investing the funds in new real investments in the developing countries, where they have their greatest potential, would, on the other hand, protect their real value while adding to the real wealth of the world and discouraging inflation[25].

However, it must be stressed that while there are good investment opportunities for OPEC funds in the developing countries, the climate for such investment is not always encouraging. The potential for direct investment in the developing countries is hampered by physical and institutional constraints. The efforts of OPEC and other donors in the form of aid could no doubt help unblock these bottlenecks, by combining the soft financing of infrastructure projects with the commercial financing of new investments. A frank exchange of views between the holders of surplus funds and the countries in need of investment should be followed by effective measures to facilitate such investment for the benefit of both parties.

(b) Trade

Although trade between OPEC and other developing countries has increased considerably since 1973/74, there is room for greater expansion. The value of OPEC exports to other developing countries grew at an average rate of approximately 30 per cent per annum in the period 1973/78. At the same time, imports from other developing countries rose significantly, at an average rate of 35 per cent per annum[26]. OPEC countries have a low level of industrialization and this situation accounts for their meagre demand for the raw materials and semi-finished goods of the other countries of the Third World. As their development plans are implemented, however, this obstacle will be gradually removed. New mechanisms, including export credit arrangements, should also be developed to ensure greater economic exchange among developing countries as they continue their development process.

(c) Labour Migration

Labour migration to eight Arab OPEC countries accounted for remittances to ten developing countries amounting to $6.5 billion in 1977, according to the World Bank[27]. Although many benefits are derived by both the labour exporting and host countries, there are also certain social costs to be borne by both sides. Improved planning and management of labour migration is badly needed to minimize such costs and to ensure optimum benefits to the economies of all the countries concerned.

(d) Technical Co-operation

There seems to exist scope for much greater technical co-operation between OPEC and other developing countries. Some OPEC countries could contribute to the development of energy resources in other developing countries on the strength of their acquired experience in the oil sector. OPEC countries also stand to benefit from this kind of co-operation in other sectors given the disparate technical capabilities in various developing countries and the recent technical achievements of some of them.

Apart from the areas of possible expanded co-operation between OPEC and the rest of the developing countries, OPEC has been using its relative strength to gain ground for the reform of international financial institutions and, more generally, to lay a foundation for the long-sought New International Economic Order. Ample evidence of this could be discerned in the active role played by OPEC countries in the relevant special sessions of the UN General Assembly and in the CIEC (the Paris Dialogue). Some fruits of these efforts have already materialized in the establishment of the International Fund for Agricultural Development (IFAD) and the Common Fund as new international financial institutions where developing countries have the stronger say[28].

The conclusion to the negotiations over the establishment of IFAD was reached after OPEC countries pledged, through the OPEC Fund, to contribute more than 40 per cent of the initial resources, provided that the developing countries, as a group, acquired two thirds of the voting power while the non-OPEC developing countries remained under no obligation to contribute to IFAD's resources. Through the large financial contribution of the OPEC Fund and the active role played by representatives of the OPEC countries in the negotiation of the Agreement Establishing IFAD, a new chapter in the history of international financial institutions was launched.

The prolonged negotiations on the establishment of the Common Fund quickened pace when the OPEC Fund, on its own initiative, agreed to meet the contributions to the Common Fund of all the Least Developed Countries and to make a sizeable voluntary contribution to this Fund's "second window" as well. The measures which were meant to accelerate the process of negotiation and to strengthen the hand of developing countries in this process have yielded positive results, despite the strong initial objections of some industrialized countries to the very principles on which the Common Fund is based.

The proposal of OPEC's Long-Term Strategy Committee to establish a new Joint Energy and Development Fund marks yet another step through which the OPEC countries may achieve a dramatic development for the benefit of other developing countries. Other details of the report of this Committee are based on the same principle of using realistically the position of the OPEC countries as the main exporters of oil and the holders of large financial assets, to secure better bargains for the underprivileged South in its attempt to improve its lot in the world economic order.

Conclusions

All those who have the interests of the Third World at heart realize that a strong OPEC is to the advantage of the Third World as a whole. The strength of OPEC represents a unique opportunity for developing countries. But we all have to realize that this strength is based on the transient facility for extensive oil-production and the resulting accumulation of net liquid assets. Through solidarity among developing countries, mutual benefits can accrue to all before this opportunity is lost. The surpluses of the oil-producers should be seen, however, in their true perspective: as a monetary form of a depleting asset that does not necessarily add to the wealth of oil-producing countries. It is in the interest of these countries, and of the world at large, that practical mechanisms be established for the transformation of these assets into new real investments which would provide them with revenues in the post-oil era. To the extent that these investments are implemented in other developing countries, OPEC will also play a major role in the international redistribution of income to the benefit of the poorer countries. This redistribution has already started and is becoming a social imperative on the international scene. The sooner it is achieved in an orderly manner, the happier the inhabitants of this planet will be.

CHAPTER 3

THE OPEC AID RECORD

Based on a paper submitted to "The Experts Meeting on Alternative Solutions to the External Public Debt Problem of the LDC's" held in Mexico City on 27-30 October 1977. First published by the OPEC Fund in January 1978 (in English and then French) it also appeared as a chapter in "LDC External Debt and the World Economy (1978)" in English and Spanish; as an article in "Oil and Arab Co-operation", Vol. 4, No. 1, 1978 (in Arabic) and in "World Development", Vol. 7, No. 2, February 1979 (in English). This paper was written by the Author in collaboration with Dr Robert Mabro, Director, Middle East Centre, St Antony's College, Oxford.

INTRODUCTION

Financial aid from OPEC member countries to the other countries of the Third World is a novel historical phenomenon which differs in many of its characteristics from aid extended either by Western industrialized economies or by the Soviet Bloc. OPEC financial co-operation with the Third World represents a transfer of resources from some developing to other developing countries. The main donors among oil-exporting economies are admittedly endowed with large financial assets; yet their wealth is derived from a depletable natural resource, not from industrial power. These are central facts with interesting implications for both donors and recipients.

The burden of aid is heavier on an OPEC donor than apparent at first. This is because the immediate future (the period during which revenues from oil and the accumulation of net financial assets tend to increase) has a higher social discount rate than the distant future (when revenues and financial accumulation begin to decrease as oil resources become depleted). Furthermore, aid is given from oil revenues which are in fact part income and part capital, as they represent, to a large extent, the monetary form of a capital asset. The benefits from aid to recipients are also greater than apparent because OPEC grants and loans, for evident reasons, are rarely, if ever, tied to their source.

Most OPEC members are small developing countries. None of them is a "super power" with world-wide strategic interests, or an ex-colonial power, with political and economic commitments to former dependencies. OPEC members extend their aid for a different reason. They are deeply concerned with the relationships of Third World countries with each other and the mutuality of their interests.

OPEC aid has been considerably influenced, both in scope and in scale, by the oil revolution of 1973. Further questions arise here. Do increases in the export prices of a certain commodity create a case for aid giving? Should the beneficiaries of price increases compensate in some way those who carry the burden of the additional import bill?

The subject tackled in this paper is important. OPEC aid is not a minor phenomenon. The flows of financial assistance from oil-exporting countries in recent years have become very substantial. Commitments of funds and amounts actually disbursed represent an unusually high proportion of the gross national product of major OPEC donors. The share of OPEC member countries in the total flow of official assistance to the Third World is large. Many an important developing country critically depends today on OPEC aid. Major international development institutions have also come to depend on oil-exporting countries for substantial borrowings. More interesting perhaps than these indications of quantitative significance, is the fact that OPEC aid has taken a variety of forms, some newly conceived or hitherto untried.

The purpose of this paper is to establish and evaluate the record of OPEC aid. This analysis will attempt to highlight aspects of it which are original and novel, and those features of it which are distinctive. Another purpose is to draw some tentative lessons from the experience of providing aid and to assess the prospects of OPEC aid in the coming years. The history of OPEC aid is perhaps sufficiently long by now to justify the attempt to appraise it; and yet far too short for any appraisal undertaken at this stage to be anything but tentative in nature.

THE RECORD

Opec Aid before the Oil Revolution

The history of financial co-operation between member countries of
OPEC and other developing nations began soon after the foundation
of that organization in 1960. This process started with the creation in
1961 of the Kuwait Fund for Arab Economic Development. The
chronological coincidence of these events may be considered as
accidental; there was no necessary link between the actions of the five
oil-exporting countries which decided in 1960 to join together in
order to defend vital economic interests threatened by the erosion of
petroleum prices, and the separate decision of Kuwait in 1961 to
establish a Fund for external development aid. Yet, in a subtle sense,
one may now recognize in these diverse actions the features of a new
and important phenomenon: the emergence of effective solidarity in
the Third World both within a group of countries with similar
economic interests and between members of this group and other
developing nations. The point of interest in the context of this paper
is the birth, as early as 1961, of a new concept in foreign aid in which
both donor and recipient are developing countries.

The Kuwait Fund during the 1960s was, by present standards, a
fairly modest aid institution. Yet, Kuwait was in this period
transferring in foreign aid every year a percentage of its Gross
National Product higher than that of any other donor country.
Cumulative disbursements from the Kuwait Fund between
1962/1963, the first year of operation, and 1970/1971 were of the
order of KD60 million or approximately $200 million (US). Other
aid institutions sprang up in OPEC member countries early in the
1970s, prior to the oil events of 1973. The Abu Dhabi Fund for Arab
Economic Development was launched in 1971, and the Arab Fund
for Social and Economic Development, established in 1968, became
operational in 1972. The Abu Dhabi Fund, like the Kuwait Fund, is a
national institution owned by one OPEC member country. The
Arab Fund is a regional institution founded by a group of countries
not all of which are members of OPEC. These funds were mainly
concerned with the granting of project loans on concessional terms
to Arab countries.

Aid from OPEC member countries before 1973 was not uniquely
channelled through development finance institutions. Late in the

1960s three Arab oil-exporting countries, Kuwait, Libya and Saudi Arabia, began to extend substantial grants to Egypt, Jordan and Syria pursuant to a resolution adopted in the Khartoum Summit of August 1967. There are considerable differences between this particular type of aid and that provided by the Funds. The payments were in the form of grants, not loans. They were not tied to projects nor to plans but given as straight budgetary support. They were benefiting only three Arab countries while the Funds had, from the beginning, a much wider vocation. They were motivated by a strong political imperative: the need to support the states victim to the Israeli armed attack of June 1967 and to the military occupation which resulted from it.

Estimates of actual disbursements of OPEC members in the years 1970 to 1973 are as follows (US$ million):

1970	1971	1972	1973
443.5	630.9	688.9	1740.0

Sources: 1970-1972, World Bank; 1973, OECD

The data suggest that OPEC aid, even with the exclusion of the Khartoum payment, was already substantial before 1973. The oil events of that year enabled OPEC countries to inaugurate a new chapter in their record of aid provision, but they did not mark an absolute beginning. Institutions with proven capabilities in the provision of financial assistance were in existence before 1973. Governments had already recognized the need to express solidarity with other developing countries, beginning with immediate neighbours, through foreign aid. Large disbursements in the form of grants and soft loans for budgetary support were being made since 1968. And the scope of aid in terms of objectives, geographical extent and scale of disbursements had broadened significantly in 1971.

OPEC Aid after the Oil Revolution

There are at present two sets of comprehensive data on flows of resources from OPEC members to developing countries. One set is compiled by OECD and the second by UNCTAD. The two sets display significant differences in both aggregates and detail; yet these sources are not totally independent of each other. There is now a greater exchange of information between researchers in these two international organizations than was the case in the past, and all rely to a large extent on the same sources. Differences in estimates of aggregate flows seem to arise primarily because of definitional issues. OECD applies special criteria evolved for its Development Assistance Committee (DAC) flows and has less contact with primary sources than UNCTAD in the identification of OPEC aid flows.

The main data recently collected by both sources are summarized and compared in the table below.

Estimates of net disbursements of concessional aid (multilateral as well as bilateral) made by UNCTAD and OECD are basically very similar for all years except 1973[1]. The major difference between the two sources seems to lie in estimates of non-concessional multilateral flows. OECD does not consider payments to the IMF oil facility as part of the relevant flows while UNCTAD does[2]. The OECD argument is essentially that these payments did not constitute long-term financial flows, but rather short to medium-term balance of payments assistance and did not diminish the donors' resources since they were able to draw on them whenever their own payments position so warranted. The UNCTAD argument holds that OPEC flows to the IMF oil facility exceeded the facility's flows to developing countries which could be considered as exclusively financed by the OPEC donors, and that the duration of the facility's loans (up to seven years) constituted as much relief for the recipients' balance of payments as any bilateral non-concessional loan subject to similar terms. The IMF oil facility was indeed conceived by OPEC countries as a form of assistance to other developing countries. Flows may have been diverted to other recipients by the intermediary in ways that did not necessarily correspond to the donor's intention. This, of course, is an inherent feature of multilateral aid, especially when little control is exercised by donors on the final allocation. To distinguish disbursements from receipts becomes legitimate when there is such diversion of flows. Disbursements are an indicator of the donor's effort; receipts a measure of development aid. Such an argument implies that the UNCTAD figures correspond to a meaningful concept(disbursements) while the OECD data may underestimate both outflows from OPEC and inflows to developing countries.

Having interpreted the conceptual differences of the sources, we may now turn to the figures. The picture, however looked at, is clear: net disbursements from OPEC countries increased manifold

Net Disbursements of OPEC aid 1973-1976. Estimates by UNCTAD and OECD (US$ millions)

	1973		1974		1975		1976	
	UNCTAD	OECD	UNCTAD	OECD	UNCTAD	OECD	UNCTAD	OECD
Disbursements								
Concessional:	1145.5	1307.6	3504.2	3445.6	5472.8	5511.9	5239.4	5182.0
Bilateral	1043.0	1208.0	3038.3	3015.1	4920.9	4947.1	4405.5	4386.5
Multilateral	102.5	99.6	465.9	430.5	552.0	564.8	833.9	795.5
Non-Concessional:	445.9	432.4	4057.0	2506.3	5984.3	2651.6	3738.6	2773.2
Bilateral	142.2	138.3	688.7	981.5	1486.7	1497.3	1106.2	1592.5
Multilateral	303.7	294.1	3368.1	1524.8	4497.6	1154.3	2632.5	1180.7
Total	1591.4	1740.0	7561.3	5951.9	11457.1	8163.5	8978.1	7955.2

Sources　UNCTAD, statistical tables dated 4 November 1977 (mimeographed)
OECD, statistical tables dated 4 November 1977 (mimeographed). The OECD figures will appear in the
1977 DAC Annual Review and reflect a revision of the data published in earlier DAC reports.

in 1974 and 1975 above the high levels achieved in 1973. There is a dip in 1976 much more marked by the UNCTAD than the OECD figures. Once again, the IMF oil facility is the main cause of the apparent difference in behaviour. Interpreting the data in terms of disbursements and receipts, it would be fair to say that outflows from OPEC member countries declined in 1976 if compared to 1975 but that receipts by developing countries attributable to OPEC bilateral and multilateral contributions decreased much less in this period than the figure of the decline in outflows would indicate[3].

The magnitude of OPEC aid can be assessed in different ways. First, the comparison with the official development assistance of the industrialized DAC countries, though uncalled-for because of the structural differences between the two groups of donors, yields striking results in favour of the OPEC group. OPEC aid, according to the lower estimate, represented 44 per cent of DAC official disbursements in 1974. In the peak year, 1975, the low OECD estimate corresponds to a ratio of 49 per cent, the higher UNCTAD figures indicate a ratio of 67 per cent. Two OPEC countries, Saudi Arabia and UAE, ranked in 1976 among the six largest bilateral aid donors in absolute terms, Saudi Arabia being second only to the United States.

Net Disbursements, OPEC and DAC, 1974-76[*]

Concessional and non-concessional official flows US$ m.

	1974	1975	1976
DAC	13500	16609	17030
OPEC			
(OECD estimate)	5952	8163	7955
(UNCTAD estimate)	7561	11457	8978

[*]Official flows only; excluding flows to Southern European recipients, but including contributions to IMF Oil Facility.

Comparison of disbursements to the GNP of the donors is even more revealing. In 1974-76, official development assistance (concessional flows) from DAC countries to developing countries was equivalent to 0.33-0.35 per cent of their collective GNP. In these years, Sweden and the Netherlands shared the best record, reaching on occasions the 0.82 per cent mark. The comparable OPEC averages[4] in 1974-1976 (net disbursements of concessional aid, using OECD estimates) range between 2.01 and 2.7 per cent of the collective GNP. In 1976, OPEC countries occupied the top six places among all the donor countries of the world as regards the proportion of aid to GNP. In the peak year of 1975, OECD sources record 15.6 per cent of the GNP figure for Qatar and 11.8 per cent for the UAE. If non-concessional official flows are added, net disbursements (excluding IMF oil facility) represent 3.4 to 4 per cent of GNP in 1974-1976, according to OECD estimates. In none of these three years did total disbursements of Kuwait, Qatar and the UAE fall below ten per cent of GNP. These percentages are the lowest possible estimates, being based on the OECD figures and on a definition of OPEC donors which include countries such as Algeria and Nigeria which, while doing their best in aid-giving, have per capita incomes lower than in many an "assisted" developing country. To illustrate the differences in results if alternative definitions are adopted the following calculations were made for 1975:

As Percentages of GNP
(OECD Estimates)

Net disbursements of OPEC countries (total official)	4.01%[5]
Net disbursements of OPEC countries (excluding Algeria and Nigeria)	7.21%
Net disbursements of four OPEC countries making the highest disbursement/GNP ratio (Kuwait, Qatar, Saudi Arabia and UAE)	12.3%

In 1975, if contributions to the IMF oil facility are included, the net disbursement/GNP ratio would rise from 7.4 to 10.9 per cent for Saudi Arabia and from 11.4 to 14 per cent for Kuwait.

These percentages, already higher than any aid ratios previously known, would become all the higher if the nature of oil revenues, as basically a new form of capital wealth and not a net income, is taken into consideration. Even at the low 30 per cent "depletion factor" suggested for the GNP of the major oil-exporting countries by Mr McNamara in his September 1974 address to the World Bank Board of Governors, the 10.9 per cent disbursement/GNP ratio for Saudi Arabia would become 16 per cent and the 11.5 per cent for Kuwait would become 17.4 per cent, etc. Such ratios become much higher, of course, if we take the UNCTAD figures as a basis of calculation[6]. In all cases, including the most conservative estimates, the ratio for OPEC aid exceeds by several times the target long sought by developing countries and interested international organizations.

From the beneficiaries' point of view what matters most, however, are the amounts received and the terms on which aid is extended. The OECD estimates that the overall grant element in the concessional commitments of OPEC countries is as follows[7]:

1974	1975	1976
79%	72.3%	79.3%

The OECD/DAC practice in measuring the grant-equivalent of official development assistance is to use a rate of discount of 10 per cent. But no allowance is made for factors other than the specified terms of grants and loans. Yet the value of a loan to the recipient does not depend only on the rate of interest, the maturity and the grace period of the loans. Aid which is not tied to source has greater value to the beneficiary than aid given for purchases of goods and services from the donor country. Similarly, aid tied to a project may be (though the issue is extremely complex in this case) of less real value, in terms of volume, than the same amount given for balance-of-payments support. The World Bank calculates a "commitment deflator" on project loans, which is an index designed to take into account the fact that commitments in a given year will be disbursed over a number of years, five on average, thus reducing sharply their real value in a period of rapid inflation. Professor Henderson, among others, argued also that an allowance should be made, when measuring the grant element of aid, for tying the aid to source, as well as for such other factors as "the quality of technical assistance provided, the continuity and predictability of funds and the administrative efficiency of the agency which handles the aid programme in the donor country"[8]. However, all recognize that it may be difficult in practice to make even the roughest allowance for such qualitative factors.

When comparing the grant element of OPEC with DAC aid, figures for DAC should thus be reduced to allow for the costs of tying to source and probably to a lesser extent, because of tying in use. Comparability calls for further adjustments. The grant element is calculated for commitments, not disbursements. There is a larger discrepancy between volume committed and amounts disbursed in the case of OPEC (because of the sudden increase in OPEC aid in 1974) than in the case of DAC. Terms of the total OPEC committed aid tend, in fact, to be harder than the terms of the aid actually disbursed because recipients cash straight grants and budget support aid with greater ease than they draw on allocated loans for projects or other purposes[9]. In short, the grant element in OPEC aid is probably greater, in fact, than it may seem to be if one considers the commitments figures only.

Let us finally note on this issue of the terms of aid that official non-concessional flows represent a much larger proportion of OPEC than of official DAC aid. The concessionality element involved in some forms of OPEC financial assistance (such as direct deposits from the donor's to the recipient's Central Bank) tend to be grossly understated. The value of these deposits is greater than apparent from their terms as, in most cases, their effective duration is much longer in practice than their formal maturities. This allows recipients to avoid the tough liquidity problems which arise in connection with short-term commercial loans.

If the suggested adjustments were made it would probably appear that by 1976 the terms of OPEC aid had become at least as favourable to developing countries as those of DAC countries' official assistance where the grant element is estimated by OECD as follows:

1974	1975	1976
86.0%	88.6%	88.9%

The geographic distributional characteristics of OPEC aid after 1973 are of interest. There was an increase in the number of both donors and recipients immediately after the oil price adjustment. Before 1973 donors numbered three or four. Today, ten OPEC members have become international donors of some significance, and all thirteen members have contributed to the OPEC Fund. Some of the new donors have fairly low per capita incomes; several experience balance-of-payments difficulties, and a few are regular borrowers of foreign exchange on non-concessional terms in international financial markets.

The total number of recipients of OPEC concessional disbursements in the period 1970-1973 was 23 developing countries, including three low-income OPEC members. This number is estimated by UNCTAD at 42 in 1974, 55 in 1975 and 63 in 1976. Recipients of assistance from the OPEC Fund alone have so far been 60 developing countries. The high concentration on recipients neighbouring the major donors is now giving way to a larger geographic distribution, as shown in the following figures on bilateral concessional disbursements measured in terms of the proportion of funds received by Arab countries to the total:

	1973	1974	1975	1976
OECD	96.3%	73.9%	81.9%	64.5%
UNCTAD	96.6%	74.5%	80.5%	63.1%

A clear example of this trend to widen the geographic distribution of OPEC bilateral aid is manifested in the spheres of operation of the Kuwait Fund and the Abu Dhabi Fund which, restricted before 1974 to Arab League members, have been extended since that year to cover all developing countries. The Saudi Fund for Development, the Iraqi Fund for External Development and the Iran Organization for Investment and Foreign Assistance have from their inception included all developing countries.

In addition, there has been, after 1973, a considerable expansion of financial flows from OPEC countries to multilateral institutions which no doubt have also broadened, indirectly, the geographical spread of OPEC aid.

The second distributional characteristic of OPEC aid worth commenting upon is the allocation by purpose. Understandably, the share of technical assistance is very small. The equivalent for OPEC countries to commodity aid extended by DAC countries would be the concessional credits for the sale of oil extended by some OPEC countries, notably Iraq, Iran and Saudi Arabia. Other OPEC countries have arrangements to supply oil at reduced prices (e.g. the Venezuelan part-financing of oil sales to Central American countries), but this form of aid is very limited in scale. There are also some examples of support for the stabilization of the export earnings of recipient countries through such mechanisms as the special fund considered by Venezuela to finance the stockpiling of Central American coffee beans. The distinguishing feature of OPEC aid is, however, the very large share of budget or balance-of-payments support assistance. In bilateral concessional aid two-thirds of the disbursements in 1975 and four-tenths in 1976 was for general support assistance, compared with DAC's 11 per cent share in 1975.

The third, and perhaps more remarkable, characteristic is the diversification since 1973 of channels and modes of financial cooperation between OPEC members and other developing countries. The institutional channels for the granting and distribution of funds now consist of the following:

(i) National funds created for the purpose of providing external assistance, such as the Abu Dhabi, the Kuwait, the Saudi and the Iraqi Development Funds, and similar agencies which combine the task of foreign aid with investment at home, such as the Iran Organization for Investment and Foreign Assistance and the Venezuelan Investment Fund.

(ii) The OPEC collective aid facility, namely, the OPEC Fund.

(iii) Multilateral institutions established by some OPEC members and other developing countries such as the Arab Fund, the Arab Bank for Economic Development in Africa (ABEDA) and the Islamic Development Bank.

(iv) Nationally financed trust funds administered by multilateral institutions such as the Algeria Special Fund and the Nigeria Special Fund, administered by the African Development Bank and the Venezuela Special Fund administered by the Inter-American Development Bank.

(v) New multilateral institutions involving other developing and developed countries in the creation of which OPEC countries played a leading role, such as the International Fund for Agricultural Development (IFAD) and the projected Common Fund for commodities.

(vi) Existing multilateral institutions such as the World Bank, the IMF, UNDP and others, in receipt of contributions, grants or loans from OPEC member countries.

(vii) Central Banks and national Treasuries.

OPEC aid, through these channels, is taking a variety of forms. Bilateral aid includes long-term and medium-term balance-of-payments support grants and loans, project aid, central bank to central bank deposits, and banking guarantees under-writing commercial loans to developing countries. Multilateral aid involves straight contributions to international development agencies, as well as the creation of new multilateral institutions. Financial co-operation between OPEC and other developing countries has led to the establishment of joint companies for financial placements and direct investment in the Third World. Such bilateral arrangements have often involved third parties from the developed countries, thus widening the scope of the emerging phenomenon of "trilateral co-operation".

THE EXPERIENCE

Four years have elapsed since the dramatic events of October 1973, which inaugurated a new and important chapter in the history of OPEC aid. The time may have come to appraise, and to attempt to formulate the questions raised by this short but fruitful experience.

One, perhaps the most important, issue relates to the donors. What is prompting them to give aid? What are the motives, the justification, the legitimate interests? An explanation of the origins of OPEC aid may provide some useful clues. The first chapter of the history of OPEC aid concerns the emergence of Kuwait as a donor in the 1960s. In these early days Kuwait was already accumulating part of its oil reserves in the form of liquid assets and thus had the means to engage in financial co-operation with other developing countries. Yet the availability of funds is just an enabling factor. The motivation, surely, must involve the interests of the State in its international relations. Kuwait was a small country which was rapidly achieving economic prosperity and which had just acquired full political independence. The granting of aid was probably perceived as the instrument of an enlightened foreign policy, allowing the State to play a positive role in the area surrounding it and to achieve a measure of international recognition for the prosperous, peaceful and newly independent nation.

A second chapter opens in 1967 at Khartoum when Arab oil-exporting countries pledged themselves to provide Egypt, Syria and Jordan with substantial annual grants. The motivation here is readily understandable. The need to consolidate the Arab front in the context of a violent and much damaging regional conflict. Aid in this situation is a necessary act of solidarity linking a small group of neighbours sharing a vital common interest and a deeply rooted sense of community.

The third and major chapter in the history of OPEC aid begins as shown in earlier sections of this paper after the oil events of October 1973. The various sets of objectives and motivations which inspired earlier acts of financial co-operation continued to operate, acquiring, indeed, greater significance. A large component of OPEC aid, after 1973, is accounted for by the support given to Egypt and Syria by Arab oil-exporting countries. And it could be argued that a number of the smaller oil-exporting countries today find themselves in a similar situation to that of Kuwait in 1961, seeking through aid to play an international role commensurate with their new status as holders of the power and wealth of oil.

Aid could also be an effective instrument in creating a vested interest for the recipient countries in the continued prosperity of the donors. This factor has been strengthened by the responsible feeling of many OPEC governments of the need to strengthen the hand of developing countries during a period of immense economic stress where solidarity among all developing countries becomes all the more necessary if they aspire to reach more favourable deals in their relationships with the developed world. Indeed, the oil revolution has introduced new elements in this respect. One such element is that OPEC successes in raising the price of oil in such a dramatic and significant manner have put petroleum-exporting countries in the vanguard of the developing nations. The price of primary product exports is not simply an important economic issue for the Third World; it is a political issue which relates historically to the colonial past and the struggle for independence. Consciously or unwittingly, OPEC, by raising oil prices, has acquired a leading role in the demand for and the attempts to build a new international economic order. This role involves acts of solidarity within the Third World and the building up of networks of co-operation. Financial aid, given the availability of liquid assets in some OPEC countries, has been the natural way to express this solidarity. A further consideration may have enhanced the need to express this solidarity: the fact that the higher oil prices represent a financial burden on the oil-importing countries of the Third World. The OPEC position is that oil price increases do not create a case for compensation through aid. However, OPEC countries have been mindful of the special financial difficulties experienced by many developing countries in recent years. It would be paradoxical indeed if successful actions on the part of a group of developing countries, which correspond to deep aspirations of the Third World and which help the building up of solidarity, were allowed to develop damaging side-effects on those who are supposed to benefit. There is no case for sellers to compensate buyers for every significant price rise (at the limit, this would mean that prices should remain indefinitely fixed, which is absurd), but there is a case for alleviating burdens in the context of Third World solidarity to the extent that such a role could be played without appreciable harm to the donors.

Further, the emergence of substantial foreign exchange balances in the hands of a number of oil-exporting countries introduces an economic dimension in the donors' objectives. The difference between an OPEC and, say a Western world donor, is that the former has liquid assets in search of locations for placements, while the latter may be in search of markets for goods and services and outlets for foreign private investments. Oil-producing countries with financial surpluses have limited outlets for placements, and non-concessional flows to developing nations have come to be considered as an additional option in this area. The large component of non-concessional flows in total OPEC contributions to the Third World is largely explained by this state of affairs.

One could look at the question of objectives and motivations in a different way. Three main cases can be made to justify aid-giving: ethical, economic and political. *Ethical* considerations, however important, have in the past only explained a relatively small proportion of aid-giving activities in the world. They apply in cases of emergencies, natural catastrophes (such as famines and earthquakes) and similar distress situations (e.g. help to refugees). Ethical considerations also have begun to influence the allocation of aid, as distinct from its volume; hence, the concern recently displayed by some multilateral agencies in the plight of the absolute poor and to the problems of the Sahel countries. OPEC may, in this respect, be different from most DAC and Eastern bloc donors in that a good part of its aid is made in response to ethical and religious factors. Other motives could not explain most of the aid provided by the small members in the OPEC group to areas outside the region of direct political interest to them.

The case for aid made in terms of the donors' *economic* interest usually involves such arguments as the need to create commercial goodwill in Third World countries, or the need to strengthen and develop existing economic and trade ties and to create a favourable environment for foreign investment. It is sometimes argued by the supporters of foreign aid in industrialized countries that to foster economic growth in the Third World is enlightened self-interest, because advanced countries benefit more from economic progress than from economic stagnation in the rest of the world. OPEC donors do not, however, have an immediate interest in promoting crude oil exports – the major items of their merchandise trade. The promotion of other exports for most of them is indeed a premature exercise. As argued earlier, aid provides an opportunity for placement of funds in situations where placement on commercial terms is not always very attractive. The trade-off here is between diversification and returns. Financial co-operation between OPEC and other developing countries makes much economic sense in the area of joint ventures and investment in the productive sectors of developing economies. Some of that is taking place, but, unfortunately, not yet enough.

There are two *political* cases for aid. The first seems to apply exclusively to Western countries. It has been argued that foreign aid is the least costly course of action for governments faced with demands to help the Third World from lobbies within the donor countries. It is easier and politically more expedient to launch an aid programme than to remove trade barriers, allow immigrants in, facilitate movements of capital, etc. Whatever the relevance of that argument, it does not readily apply to OPEC aid. The second political case for aid is that its justification lies in foreign policy objectives. Broadly speaking, the existence of OPEC aid may be attributed in part to foreign policy, that is to the national interest in areas which involve other countries. This accounts in part for the large share of OPEC aid that is allocated to the donors' close neighbours. But foreign policy may be enlightened and in seeking its national goals the donor can be helping the building up of mutual interests. If financial co-operation between OPEC members and other countries, for example, contributes to the creation of a new international order, mutual interests are well served.

The experience of OPEC aid does not only raise issues about objectives but about instruments and means. Though the experience is short it is possible to seek to learn some lessons from the ways in which aid was conceived and managed and the ways in which it evolved.

There is no doubt that the suddenness with which the oil-price adjustment has taken place, and which allowed for a substantial increase in OPEC aid, has caught most donors by surprise. They simply lacked the time to elaborate an aid philosophy, to design elaborate sets of policies, establish procedures and organize all the efficient channels that the unexpected scale of aid operations required. It is remarkable that they managed what they did, but there were inevitable defects. The major drawback in such a situation is the temptation to respond fairly passively to the demands of the potential recipients, whether governments or international institutions, rather than to initiate the aid programme and implement it according to one's own priorities. The oil revolution seems to have fostered much impatience about immediate action. However, as time passes the OPEC countries are developing their own thinking on this matter through new institutions, methods and techniques.

However, the creation of a large number of new institutions for financial co-operation after 1973, necessary as it was, raises problems also. There is a danger of duplication, and manpower difficulties are often experienced. The pool of available talent is still so small in relation to the new demands for its services.

In its short experience OPEC aid faced the perennial problem of balancing the advantages of project and general support aid. The emphasis on project loans as a mode of financial assistance has known advantages and drawbacks. Project aid often involves long administrative processes with feasibility studies, economic apprais-als and the drawing-up of elaborate contracts. Donors may become victims of some illusion about the quality of the investment funded as the project-tied aid often releases other funds to finance different expenditures. The poorer and less developed countries, which are perhaps in the greatest need of aid are often least able to identify projects useful to the country and attractive to the donor. Project aid may inadvertently favour countries which have the specialized man-power resources for identifying projects and for promoting them to the donors. Donors may also find that they are committing and disbursing for project financing much smaller amounts than intended and that the distribution of their aid does not correspond to their preferred allocation. The advantages, however, are that project aid involves an element of technical assistance to the recipient; it ensures that certain standards are applied in the scrutiny and selection of projects; and it contributes in a certain way to an increase in the rate of investment in the recipient country. It also provides the donor with psychological and sometimes political rewards by associating him and identifying him to some extent with a concrete achieve-ment. However, disbursement flows in this type of aid, whatever the volume of funds allocated or committed, tend to be very con-strained. Hence, the significant recourse to general support grants and loans, which form a very large proportion of OPEC aid.

OPEC aid includes considerable contributions to the major inter-national financial agencies. One could argue that the contributors should have insisted from the outset on acquiring a role in the management of these agencies commensurate with their importance as contributors. Here again restraint was displayed suggesting that aid has not been fully used by OPEC members as a tool of foreign policy. Many developing countries are calling upon OPEC members to adopt a more aggressive policy in this respect for the promotion of the interests of the Third World in the agencies hitherto dominated by the developed industrialized countries.

Finally, OPEC members have not yet resolved in this short time the important issue of how much aid should be given on a bilateral basis and how much on a multilateral basis. At present, aid from OPEC as a group is provided through the OPEC Fund, an international account to which all member countries contribute. In this area what matters most is not the size of the collective facilities but the concerted action of member countries, which ensures a greater degree of effectiveness. Recent experience has revealed the advantages of collective and concerted efforts, especially in international fora where co-ordination among OPEC member countries has been effected through the OPEC Fund, such as in the case of the establishment of IFAD.

CONCLUSION: THE PROSPECTS

What are the likely prospects of OPEC aid in the immediate future and in the medium-term?

The volume of OPEC aid is not only large but in 1974–75 expanded suddenly at a very rapid rate. The events in the oil sector, which were associated with this expansion of aid efforts, were fairly unique and are unlikely to be repeated in the near future in the same way. Barring unforeseeable events, one should not expect, therefore, much growth in the gross volume of OPEC aid in the years to come.

It is likely, however, that the level of aid will remain high in the immediate future. Many of the forces and interests which motivated a large part of OPEC aid in recent years are not likely to disappear overnight. True, data on aid for 1976 show that commitments have declined, but this does not imply that disbursements will automatically decrease in the coming two or three years, as gross disbursements are yet to catch up with the abrupt and significant increases in commitments in 1974–1975. Since repayments are still many years ahead in most cases, the figure of net disbursements will remain close to that of gross disbursements for some years to come[10].

The prospects of OPEC aid beyond the short-term will be influenced by two factors: the manner in which aid is being channelled and the developments related to oil revenues. That part of aid which is channelled through the many institutions created by member countries will continue over time, as these institutions have their own capital endowments and are thus able to survive, even if confined to their present resources. That part of aid which is financed directly by governments may well be strongly influenced by developments related to oil prices and oil revenues. Though oil revenues and financial surpluses do not necessarily provide a case for aid giving, they are obviously the enabling factor. There is no need to indulge here in forecasts of future oil prices, as the main point is simply that stagnation or decline in revenues (if they take place) would inevitably affect the volume of aid that OPEC member countries could afford.

A further consideration is that needs of OPEC countries in respect of their own development are increasing. "Absorptive capacity", that is the ability to spend domestically on economic development, has a tendency to increase with time. As oil is a depletable asset, the priority given to domestic economic objectives becomes more, rather than less, important with the passage of time. Oil-exporting countries are increasingly aware that surplus funds at their disposal are not income but paper assets acquired in exchange for a natural asset on terms which are not, from their viewpoint, as favourable as suggested in the outside world. They depend crucially on these assets – whether financial or natural – for their economic future, and they have an important duty towards future generations in their countries, particularly since many have few or no resources other than depletable oil. Estimates of the accumulation of liquid assets of OPEC member countries as a group indicate at any rate a rapidly declining trend, and several OPEC countries have already switched from a net surplus to a net deficit position.

The medium-term may thus involve a decline in the volume of concessional flows for all the reasons mentioned unless revenues grow significantly. This decline, if it occurs, may, however, be partially offset by an increase in the volume of OPEC investments in other developing countries. Investments with adequate returns to both the OPEC investor and the host developing country may present at any rate a more balanced pattern of co-operation in the context of Third World solidarity, in view of the special nature of oil revenues and the future needs of OPEC countries. The slow pace of such investments which, by definition, require a long period of time to materialize, may, it is to be hoped, accelerate, paving the way to greater co-operation in this field. The trilateral venture formula which involves co-operation of third parties from the developed countries could help advance such a process especially when the legitimate interests of all parties are secured.

The level of sophistication of financial co-operation extended by OPEC countries, the modes of assistance and the patterns of allocation (irrespective of what happens to volumes) will also inevitably improve as the aid donors progress on the road to economic development. As there are gains to donors when the recipients' economies grow and progress, there may be gains to recipients when the donors become more developed, even if they lose, in the process, some of the false appearances of wealth.

(Annex of Tables to Chapter 3 may be found on p. 254)

CHAPTER 4

OPEC AID, THE OPEC FUND, AND CO-OPERATION WITH COMMERCIAL DEVELOPMENT FINANCE SOURCES

Based on a lecture to the "Chase World Forum on Arab Capital for Mid-East Financing and Third World Projects", New York, U.S.A., 20 September 1978. Published in The Journal of Energy and Development, *Boulder, Colorado, Spring 1979 (English) and* Oil and Arab Co-operation, *Vol. 5, No. 1, 1979, Kuwait (in Arabic).*

Among the concessionary sources of external finance available to developing countries, the OPEC Fund is probably the newest on the scene. It is, however, the one source that reflects the joint aid efforts of *all* OPEC members, that is, of practically all donor developing nations. Equally important, it is one of the sources keenly interested in the search for new solutions to the development problem. Not only does it work under more liberal articles of agreement than those governing other official aid agencies, it is also free, or, if one may say so, innocent, of the "long-standing policies" which often inhibit older institutions from trying untested ideas. Since the OPEC Fund is the collective aid facility of OPEC members, it is presented here in a wider perspective. Description of its activities will be preceded by general remarks on the assistance rendered by OPEC members as a whole to other developing countries. The analysis of the Fund's role will also be followed by an elaboration of the role Western banks can and, in this author's view, *should* play in project financing within developing nations, especially in association with the concessionary sources of finance, the traditional as well as the new.

OPEC AID

According to United Nations figures recently compiled, after a fourfold increase between 1973 and 1974, total *commitments* of OPEC donors to other developing countries increased by a further 22 per cent in 1975 to reach a figure in excess of $15 billion, which corresponded then to 7.5 per cent of the combined GNP (gross national product) of OPEC aid extenders[1]. The somewhat lower figures for 1976 and 1977 have remained, nonetheless, above the $10 billion mark. Actual net *disbursements* achieved, according to the same source, a near five-fold jump between 1973 and 1974 and were followed by a further 50 per cent increase in 1975 for a total net outflow of $11.5 billion, corresponding to 5.6 per cent of the donor's GNP (or to above 12 per cent of GNP, if we restrict the data to the four major *Arab* extenders). As a result of these developments, OPEC states occupied the first six positions in ranking among all donor countries of the world as regards the proportion of aid to GNP in 1976[2]. Two of them ranked among the six largest bilateral donors in absolute terms, Saudi Arabia being second only to the United States.

Although there is no justification for comparing the aid performance of the industrialized, rich countries with that of a group of developing nations, a few of which may be in possession now of large net liquid assets but none of which is developed in the economic sense, such a comparison yields startling results. The figure for total commitments from the DAC (the Development Assistance Committee of the Organization for Economic Co-operation and Development or OECD composed of the United States, Canada, Japan, and Western European states) has been estimated to be about $25.3 billion in 1975. All official flows from these countries reached $16.5 billion in the same year and remained roughly unchanged in real terms in subsequent years, corresponding to less than 0.7 per cent of the combined GNP of the donor countries[3]. Expressing this relationship differently, the commitments in 1975 of what amounts to less than a dozen OPEC donors represented more than 60 per cent of the DAC total, although the combined GNP of countries in the latter group was almost sixteen times as great as that of the former bloc. In 1977, OPEC members gave at least two and a half times as much as the United States did. If DAC countries were to give concessional assistance in the same ratio of aid to GNP as do OPEC members, they would have expended more than ten-fold what was actually expended in that year.

Set against this gross disparity between the aid ratios of OPEC members and DAC countries (not to mention the much poorer performance of the Soviet bloc) are two noteworthy features which provide a yet more vivid contrast. First, OPEC assistance, unlike much of the aid provided by DAC nations, is not tied to source while DAC flows are, almost inevitably, recycled back to the donors. One can say inevitably because even the un-tied DAC flows readily find their way back either to the donor country itself or to another Western economy, since DAC states constitute collectively by far the major source of procurement for the goods and services that recipients purchase. This, of course, results eventually in a much lower net aid transfer from the DAC extenders. On the other hand, OPEC aid brings no financial return to its donors. If anything, it actually helps two sources simultaneously: the developing, recipient countries as well as the developed nations from which procurements are made. (As a more cynical observer might put it, admittedly not without some exaggeration, aid may have its *recipients* in the developing world, but its *beneficiaries* are almost always in the developed world.) This distinguishing feature, coupled with the hard fact that OPEC aid is extended from revenues generated from exploitation of a commodity itself depletable (not from a renewable income yielded by industrial or agricultural production), makes the aid ratio comparisons even more disproportionate.

On the other hand, OPEC inflows, which are not and have not been meant to provide compensation for higher oil prices, accounted for the financing in 1975 of the equivalent of 99 per cent of the value of net oil imports of other developing countries as a whole. This aid exceeded the increase of the aggregate oil bills of Sub-Saharan African nations while reaching two to three times the value of incremental oil imports of many of the least developed countries. In 1976, OPEC inflows financed directly up to 26 per cent of the current account deficits of non-oil, developing states. In a broader sense, as the recent UNCTAD report used in this article confirms, "the entire deficit may be thought of as having been financed by OPEC capital exports recycled via the Eurocurrency and other financial markets."[4]

This OPEC aid is, of course, a relatively novel phenomenon in that it represents a transfer of resources from one group of *developing* countries to another. It is novel also because it has been swiftly extended through a broad range of channels combining bilateral, regional and multilateral sources. The OPEC Fund is just one among these channels. Although it has its own characteristics, its creation represents only the most recent of several initiatives taken by OPEC members to consolidate their position within and solidarity with the rest of the developing world.

THE OPEC FUND

Constituted in 1976, the OPEC Fund is the aid facility of the thirteen members of OPEC which have all signed its establishing agreement and contributed to its resources. The Fund began its operations in August 1976 with initial contributions of approximately $800 million. Subsequent contributions, some of which are earmarked for transfers to various international aid agencies, have brought the total contributions to date to something in excess of $1.6 billion. The transfer of funds to other agencies amounted to $481 million, thus making the net resources available to the OPEC Fund for its direct operations over $1.2 billion.

Basically the Fund is entrusted with two functions: that of co-ordinator of the joint OPEC members' policies and activities in the field of external assistance and that of a collective aid donor in its own right.

Briefly, in its *role of co-ordinator*, the Fund, or rather its Ministerial Committee and its Governing Committee, constitute the voice through which OPEC states have chosen to speak on various aspects of their external aid policies. Generally, the Fund has tried, since its foundation, to play a positive role in supporting new institutions and in developing appropriate policies to effect changes in international economic relations. The main objective is to achieve the establishment of the "New International Economic Order" through a maximum of action and a minimum of rhetoric. The participation of the Fund in the creation of the International Fund for Agricultural Development (IFAD), for example, was an effort in partial fulfilment of this objective. OPEC members contributed through the Fund $435.5 million (or almost half the initial capital subscriptions to that newly created institution), thus securing two-thirds of the voting power in IFAD's governing bodies for developing countries. Another instance is the interest shown by OPEC states in UNCTAD's Integrated Programme for Commodities and its main feature, the projected Common Fund. The primary purpose of the Common Fund is to provide assistance to individual commodity organizations for purchase and stocking of commodities when prices fall below an agreed level. Price support would then be provided when supply and demand conditions adversely threaten price and other economic effects to producers. The OPEC Fund was entrusted with the responsibility of co-ordinating the efforts of OPEC members in the negotiations for the establishment of the Common Fund. The financial contribution of these countries to the Common Fund will also be made eventually through the OPEC Fund. In another development, the Ministerial Committee, which oversees the activities of the Fund, was instrumental in arranging for the donation of the profits accruing to a number of OPEC states from the International Monetary Fund (IMF) gold sales to the OPEC Fund, which in turn donated these profits to the Trust Fund administered by the IMF. An arrangement with the United Nations Development Programme (UNDP), also in the form of a collective donation through the Fund, has been made to finance a number of the UNDP technical assistance regional projects. Yet another important facet of the Fund's role as co-ordinator concerns the activities of *national* aid agencies of the individual OPEC states. The task of co-ordinating the policies and programmes of these agencies is now entrusted to the Governing Committee of the OPEC Fund which has just started to play an active role in this field as well.

The Fund's major role as aid donor on highly concessional terms is, of course, the main reason for its coming into being. The Fund conducts basically two sets of lending activities: (1) it provides balance-of-payments assistance to countries with severe deficits in their current accounts and (2) it extends loans for economic development projects. All Fund loans have long maturities and all but a few of them have been granted free of interest.

Balance-of-payments loans, sixty of which have so far been made, are now generally extended on a smaller scale than in the past. At present, two criteria must be satisfied by an applicant country to benefit from this type of assistance: (1) the current deficit factor just mentioned and (2) the absence of quick-disbursing projects suitable for financing. Generally, when the Fund extends a balance-of-payments loan, the borrower (which in all cases is a government) agrees to deposit an equivalent amount in local currency to be used within a reasonable period of time for local cost financing of one or more development projects. When no such use is made of counterpart funds mobilized under balance-of-payment loans, the maturity of the loan itself is considerably reduced. This shortening of the loan repayment period is, in effect, an incentive to the governments concerned to mobilize domestic financial resources for the internal financing of projects that may not otherwise be realized. By and large, the Fund's experience with this type of assistance has been successful thus far as loan proceeds have been swiftly disbursed and, in the vast majority of cases, governments have opted to mobilize and use local counterpart funds for domestic projects. In fact, to date, some sixty-five projects in thirty-seven countries have been approved for financing with local funds totalling $160 million. Most of these projects were co-financed by other external sources and a few of them have benefited from additional foreign exchange financing from the Fund itself.

The second type of assistance extended by the Fund is in the form of direct project lending which has now become the Fund's major operational activity. This type of undertaking is carried out under a philosophy expressly propounded by the authors of the agreement establishing the Fund. They have taken great care to avoid creating another bureaucracy duplicating organizational structures and activities of other institutions. Rather, they have sought to create an institution empowered with swift decision-making capabilities, while maintaining a lean staffing structure to avoid the bottlenecks and delays so characteristic of larger, more formally structured bodies. Typically, when a well-studied project is submitted for the Fund's consideration, the time lag between receipt of the documentation and final approval is rarely more than three months. Some of the projects the Fund co-finances may be non-revenue earning and essentially social in character, or they may be of a commercial nature. In all cases, economic and social criteria are the paramount considerations in the decision to finance a project. Technical considerations, of course, are taken into account to evaluate the soundness of a project and in the case of revenue-earning projects, particularly those of a commercial nature, assured financial viability is also a requisite for the go-ahead decision. Up to the close of 1978, the Fund has committed $378 million for the financing of 107 projects (including the 64 projects financed by local counterpart funds). These commitments under our project loan portfolio have covered some sixty-one countries in the developing world, with "repeater" projects even in some of them, despite the relatively short period in which the Fund has been in operation. The projects financed have covered practically all economic sectors, with power having the largest share (30 per cent) followed by industry (27.3 per cent), agriculture (18 per cent), transport (14 per cent), public utilities (9.5 per cent), and telecommunication (1.2 per cent). Some of these projects are self-liquidating with their debt obligations serviced from cash-flow earnings; others are so-called "green-field" investments, that is, of a commercial nature but requiring complementary financing for basic infrastructure support, but most are simply infrastructure projects.

Project-related assistance has been extended swiftly, as attested by the number of projects so far financed. This is largely a result of the close working relationship established by the Fund with almost all the international development aid agencies, be they worldwide or of regional character, as well as with national aid agencies belonging to OPEC members. The essence of this relationship was laid down in the agreement establishing the Fund which specified that appraisal of projects to be financed by the Fund must be undertaken by "an appropriate international agency or by an agency of a member country". Again, the authors of the agreement, being fully aware of the danger of duplicating efforts in the field of international development assistance, directed the Fund to draw heavily on the talent and services of other established agencies for the administration of its loans. Implicitly, this has meant that the Fund would give priority to co-financing arrangements and, in fact, this has been the case in practice[5]. The advantages of co-financing arrangements are not restricted to the Fund's considerable savings in time and cost, although it should be mentioned here that the Fund incurs no cost for the appraisal and project-monitoring activities carried out by other institutions on its behalf. More importantly, co-financing allows for the immediate implementation of projects which might otherwise be indefinitely postponed until the financing gap could be filled. As is well known, such a postponement, if not avoided, almost always entails a widening of the very gap it was meant to help bridge due to cost overruns. For the Fund, this role of "gap financier" also makes it, in fact, a lender-of-last-resort and thus unlikely to be found in competition with other sources of finance for a given project. Being drawn in rather late in the project preparation cycle, the Fund is in a better position to give objective consideration to the merits of projects submitted for its partial financing. Moreover, the Fund has also been involved occasionally in the partial financing of "virgin" projects where it played a catalytic role seeking complementary financing from other sources, especially those to which it is closely linked.

Once a go-ahead decision for a particular project is made, co-operation with the other aid agency which has prepared and appraised the project is not terminated but extends to cover the project implementation period. The framework of this co-operation at the post investment stage is detailed in a letter of co-operation signed by the Fund and countersigned by the other aid agency which, in so doing, assumes the responsibility for administering the loan on behalf of the Fund. The first such co-operation was implemented in conjunction with the World Bank, and it now exists with almost all regional aid agencies and with practically all the national development funds of OPEC members. In each case, the loan administrator conducts the normal supervisory work required to monitor the overall progress of project implementation with the same diligence it would in administering its own loans. The Fund maintains the right to participate in supervisory missions for which it receives, in any event, both the terms of reference and the project progress reports. The loan administrator reviews withdrawal applications for the Fund loans and issues appropriate consent on which basis the Fund directly handles the disbursement process. Usually, there is provision for consultation on a regular basis among co-financiers and both parties agree to refrain from such unusual action as suspension or cancellation of the loan without mutual consultation. From the borrower's viewpoint, the absence of duplication of effort under such loan administration arrangements translates into obvious considerable gains.

CO-FINANCING AND ROLE OF COMMERCIAL BANKS

Co-financing of development projects in the Third World is a rapidly changing activity the rise of which in recent years has been limited mainly to sources of a concessionary nature. However, a number of these sources have been encouraging co-financing with private sources of funds, either through public issues by borrowing countries in the principal capital markets, through private placements by institutional investors, or by associating their financing with private bank loans.

Demand for capital from private institutions and commercial

banks in particular will, in my view, be increasing in the future. The reason is relatively simple. The capital requirements for infrastructure and commercial investments have grown and will continue to grow – as a result of increasing economies of scale reflected in project design, as a result of the rapid technological change which often translates into higher capital, and last, but certainly not least, as a result of the ever-present inflation. In fact, the increase in capital requirements of individual projects is becoming such that many investment undertakings are escalating beyond the financing means of any single source. For instance, the two most recent projects approved for co-financing by the Fund (the Arab Potash project in Jordan and the Guelb Iron Ore project in Mauritania) each required close to half a billion dollars in financing. Incidentally, the financial plans of both of these projects included substantial credits from commercial sources.

Looking into the future, the parade of projects where co-financing is not only feasible but perhaps mandated by capital needs and shortages seems endless. The trend towards higher commodity prices despite the currently flagging economic situation, with recovery in industrialized countries yet to gather pace, will improve the export performance of developing nations. This, coupled with the current trend of tighter economic and fiscal policies in the Third World economies and greater discipline in their economic management in general, will, it is hoped, bring about a decrease in lending risks and at the same time an increase in capital investments and requirements for economic development.

For these reasons, it would seem that project financing in developing countries by commercial banks offers significant potential. While the magnitude of external financing which may be or should be forthcoming from commercial banks can only be a subjective exercise at this time, there is no doubt that an acceptable level of external financing for developing nations, particularly those in the middle-income group, will only be achieved if commercial banks increase their exposure by substantial absolute amounts over the next several years.

On the macro-economic level, the surplus from which all sources of external finance draw could well be directed towards new productive investments in the deficit countries, if only to avoid continuous inflation as a mechanism for maintaining global balance. In other words, to the extent that the savings realized in certain regions do not result from dissavings in other regions, they will either have to be matched up with new real investments or lead the way to further inflationary pressures[6]. There is increasing evidence, however, that under full international exchange the relatively advanced developing states will have a clear advantage as the place for many types of new investment. Large commercial banks in the West share with aid agencies the role of intermediaries between surplus and deficit regions. Thus, in so far as they may succeed either directly or indirectly in the mobilization of surpluses for investment purposes in the developing world, they will be helping the strategies for maintaining a healthy world balance and achieving global development; there is also the probability of making a good profit in the meantime.

How, then, can the increase in commercial bank exposure come about without jeopardizing the financial position of these institutions in whose well-being we all share an obvious interest? In answering this question one must not lose sight of the special disadvantages of banks in terms of access to information about a country for purposes of risk assessment. Multilateral institutions, such as the IMF and the World Bank as well as the regional OPEC aid agencies, all with more ready access to the necessary information, should do their part by making available data on the extent of debt and other critical performance indicators in individual cases (with the consent of the governments concerned) and by encouraging exchange of views between commercial bankers and concessionary aid donors. The same concessionary sources may also play a more active role in involving commercial sources, be they in Western or OPEC countries, in their activities, at least in the cases where co-financing with the latter sources is likely to produce additional benefits to recipient nations.

Commercial and investment banks, on the other hand, could do their part by introducing some flexibility into their lending terms. Experience has shown that the success of commercial projects is more sensitive to cash flows than to the cost of borrowing for such projects. If commercial banks could grant longer maturities, the viability of projects, particularly large, capital-intensive projects with a very gradual cash flow build-up, might be enhanced. This, of course, raises the issue of the short-term nature of many OPEC deposits which, some will argue, stands in the way of allowing the banks to go into long-term lending. Such an argument, however, may be true for a particular bank but cannot be true for the banking system as a whole. It should, therefore, be possible for commercial banks to harness collective action under the guidance, or, if preferred, with the co-operation of the central bank on the national level and with the IMF on the global level, to help protect the banks against the risks involved in situations in which they receive short-term deposits but extend long-term credits. Efforts should also continue towards creating more favourable objective conditions and more flexible banking techniques that would make longer-term deposits a more attractive investment proposition.

In any event, the paramount benefit of co-financing is the increase in external assistance it brings. Strictly from this perspective, changes in maturities and even in interest rates that could result from co-financing may be of secondary importance. The OPEC Fund's experience, in a way unique, since co-financing has become the norm in its activities, has indicated certain areas in which co-financing with commercial banks may be desirable if not, indeed, ideal. One example is the case of "green-field" commercial investments for which basic infrastructure support is required. In these projects, commercial investments and development aid can be pooled for the benefit of all. Within appropriate financial packages, a project may be structured into different components depending on the type of financing required for each. The commercial component can be financed with equity and commercial loans, while the infrastructure component can be financed with concessionary aid. The overall return on the total amount of capital employed will be such as to ensure a strong incentive for all parties on the basis of the project's merits alone. Other benefits of this scheme are obvious; the concessionary sources would benefit from the opportunity of diversifying their aid, both within a borrowing country, if they have definite allocations for each nation, and, more generally, within the geographical sphere of their lending activities. The commercial banks would still get a fair return on their investment. And the developing countries could benefit most from this marshalling of greater amounts of external capital, with the obvious advantages of increased investment, speedier and more efficient disbursements, and savings in time and procedures.

One must realize, nonetheless, that a blanket increase in financial co-operation among concessionary and private sources of finance is easier said than done. It has been mentioned earlier that commercial banks do face particular problems in increasing their exposure in developing countries. Indeed, many of them already entertain the

view that they may have over-exposed themselves. The first difficulty is, of course, risk and, therefore, its appropriate assessment and
trade-off with reward. This article has touched on the contribution
that international aid institutions could play by disseminating, with
the approval of governments, the information at their disposal.
Another technique which could be applied more consistently is to
include a cross-default provision in the loan agreements of concessionary co-financiers which may enjoy a stronger security than
commercial banks for their investments. One could assume, however, that such a technique would be used only to stimulate the flow
of additional resources which would not be available otherwise on
reasonable terms.

So far, other banks have tried to cover the additional risk of
lending to developing countries with lower credit ratings mainly
through applying higher interest rates, the higher spread being a
self-insurance premium against default. One may ponder whether
the benefits, in the terms of cost savings to consumers, which have
resulted from the introduction of group plans in the insurance industry could be duplicated in the field of banking. Specifically, could not
the self-insurance sought individually by banks through their higher
interest rate be transformed into a collective insurance pool,
whereby risks would be uniformly spread in the industry and the
cost to the borrowers reduced accordingly? It is hoped that collective
self-interest would induce banks to work together for the establishment of such a scheme, which probably would receive also the
support of concessionary sources of finance. These in turn could
consider the possibility of guaranteeing commercial credits, again
substantially reducing the risks to commercial lenders. However,
this latter type of co-operation must translate into net additional
benefits to developing countries, in the form of reduced cost of
borrowing and incremental increases in capital transfer from commercial sources.

One should not minimize unduly the risks facing commercial
banks. The risks in commercial bank lending are real, although in
reality I think that the whole problem of the indebtedness of less-
developed countries (LDCs) is being magnified in the tendency to
treat all developing nations as a single homogenous group. Some
countries, no doubt, have relatively large outstanding debt burdens,
and some may even already have borrowed beyond their prospective
debt-servicing capacity. It is admittedly unfair, and, at any rate,

unrealistic to request commercial banks to increase their exposure in those countries. Such countries, unfortunately, may have to remain for a considerable time to come the favoured clients of the most concessional sources of finance. Yet, just as a sneeze does not necessarily mean pneumonia, the problem of a few should not be interpreted as the widespread problem of all. It is tempting to think at times that bankers are partly responsible for this tendency to generalize on the debt problem of LDCs. Nonetheless, when one reads that Chase Manhattan earned 65 per cent of its profits abroad in 1977 and Citibank a staggering 82 per cent, one cannot help but feel a bit uncomfortable with the perpetual single reference to the problem of debt on the part of LDCs as a constraint to more lending. These earning figures suggest, to this writer at least, that banks will maintain their outward-looking policy with regard to the developing world. The challenge now before them is whether they will be forward-looking as well.

While project co-financing between concessionary aid sources and commercial banks can be of mutual advantage to both types of institution, it does not offer the only appropriate channel for commercial banks to increase their project financing. Commercial banks are encouraged to embark unilaterally as well as more aggressively in project financing, even if it means diverting for this purpose part of their lending portfolio where the proceeds are generally not earmarked, and, as a result, the productivity is, at best, questionable. In fact, banks and similar financing institutions could focus their lending on well-chosen, self-liquidating projects where potential risks are certainly not greater than they would be in the case of general purpose lending. In addition to government guarantees for the loan, the tying of the repayment to project earnings provides further security. Some banks have built up impressive internal staff and capabilities to expand the finance of venture capital. Whether or not this will become a trend will depend on such factors as the initial success of the banks which equip themselves for this relatively new field of business; and on the co-operation they provide and receive from the larger multilateral agencies for aid, and from the borrowing countries themselves. The truth remains that an increase in project lending translates into greater real investment which, if related to sound priority projects, seems to offer, on a global basis, the solution to the problem of a world economy troubled with gross imbalances.

CONCLUSION

There has been much talk in the recent past about the interdependence of our world. International financial markets also have become sophisticated enough to dispense with the traditional classifications of "developed" and "developing" countries or "creditor" and "debtor" nations. International flows abound at present in all directions, at times by-passing the poor and helping the rich and at times leaving the former in the awkward position of financing the latter, as is often the case in domestic markets. It is indeed the responsibility of all sources of finance to see to it that adequate and enlightened management policies are developed to ensure not only the continuity and stability of such flows but their rational utilization as well.

Social justice and long-term stability dictate the imperatives of economic development in the less fortunate countries of the world, which still constitute the vast majority. Just as interdependence among countries is real, the plight of the developing world is real and should not be considered as a distant fading image that will eventually disappear through the work of unknown forces.

Greater access to capital is a complement to, if not a prerequisite of, the goal of expanded trade that will fuel economic growth in both the developed and the developing countries. Sound and fair trade policies are invariably essential also. But foreign exchange earnings will contribute only a portion of the financing required for economic growth in developing countries – a growth that must take place and will take place only with continued access to external finance. Hence, the great need for closer co-operation between the two types of institutions involved – the agencies in charge of financial assistance and those in charge of capital markets.

CHAPTER 5

THE WORKING RELATIONSHIP BETWEEN THE OPEC FUND AND OTHER DEVELOPMENT FINANCE INSTITUTIONS

First published in the OPEC Review, *Volume II, No. 3, Vienna, Austria, June 1978.*

INTRODUCTION

One of the major, though less noticeable, achievements of the OPEC Fund for International Development is its success in establishing, in a short operating period, dynamic working relationships with almost all the major international development finance institutions and the external development finance agencies of OPEC member countries. Such a working relationship did not merely involve the usual exchange of information and attendance of annual meetings. It covered, in fact, a variety of financial transactions, ranging from the Fund's active role in the setting up and financing of other development agencies to the pooling of resources in the financing of development projects. It also included the appointment of some of these agencies as loan administrators or disbursement agents of the Fund's loans. Such detailed arrangements were not preceded by general "frame-work agreements" of the type familiar in the practice of co-operation among international organizations. The latter agreements are often concluded after lengthy negotiations but generally require for their implementation the adoption of subsequent measures subject to further discussions and approvals. Co-operation between the OPEC Fund and other agencies was effected in most cases by a simple exchange of letters covering the specifics of the particular case to the satisfaction of the parties involved and according to agreed patterns that have gradually taken more or less standard forms.

The purpose of this short essay is to relate the experience of the OPEC Fund in this respect, which reflects its basic approach in assisting developing countries according to the most appropriate and the speediest channel available that would in each case serve the best interests of the recipient country. The great measure of flexibility maintained in the Fund's Articles of Agreement and adopted in the work of the Fund's Governing Board has paved the way to the successful implementation of this approach.

THE OPEC FUND AND NATIONAL DEVELOPMENT FINANCE AGENCIES

According to the Agreement Establishing the Fund, each Contributing Party (meaning, at present, each OPEC member country) designates a national institution to act as the Executing National Agency (ENA) of that country for the purposes of the Agreement. The ENA establishes in its records a separate account in the name of the Fund. In the initial period of the Fund's operations, disbursement of the proceeds of the Fund's loans were effected from such accounts to the Borrowers, either directly, or through the Fund's Central Account which was established by the Governing Board to facilitate disbursement of the proceeds of project loans, both the payment of loan proceeds and the repayment of loans are made through the Fund's Central Account.

In practice, most member countries which have national institutions for external assistance have designated these institutions as their ENAs (others have designated their Central Banks or their Ministries of Finance). As a result the Fund developed, almost automatically, a working relationship with each of the Abu Dhabi Fund for Economic Development, the Kuwait Fund for Arab Economic Development and the Saudi Fund for Development in their respective roles as ENAs for the UAE, Kuwait and Saudi Arabia. These institutions as well as the ENAs of other member countries were responsible for the direct disbursement to Fund Borrowers of almost $200 million representing the proceeds of the first fifty balance of payments support loans extended by the Fund. Furthermore, they were, in some instances, responsible for the investment of the balance of the Fund's accounts held by them pending the disbursement of loan proceeds.

Three ENAs – the Abu Dhabi Fund, the Kuwait Fund and the Saudi Fund – have also assumed the role of loan administrator on behalf of the Fund Management for projects in which each of them was involved, both as the appraising agency and the co-financier of the project. This expanded role was effected in the same mode of co-operation with international development institutions as under the co-financing and loan administration arrangements elaborated upon later in this paper.

THE OPEC FUND AND IFAD

The International Fund for Agricultural Development (IFAD) which started its operations on 13 December, 1977, is the most recently established international development agency. The concept of establishing this agency, with its distinctive characteristics, emerged from the resolutions of the World Food Council. The timely realization of the concept would not, however, have been possible but for the initiative taken by the OPEC Fund in committing $435.5 million for this purpose. This commitment, along with the pledge of $200 million from the US, paved the way for further commitments by other countries which finally enabled IFAD to reach, and even exceed, its declared target of $1 billion in initial resources. The contribution of the OPEC Fund was made under an Article in its Constituent Agreement which authorizes the utilization of the Fund's resources, inter alia, for "making contributions by Parties to this Agreement to international development agencies, the beneficiaries of which are developing countries".

The decision of the Governing Board of the OPEC Fund to grant to IFAD what amounted to more than half of the Fund's initial resources was specifically meant to help channel, in an acceptable institutional framework, additional and greater amounts from developed countries for the agricultural development of the Third World. It was also designed to enable IFAD to come into existence as the first feature of the long-sought New International Economic Order. Indeed, IFAD is not only the first universal financial institution practically under the control of developing countries, where they enjoy two-thirds of the voting power in the governing bodies, but it is also the only institution of its kind that places no obligation on developing countries to make financial contributions to its capital resources. The innovative voting structure in IFAD's councils, and the optional financial participation on the part of developing countries, were only achieved thanks to the massive contribution made by OPEC member countries through the OPEC Fund.

Although the OPEC Fund has no direct role in the functioning of IFAD (being merely the source of financial commitments made in the name of twelve OPEC member countries), it has provided the forum for co-ordinating the policies and the views of the representatives of these countries in IFAD's governing bodies. With one-third of the voting power vested in them, OPEC countries have thus followed a concerted and co-ordinated approach in IFAD's Preparatory Committee and Executive Board. This approach has definitely enabled the OPEC countries to play a leading role in shaping the policies of IFAD. As they are themselves developing countries with no self-serving interest in the financing process, they are playing this role for the sole purpose of enabling IFAD to reach the objectives stated in its Articles of Agreement.

The commitment of a large portion of the OPEC Fund's resources to IFAD did not preclude the former from directly financing agricultural projects in developing countries. Thus, the possibility of future co-operation between IFAD and the OPEC Fund in the co-financing of development projects and programmes presents a new opportunity for a working relationship between the two institutions.

THE OPEC FUND AND THE IMF

The OPEC Fund has greatly benefited from the experience of the IMF in devising its first lending programme which involved providing balance of payments support loans to the most seriously affected countries. Furthermore, it continues to draw from the IMF's data on balance of payments, debt service and current accounts of developing countries and their situation with respect to reserves. But co-operation between the two institutions was not limited to this one-sided relationship. A few months after the OPEC Fund started its operations, eight OPEC member countries indicated their willingness to donate to the OPEC Fund the profits accruing to them from the IMF sales of gold, with the understanding that the OPEC Fund Governing Board will in turn authorize the donation of these profits, as they accrue, to the Trust Fund to be administered by the IMF.

This initiative, so far taken by six OPEC member countries, helped implement the decision establishing the IMF Trust Fund, which had received from the OPEC Fund on 31 December 1980 more than $110 million, representing the profits accruing to Iraq, Kuwait, Qatar, Saudi Arabia, UAE and Venezuela from the IMF gold auctions undertaken before that date. Larger amounts are yet to be transferred to the IMF Trust Fund under this arrangement. A noteworthy feature of this relationship between the OPEC Fund and the IMF is that OPEC Fund members have willingly transferred resources from an agency where they have exclusive control to an agency subject to the control of the IMF Executive Board, where OPEC countries exercise only a marginal voting power. The objective was to allow for a speedy implementation of the decision to establish the IMF Trust Fund through which eventually larger amounts would reach developing countries facing acute foreign exchange difficulties.

THE OPEC FUND AND THE UNDP

In the early stages of its operations, the OPEC Fund was approached by the UNDP for financial assistance to help fill a gap in its projects' budget. The Governing Committee of the Fund, in an initiative meant to promote co-operation among developing countries through the institutional framework of the UN, decided to grant $20 million for specific UNDP projects of regional or global character. Seven of these projects have already been selected by the Governing Committee from the list of projects submitted by UNDP. They include projects in different regions of the world related to such fields as energy, food production, rural and urban development and training activities. The UNDP "project document" for each of these projects is discussed with the OPEC Fund Management before it is signed with the beneficiary countries and the OPEC Fund maintains a role in the follow-up and the supervision of its implementation. As the execution of the projects involves, in many instances, other UN executing agencies, this arrangement has also opened up several opportunities for co-operation between the OPEC Fund and UN specialized organizations. Through its participation, the OPEC Fund attempts, in particular, to speed up the process of implementing some UNDP projects which, despite their importance, have experienced some delays.

CO-FINANCING AND LOAN ADMINISTRATION IN PROJECT LENDING

The authors of the Agreement Establishing the OPEC Fund were fully aware of the danger of duplicating efforts in the field of international development assistance. Far from intending to create a new bureaucracy, they meant the Fund to be managed by a small, but efficient staff that would speedily channel financial assistance to other developing countries under the collective name of OPEC. In so doing, the Fund would benefit to the utmost from existing facilities, both international agencies and national institutions of member countries, rather than build up a large administrative structure of its own with the inevitable results of high cost and slow performance. Under the Agreement, the appraisal of projects to be financed by the Fund has thus to be undertaken by "an appropriate international development agency" or may be entrusted to an ENA or any other agency of an OPEC member country as the Governing Board may decide. Once a project is approved for financing by the Fund, the Governing Board must entrust again an ENA or "an international development agency of a world-wide or regional character" with the task of the day-to-day administration of the Fund's loan. (After the amendment of the Agreement Establishing the Fund on 27 May 1980, the Fund was also given the power to appraise directly and administer directly project loans.)

Within this framework, the Fund's Governing Board gave clear priority to the co-financing of projects, on a joint or parallel basis, with other development finance agencies. Through such co-financing arrangements, it was possible for the Fund to finalize, in less than one year, twenty-six project loans in twenty-four countries in Africa, Asia and Latin America. Many of these projects involved more than one co-financier, allowing the Governing Board a greater choice in selecting the loan administrator of the Fund's loan. Only in a few cases, such as the Fisheries project in Vietnam and a power project in Ghana, was the Fund the sole external financier for reasons irrelevant to the soundness of the project and the seriousness of the Borrower's development efforts. Nevertheless, it was possible in these particular cases to entrust the tasks of appraisal and loan administration to the other international development institutions which readily undertook to perform these tasks on behalf of the Fund.

The advantages of co-financing arrangements are not restricted to the great saving in time and cost to the Fund. (All appraisal and administration work is done at no cost to the OPEC Fund). It allows for the immediate implementation of projects that may otherwise be indefinitely postponed until the financial gap is filled, a postponement that almost certainly leads to the widening of the gap due to the rise in cost in the meanwhile. By providing the complementary financing required, which may involve a relatively small portion of the entire cost of the project, greater available resources would be put to good use. Such arrangements also allow for a greater contact among various sources of external assistance. In turn, through this contact the newer agencies stand to benefit from the experience of the previously established agencies and may at times positively influence their future policies. Both these aspects have already been demonstrated in the short experience of the OPEC Fund, especially when it has been involved in the early stages of loan negotiation and in cases of extending lines of credit to local development banks.

Co-operation with each of the loan administrators has been simply effected by virtue of a letter sent from the OPEC Fund Management to the agency requested to administer the loan. The letter specifies the mutual rights and duties of the OPEC Fund and the loan administrator and is counter-signed by the latter as evidence of the acceptance of its contents. The first letter of this type was negotiated between the OPEC Fund and the World Bank. Identical letters, with minor modifications, were readily accepted by other agencies. Each international development finance agency requested to perform the administration of OPEC Fund loans has undertaken to do so "with the same degree of care as it uses in the administration of its own loans". The loan administrator receives the withdrawal applications (of which a copy is always sent to the OPEC Fund) and upon processing them requests payment from the OPEC Fund to the Borrower. The OPEC Fund maintains a close supervision of the disbursement process, the right to participate in the supervision of the project implementation and the right to terminate the administration arrangement.

CONCLUSION

In less than five years of operations, the OPEC Fund has directly provided 112 loans, 95 of which are directed towards financing the foreign cost of development projects and are administered by such agencies as the Kuwait Fund, the Saudi Fund, the Arab Bank for Economic Development in Africa (BADEA), the Asian Development Bank (ADB), the Inter-American Development Bank (IDB), the International Development Association (IDA), the Islamic Development Bank (IsDB) and the World Bank (IBRD). The OPEC Fund has also participated in meeting the local cost of 110 projects, in 78 of which other external development agencies are involved as co-financiers. It has also helped create IFAD, has participated in the financing of the IMF Trust Fund and has committed grants for seven regional UNDP-sponsored projects. Simultaneously, it maintains close contacts with UNCTAD, for the promotion of the Common Fund for Commodities; with UNIDO, for the promotion of new industrial projects in developing countries; and with FAO, IFAD and the World Food Council, for the development of the agricultural sector in the Third World. In terms of the type and volume of operations and the pace of commitments and disbursements, the OPEC Fund may well have served some of the purposes for which it has been established. A good part of this achievement is due to the working relationship the OPEC Fund was able to develop with other international development finance agencies and with the external assistance agencies of OPEC member countries. The co-operative spirit expressed by all such agencies in their transactions with the OPEC Fund and the smoothness and efficiency which has characterized this co-operation must be acknowledged as a major factor in enabling the OPEC Fund to generate a wide impact in such a short span of time.

CHAPTER 6

THE OPEC FUND AND THE
NORTH-SOUTH DIALOGUE

Based on a lecture before the Austrian Society for Foreign Affairs, Vienna, Austria, 25 April 1979. First published in Third World Quarterly, *Volume 1, No. 4, London, October 1979.*

When I use the words "North-South Dialogue", I do not simply mean the Conference on International Economic Co-operation (CIEC) held in Paris in 1975-7, which brought together eight industrial countries and nineteen developing nations. The protracted talks at that Conference made the headlines for a while, but soon receded into oblivion. I am concerned more with the whole gamut of continuing discussions between the developed countries of the West and the developing countries of Africa, Asia and Latin America. In terms of peoples (rather than states), this represents a relationship between a population of approximately 700 million, partaking in 1977 of a GNP close to $5,000 billion (or about $7,000 per capita), and a population of over 2 billion, but sharing a GNP slightly above $1,000 billion in the same year. The last figure would be even lower if we exclude the relatively high income (above $1,000 per capita) countries among the developing nations, as it would leave an aggregate GNP of only $450 billion for a population of more than 1.6 billion (about $280 per capita). This great disparity in relative wealth is even more drastically reflected in the marginal share of the South in the world's economic activities. Even after including China, the South, with seventy per cent of the world population, accounted in 1977 for only nineteen per cent of total gross world product, twenty per cent of world trade and investment, seven per cent of world industry and less than one per cent of research and services.

The issues that have divided the "have" countries of the North and the "have not" countries of the South, cover a wide range. They are adequately spelled out in the resolution on Development and International Co-operation adopted by the UN General Assembly's Seventh Special Session in September 1975. This resolution invited all countries to join in the search for solutions to world problems, pointing in particular to: international trade; transfer of real resources to developing countries; international monetary reforms; science and technology; industrialization; food and agriculture; co-operation among developing nations; and restructuring the economic and social sectors of the UN system[1].

Ironically, the lengthy discussions of these issues have been generally characterized by a lack of real dialogue. In fact, it has been more in the vein of a "collective monologue", where each participant speaks only of his own worries, assuming that the matter must be uppermost in the minds of his interlocutors.

LOOKING BACK AT PARIS

A few comments on the Paris Conference may help in placing the North-South parleys in their proper perspective. Although the Conference did not signal the beginning or the end of the dialogue, nonetheless it had the merit of constituting a forum where the problems, though by no means solved, were thoroughly examined and articulated. It helped focus world attention, in particular, on the problems of development aid, primary commodity exports, external debt and, in general, on the increasing gap between North and South. The Group of Nineteen came to Paris with the optimistic expectation of implementing the challenging recommendations of the UN Seventh Special Session. To their chagrin, the outcome of the Conference lagged behind the goals conceived for a broad and fair programme leading to the creation of NIEO. The rich countries, on the other hand, did not offer any support for proposals dealing with structural changes in the international economic system. Their commitments, as perceived by the developing countries, were mostly concerned with minor concessions on the subject of international aid and trade.

With respect to the issue of financial and development assistance to the South, the industrial nations agreed to contribute $1 billion in a "Special Action Programme" in order to help to meet, on highly concessionary terms, the urgent needs of the low income countries "facing general problems of transfer and resources". Of this amount,

$385 million was later entrusted by the EEC to IDA for use in future project and programme assistance to be disbursed over a number of years. Sweden and Switzerland have since cancelled some debts of the least developed countries totalling $55 million. The developed North also concurred, without specific commitments, in the necessity of increasing official development assistance in real terms. Part of this assistance was to be assigned for the expansion of food production in developing countries. Specifically, it was agreed only to set up a minimum target of ten million tons of grain per annum for food aid, a target which remains unfulfilled to date.

In the area of trade, the agreed arrangements were expressed in general, if not vague, terms, including such points as:
(a) further co-operation in primary commodity marketing and distribution;
(b) assisting developing countries in their attempts to diversify domestic production and exports;
(c) working out measures to cope with the problem of synthetic goods so as to ease their impact on natural products;
(d) establishing a generalized system of preferences more favourable to the developing countries;
(e) giving special and advantageous treatment to the developing nations in Multilateral Trade Negotiations (MTNs)[2].

One important commitment in this area of trade, which would later lose much of its original comprehensive content, was agreed upon in principle by the industrial countries, namely the agreement to establish a Common Fund, to finance buffer stocks for certain primary commodities of export interest to the South.

Finally, in the field of energy, no more than a restatement of the obvious was made, spelling out the importance of energy availability and supply, recognition of the depletable nature of oil and gas (and the necessity of a gradual shift from an "oil-based energy mix to more permanent and renewable sources of energy") and the significance of conservation and increased efficiency of energy use and, lastly, the need to develop all forms of energy.

At the conclusion of the Paris Conference it was not surprising, therefore, to see the developing countries express their regret on having most of the proposals for structural changes, and some other suggestions dealing with crucial questions, discarded by the North. As to the latter, its expression of regret mainly centred on the lack of agreement on issues related to "co-operation" on energy.

Following the Conference, the negotiations between the industrial and the developing countries were scattered among several bodies. The issue of commodities was left to UNCTAD; compensatory financing to the IMF-IBRD Development Committee; the matter of external debt to both UNCTAD and the Development Committee; development and balance of payments to IMF and IBRD; and the question of access by developing nations to industrial markets to GATT.

In all of these assemblies, and on most important issues, the developed countries generally reacted in a negative way to the demands of the developing countries[3]. Whenever their response was positive, it came late, offering at times too little. At the root of this failure lay the seemingly incompatible North-South differences, as each saw the world through different lenses: the developing nations calling for fundamental and structural changes in the existing production and exchange systems, and the developed countries favouring only marginal adjustments. A broad consensus among both sides on principles and objectives, therefore, remains a remote target.

THE OPEC FUND

The adjustment of the price of oil and the financial surplus it generated, coupled with the growing scarcity of supply of this strategic commodity, have all given the oil-producing countries of the South a new bargaining position, placing them, at least temporarily, in the vanguard of developing countries in their quest for a new world economic order. Developed countries became willing and, indeed, anxious to negotiate the energy issue with the oil-producers. The latter, in turn, took this unique opportunity to ask for a reconsideration of the whole range of issues of particular interest to developing countries. They played a leading role in the Sixth Special Session of the UN General Assembly which resulted in the adoption of the Declaration and Programme of Action on the establishment of NIEO. When invited later to discuss energy problems with the major consumers, they insisted that the Paris Conference be a forum for a comprehensive North-South Dialogue and not merely a meeting of oil producers and consumers. The "Solemn Declaration of Algiers" issued by the heads of state of OPEC countries in March 1975 outlined the strategy which OPEC countries were to pursue in this respect and put particular emphasis on their role in strengthening the solidarity of the Third World.

The OPEC Fund has appeared in this context as a response to the need for a greater degree of co-operation among developing countries. Behind its creation was the necessity to promote more successfully their demands for the establishment of a new system which would lead to rapid economic development and better prospects for the gradual and effective elimination of poverty.

The OPEC Fund is a manifestation of the joint aid endeavours of all OPEC member countries. It is their collective financial facility for providing concerted support to other developing countries, in addition to the existing bilateral and multilateral channels through which they have individually extended considerable and diversified assistance.

OPEC AID IN GENERAL

It may be relevant, at this point, to see what OPEC aid consists of. According to recent UNCTAD data, OPEC aid in terms of total commitments increased fourfold between 1973 and 1974. It rose by another twenty-two per cent in 1975, reaching a level in excess of $15 billion. This level represented 7.5 per cent of the OPEC donors' aggregate GNP, or sixty per cent of the estimated commitments of the developed countries in that same year. In 1976 and 1977, OPEC commitments were somewhat lower than in 1975, but they remained above $10 billion a year[4]. Owing to these developments, some OPEC countries now occupy a very high ranking among all donor countries of the world both in absolute terms and, more particularly, with respect to the ratio of aid to GNP. They fill the top six places in terms of the proportion of aid to GNP, and two of the six highest positions in absolute terms. On the basis of the second indicator, Saudi Arabia now holds the second place among all donors, preceded only by the US.

What should be kept in mind is that this assistance is provided by a group of developing countries which identify themselves with the interests and aspirations of the recipient countries, and still face many of their problems.

In the context of the "Second Development Decade" which began on 1 January 1971, it was envisaged that net flows of financial resources from developed countries, amounting to one per cent of their GNP, would be needed in order to sustain in developing countries a minimum average rate of growth of six per cent per annum. It was also recommended that seventy per cent of the net capital flows should be in the form of Official Development Assistance (ODA). These guidelines were accepted in principle by the DAC countries (OECD members). However, the performance remained far below the target figures, as DAC flows represented only an average of less than 0.4 per cent[5] of the GNP of these countries. The authors of DAC's *Development Co-operation Report* themselves qualified the record of DAC aid as "disappointing". Official statements supporting increased commitments have been made by several governments in the industrial countries, but the overall record of development assistance has actually shown a decline in real terms. The latest available figures from OECD sources show that aid disbursements fell in 1977 to 0.31 per cent of the GNP of donor nations. Development assistance of the socialist countries in the form of credits to the South is even less substantial and has been diminishing; in 1975-6 it represented only two per cent of total net financing aid as compared with seven per cent in 1971.

The main impact of these trends has been to slow down the pace of growth in the developing countries, particularly the poorer ones which rely heavily on ODA to add to their scarce domestic resources.

It is relevant here to note also an important characteristic of OPEC aid: the assistance provided is not tied to any given source of procurement. There is an increasing awareness of the favourable impact of such non-tied aid for the economic advancement of the recipient countries. Undeniably, the attempt to achieve trade promotion for the donor through aid reduces the real value of the assistance and often fails to meet the best interests of the aid beneficiaries. At least half of the aid from DAC sources remains tied to procurement in the donor country, resulting ultimately in a lower net aid transfer to the developing nations.

OPEC aid is not only non-tied, it is also positively used to finance procurement from other countries, generally the developed countries of the North. In other words, the financial co-operation between two groups of developing countries inevitably involves substantial and, at any rate, unquestionable benefits to the advanced countries, in view of the inability of the economies of the OPEC donors (which are developing countries themselves) to provide the goods and services in demand.

OPEC FUND ASSISTANCE

The role of the OPEC Fund as an aid donor should be seen within the framework of OPEC aid in general. The OPEC Fund is not only one of the many facilities through which OPEC countries extend their assistance to the rest of the developing countries; it is also the instrument of co-ordination among such national facilities.

First of all, the OPEC Fund extends direct concessional loans to developing countries other than OPEC members. Since the start of its operations in August 1976, the OPEC Fund has launched three lending programmes including both balance-of-payments support loans and project lending assistance. Total OPEC Fund resources so far amount to about $1.6 billion and out of this sum over $742 million has been approved under the three lending programmes. Of this latter amount, $447 million (representing 113 loans extended to 66 countries) has actually been committed and about fifty-eight per cent of the committed amounts has already been disbursed. In addition, fourteen loans involving close to $90 million will soon be signed.

The First Lending Programme was undertaken in the form of a balance-of-payments support programme, involving an amount of $200 million allocated for the purpose of assisting the Most Seriously Affected (MSA) countries in the world. All the recipients represented countries with an average income per capita of below $200 in 1974. They all depend overwhelmingly on agriculture and face conditions of serious economic instability. In March 1977, the OPEC Fund took on its first major project lending operation after the allocation by its Governing Committee of about $142 million for this purpose. The countries which were to benefit from these funds numbered thirty-eight and were distributed over a wide geographical area encompassing Africa, Asia and Latin America. The Third Lending Programme was initiated with $400 million and its implementation began in July 1978. It covers both balance of payments support loans and project loans to some sixty-five countries with a per capita income of less than $750 in 1975. All loans have long term maturities, and all but a few have been provided interest-free. Owing to the softness of the terms, the overall grant element of OPEC Fund aid, on the basis of the customary discount rate of ten per cent, has been very high in most cases, ranging between sixty and seventy per cent.

The figures just cited may not indicate much in terms of magnitude, especially when related to the huge needs of the developing countries concerned. Nonetheless, the OPEC Fund, together with the other aid facilities of OPEC countries, in the last two years has been channelling nearly thirty per cent of the total amount received by these countries on ODA terms. The OPEC Fund places particular emphasis in its project loans on the financing of energy and food production to lessen the dependence of developing countries (whose precarious situation is particularly vulnerable) in these two vital sectors.

In addition to its lending activities, the OPEC Fund has contributed substantially to international institutions and mechanisms which promote the objectives of NIEO. These have so far included the International Fund for Agricultural Development (IFAD), the Common Fund and UNDP. If endowments to various international organizations are included, actual OPEC Fund commitments stand close to $1 billion.

THE OPEC FUND AND IFAD

An important step was taken in November 1974 in Rome by the UN sponsored World Food Conference. It adopted a resolution related to the establishment of IFAD to finance agricultural development projects primarily for food production in the developing countries. There is little doubt that this resolution would have succumbed to the same fate that has befallen a number of other international schemes, were it not for the OPEC Fund. Through a sizeable commitment of $435.5 million, the OPEC Fund helped to turn the idea into a reality. Its contribution served as an effective catalyst in the mobilization of other capital, since it was made conditional on the contribution by developed countries of at least sixty per cent of the $1 billion target.

OPEC Fund involvement in IFAD stemmed from the recognition of the urgency of a very rapid increase in food production in the developing world. The problem of matching food demand and supply is very acute. A substantial investment, both technical and financial, is required in order to deal effectively with the issue at hand.

Significantly, IFAD represents, on the other hand, the first multilateral aid institution where developing countries have a controlling role. Holding two-thirds of the voting power in the governing bodies, these countries are more certain to exercise a major influence on investment decisions for the resolution of their problems. The structural innovation is that voting power is shared equally by three categories of members: developed countries, developing donor countries (namely, the OPEC group) and other countries. This structure provides an interesting example of an international financial undertaking to mobilize additional concessional funds for agricultural development within an institutional framework more suited to the requirements of NIEO.

The agreement establishing IFAD came into force in November 1977. The OPEC Fund has followed the progress of this important forum closely. It acts as the co-ordinator among OPEC member countries on issues towards which they have adopted a unified approach, and by so doing attempts to ensure a more decisive role for these countries to the benefit of the rest of the developing world.

THE OPEC FUND AND THE COMMON FUND

At UNCTAD IV in Nairobi (1976), an Integrated Programme for Commodities (IPC) was adopted in recognition of the need for "an overall approach" to commodity problems, as opposed to the earlier partial efforts or commodity-by-commodity approach which had failed to produce acceptable results. The key IPC proposal was concerned with the setting up of a Common Fund to finance commodity schemes of export interest to developing countries. The Common Fund thus came to be considered by the developing countries as an integral part of NIEO[6]. Their hopes were somewhat raised when in June 1977 the nations participating in CIEC in Paris agreed that a Common Fund should be created as a new entity that would be instrumental in achieving the agreed targets of IPC. Soon, however, the Third World came to realize that the way to an agreement that would lead to decisive action was long and difficult. By November 1977, at the end of the Second Session, there was still no agreement even on the most basic elements.

In its efforts to promote the establishment of the Common Fund as a basic feature of NIEO, the OPEC Fund has been present, though officially only as an observer, in the negotiations related to this issue. This participation was to reflect the willingness, expressed since UNCTAD IV in Nairobi, of OPEC member countries' to lend their full support to the Common Fund. Accordingly, in March 1977, the OPEC Ministerial Committee of Financial and Monetary Matters determined that co-ordination among OPEC countries in the course of negotiations for the creation of a Common Fund was to be accomplished through the OPEC Fund. In August 1977, the same Committee stipulated that future contributions by OPEC countries to the Common Fund would be made through their collective aid facility, namely the OPEC Fund.

This support is motivated by the concern of OPEC countries with the stabilization of export commodity prices which is in the interest not only of the developing countries, but also of the world as a whole. The Common Fund is meant to enable all countries to cope effectively with the cyclical vagaries of supply and demand, and thus bring about stability, a necessary condition for sustained growth.

Despite the lack of success in a number of successive UN negotiating conferences, UNCTAD maintained its optimism as to the achievement of a workable compromise. In November 1977, it declared that it would meet the contribution of all OPEC countries to the Common Fund and called for the adoption of a realistic approach in determining the size and role of that Fund. A year later, the OPEC Fund, perceiving the need to boost the developing countries' concept of a Common Fund endowed with its own capital resources, announced a new initiative. It declared its readiness to provide financial support to all the least developed countries to help them meet their contributions.

The UN Negotiating Conference resumed its deliberations in March 1979, after the Group of 77 had redefined its position more realistically. The participants finally agreed to set up the Common Fund with $400 million to finance buffer stocks (the so-called "first window") and $350 million to promote research and development with regard to improved marketing conditions for raw materials (the "second window"). Each member country must initially subscribe $1 million, plus an additional contribution on a scale in line with its size and wealth. The initial subscriptions are supposed to bring in cash $150 million, on the optimistic assumption that 150 countries will participate in the Common Fund. Out of this $150 million, $80 million will go to the "first window" and $70 million to the "second window". It leaves $320 million for the buffer stock fund which will come from additional contributions and $280 million for the "second window" to be met by voluntary donations.

No one can claim that the amounts of money now involved will allow for an effective Common Fund with the comprehensive mandate envisaged for it in Nairobi three years ago. Compared to the original proposal for a $6 billion Fund, what is offered now is a Fund which cannot be "common", and can hardly be the sole banker of the commodities involved. Even the voting structure which reserves to the developing countries forty-seven per cent of the voting power, has been adopted with reluctance by the industrial countries, with the US already planning to seek a revision of the agreement in this respect. The battle for establishing a viable Common Fund is thus not yet won. The role of the OPEC Fund in the creation of a Common Fund suited to the interests of developing countries is, therefore, yet to be fully accomplished.

THE OPEC FUND AND UNDP

Shortly after the commencement of activities, its Governing Committee, in the spirit of furthering co-operation among developing countries, approved a grant to the amount of $20 million to technical assistance projects assisted by the UNDP. This organization, which has been instructed by the UN General Assembly to assist in implementing a programme of action for NIEO, was to use the proceeds of the grant for specific regional and global projects chosen jointly with the OPEC Fund. Such projects were to promote technical co-operation among developing nations, to encourage and co-ordinate studies and programmes, and to increase technical and scientific knowledge. The regional ventures thus undertaken are related to such diverse fields as energy, mineral and fuel surveys, regional infrastructure development and manpower training as indicated by the following list:

(a) Central American energy programme;
(b) development of the Niger River basin;
(c) technical support for regional offshore prospecting in East Asia;
(d) development of the Red Sea and Gulf of Aden fisheries;
(e) Caribbean regional food plan;
(f) industrial vocational centre in the Suez Canal region;
(g) labour-intensive public works programme;
(h) UNCTAD Research and Training Centre;
(i) International Centre for Diarrhoeal Disease (Cholera) Research in Bangladesh;

(j) desert locust emergency assistance.

The new UNCTAD Research and Training Centre, about seventy per cent of whose total budget for the first three years will be funded by the OPEC Fund, presents a case in point. It will offer specialized orientation and training courses in each of the developing regions, through their own institutions, and should help raise the level of understanding of the trade and development issues. It should also contribute to the elaboration of effective action-orientated policies in the area of international economic relations and help to develop and organize programmes of research on economic questions that are of vital importance to developing nations.

The list of UNDP-assisted projects shows the concern of the OPEC Fund for operative projects that go beyond the mere preparation of studies and plans. In the details of each project, the OPEC Fund has been particularly seeking specific results of obvious advantage to the countries concerned.

OPEC FUND RESEARCH AND TRAINING

It need not be stressed that developing nations suffer from a lack of planning and research to support their efforts towards the building of NIEO. This situation underlines the urgent need for organization and adequate co-ordination in order to develop an effective strategy for these countries, individually and as a group. Compared to the developed North, the Group of 77 lacks a technical secretariat, like that of OECD. It does not have the "think tanks" which in the West are constantly busy promoting the interests of developed countries. It has not yet built the institutions which can devote themselves to systematic research and strategic planning. As a result, South faces North at every conference from a weak bargaining position, not only because of the obvious objective differences, but also as a consequence of the great disparity on the technical level. An improved organization and the setting up of machinery for research and technical support are called for to make the dialogue between the two sides more balanced. The South does not lack the talent and the human resources for research, analysis and co-ordination, that will enable it to formulate strategy and policies and develop tactics and fall-back positions when undertaking negotiations with the North. The UNCTAD Research and Training Centre may help in orientating the present scattered facilities in the South towards these goals, and in strengthening their capabilities.

To further these aims, the OPEC Fund also lent its support, in late 1977, to the establishment of the Centre for Research on the New International Economic Order at Oxford. This is an independent, non-governmental, non-profit-making institution, whose objective is to advance research on issues of interest to developing nations, and promote larger economic and technical co-operation among them.

DEVELOPMENT STARTS AT HOME

The OPEC Fund has been created by a group of developing countries which have achieved some measure of prosperity as a result of their joint action for the improvement of their terms of trade. The Fund's philosophy is based on the belief that development must start at home through serious and disciplined efforts, and that external assistance, though necessary at this stage for many developing countries, should not be an endless process. It realizes, however, that balanced economic growth in these countries is a formidable task in view of the inequities of the present world order.

The objective of the Fund's various activities has been to assist developing countries in increasing their economic independence. This is not only reflected in the speed with which the Fund has so far extended 113 loans to sixty-six developing countries, but also, more clearly, in the selection of the projects financed and in the approach followed by the Fund in promoting new institutions and concepts. Self-reliance is seen in this respect as a way to set in motion a process that can contribute to the solution of the growth problems of the developing countries. It involves the mobilization and rational utilization of domestic resources jointly with those made available by other members of the world community. Such a process should expand the capacity of the countries concerned to deal more effectively with the issues of economic development and make it possible for them to negotiate with the North in more favourable circumstances.

NIEO, as it is generally understood by the developing nations, is an order that implies a structural change, not a system that will offer more of the same. Little can be achieved in the near future for the developing countries within the prevailing economic system largely dominated by the North, Its continued inflationary pressures, increasing protectionism, and the instability of its exchange markets add to its detrimental imbalances. Until now, the North-South Dialogue has shown a lack of vision and has thus remained ineffective. It is time for serious co-operation between North and South in order to move ahead in a process that would reflect the community of interests of all nations.

The OPEC Fund, well aware of the importance of such an attitude, is making its modest contribution as a catalyst for providing the objective conditions of progress. Its creation has enriched the range of institutions that are instrumental in mapping out plans for more constructive and fruitful international collaboration. The task is by no means simple, if one considers the difficulties and frustrations that lie ahead in the course of establishing a balanced, equitable and functioning world economic system. With the lessons learned from past experience the ground may be ready now for the pursuit of a constructive dialogue between North and South, with each side showing serious concern for the problems and aspirations of the other. A continuation of the on-going "collective monologue" does not befit the sophisticated and developed countries of the North; nor is it conducive to solving the real and ominous problems which, left unanswered, will not discriminate between North and South in their serious consequences.

CHAPTER 7

THE OPEC FUND AND THE FINANCING OF

ENERGY DEVELOPMENT

The substantial text of an address delivered before the UN Conference on New and Renewable Sources of Energy in Nairobi, Kenya, on 14 August 1981.

The OPEC Fund, in operation since late 1976 and already active in most developing countries, has in fact been identified as a "Third World Fund", a "Fund for the poorer countries" and, to a great extent, an "Energy Fund":

(a) It is "a Fund of the Third World" because it has been established exclusively by Third World countries, from all three regions of the developing World. The thirteen OPEC member countries established it specifically to provide financial assistance to, and to strengthen solidarity with, other Third World countries. The people who manage it and run it also belong to the Third World.

(b) Although it has so far extended its activities to almost eighty countries, the OPEC Fund has concentrated its assistance on the poorer countries of the world and has calculated the level of its assistance to each country by reference to that country's relative economic and financial needs. Specifically, it has not acted as a compensatory mechanism for the increase in oil prices and has not, therefore, distributed its financial assistance according to the volume of oil imported by each recipient country. Had it done so, more than seventy-five per cent of its aid would have gone to only ten developing countries, of which nine are semi-industrialized countries, with relatively high income per capita. It has chosen, instead, to apply the equitable criterion of giving more to those who have less, even though it realizes that the oil imports of the poorest countries may be negligible in comparison to those of other nations. Owing to this feature of the Fund's assistance and of OPEC aid in general, the Least Developed Countries, as a group, have received since 1973 financial assistance from OPEC sources in excess of their entire incremental oil bill, despite the steady growth of their oil imports. Between 1973 and 1979 the incremental cost of the net oil imports of all the Least Developed Countries amounted to about $3.3 billion. In the same period, these countries received over $4 billion in disbursements of Official Development Assistance (mostly grants) from OPEC sources. The volume of their net oil imports increased, meanwhile, by an annual average rate of five per cent.

(c) The OPEC Fund has also become, to a great extent, an Energy Fund, as it gives priority in its project financing and technical assistance activities to the energy sector. The share of this sector in the Fund's project lending has steeply increased, from twenty-seven per cent in its first year of operation to sixty-four per cent last year. However, the growing emphasis on energy projects, especially those which make recipient countries less dependent on imported energy, has not prevented the Fund from considering projects in other development fields, especially food production projects. It was considered counter-productive to deprive countries of the Fund's assistance merely because of the absence of ready-to-implement energy projects when these countries had other priority projects in need of financing. In this way, the Fund has been able to provide a more flexible response to the needs of its recipients than it would have done if it were restricted to financing energy development.

Through its concentration on financing the energy and food needs of the poorer developing countries, the OPEC Fund has gained certain experiences that could be of some relevance to the discussion of new and renewable sources of energy. The following three points, briefly presented, may be found worthy of consideration.

The first point is that the developments which have already taken place in the area of food, though imperfect in many respects, could provide practical examples and an important source of inspiration when discussing future international co-operation in the long run in the area of renewable energy. International action in this latter area will prove beneficial, if not necessary, to the world at large and to developing countries in particular, as we approach the post-oil era, for which the world remains unprepared.

The international initiatives gradually adopted since the early

1940s to meet the world food problem have included: the setting up of global and regional fora for the exchange of views and the extension of technical assistance; the establishment of structures and agencies for providing assistance, in cash or in kind, to meet present needs or to finance development projects; and the creation of international research centres and their continued promotion under the umbrella of the "Consultative Group on International Agricultural Research" (CGIAR). The global efforts on the food front have also promoted the concept of "food security" and have created a wide awareness of the need for establishing plans and systems for the provision and distribution of food at the level of national involvement.

Although the above steps have not always been completed to the full satisfaction of developing countries and have not fully succeeded in arresting world hunger, some of them provide important examples of the advanced level of international co-operation that could eventually be developed in relation to other vital renewable resources.

It may be useful to note in this respect, however, that a large number of international financial institutions do exist and pay special attention to the energy sector within the limits of the resources available to them. In view of this, it will be beneficial to concentrate on strengthening, and, if need be, on restructuring and reorientating these institutions instead of insisting on adding new ones which may not necessarily generate additional advantages to developing countries.

The second point I wish to bring to attention is that co-operation among developing countries in the field of energy development, much as is the case, unfortunately, in many other economic fields, is still at an initial stage. Co-operation on the regional and sub-regional levels, which is necessary for the optimal development of many energy resources, is certainly below the required level and leaves many opportunities sadly unexploited. Although such co-operation is no substitute for national action, it is badly needed for the common good of developing countries.

It may be important to recall in this respect that the one area of inter-South economic co-operation that could be mentioned with satisfaction remains the financial assistance extended by OPEC member countries to other nations of the Third World.

As is probably well known, the oil-exporting developing countries, members of OPEC, have, on their own, initiated substantial aid efforts, in certain cases long before the oil price increases of 1973/1974. They have provided financial assistance, in cash and in kind, to other developing countries at levels far beyond what the developed countries have ever achieved, relative to their GNP. In fact, since 1975, the OPEC donors, as a group, have exceeded by three to five times, on average, the UN proclaimed target of ODA disbursements (0.7 per cent of GNP), with some of them exceeding it in some years by more than ten times, and in one case by more than twenty times. More recently, they have taken major steps to enhance still further their assistance efforts. It should also be noted, that, unlike other donors, OPEC countries hardly reap any economic benefits under the assistance extended, as the proceeds of their loans and grants are typically used to finance the procurement of goods and services from other countries. And unlike other donors, OPEC countries are not giving part of a renewable income but are sharing, in fact, their depleting wealth with the other developing countries, through their ODA assistance efforts which have reached to-date an annual level of $7 billion.

The third and last point which should be emphasized, is that the nature of the energy problems of developing countries and the urgent solutions required for them necessitate international co-operation which goes beyond the practice of issuing elaborate UN plans of action, which appear at times as if they have become an end in themselves, with little or no action to follow. The management of the OPEC Fund believes that developing countries will stand to benefit more from the adoption of steps which could be implemented in the immediate future, and from using the existing financial mechanisms to the maximum.

To this effect, the occasion should be taken to reiterate the continued readiness of the OPEC Fund to consider the co-financing of energy projects especially those related to the development of new and renewable energy resources in all the low-income and middle-income developing countries. The OPEC Fund will also continue its co-operation with the UNDP, the UN Fund for Science and Technology and the Latin American Energy Organization (OLADE), to finance technical assistance projects of tangible benefits in the energy field and will continue to promote a greater role in this area for regional institutions. The OPEC Fund would wish to reiterate its support for the energy account created under the auspices of the UNDP, to which it has already pledged ten per cent of the total resources required over its first three years of operation. It calls once more on the traditional donors to provide the required complementary resources to enable UNDP to expand its initiatives in the essential area of pre-feasibility work. In addition, it plans to be involved in financing the preparation of new energy projects which could in due course be considered for concessional loans both by the OPEC Fund itself and by other available sources. The OPEC Fund also stands ready to participate with other interested sources in financing and sponsoring international research centres on the various renewable sources of energy. It is, in fact, considering as a first step in this direction the co-financing of the regional Solar Energy Institute in West Africa. It will also be prepared to discuss the establishment of a new international consultative group, along lines similar to those of the CGIAR, for the promotion of the international energy research centres which are now envisaged.

CHAPTER 8

THE OPEC FUND AND THE LEAST

DEVELOPED COUNTRIES

The substantial text of an address delivered before the UN Conference on the Least Developed Countries in Paris, France, on 4 September 1981.

During an address to the UN Conference on New and Renewable Sources of Energy in Nairobi, on 14 August 1981, it was pointed out that of all existing international development finance institutions, the OPEC Fund could be most appropriately identified as a Fund of the Third World, an Energy Fund and a Fund of the Poorer Countries. It is this latter characteristic of the Fund and indeed of OPEC aid in general, that is to be elaborated on this occasion.

Even before such terms as "The Least Developed Countries" and "The Most Seriously Affected Countries" were coined by the UN, OPEC donors have concentrated their assistance efforts on the poorest developing countries. The two groups of countries just mentioned have in fact accounted for about fifty per cent of OPEC aid in general and more than seventy-seven per cent of the assistance directly provided by the OPEC Fund. According to data published in Paris by the Development Assistance Committee of the OECD, OPEC donors gave during the period 1974-1980, an average of about thirteen per cent of their total aid to the LLDCs as a group. But this refers only to bilateral assistance from OPEC countries and institutions, and does not include the indirect aid channelled through other multilateral agencies. This level of assistance to the LLDCs is, at any rate, equivalent to about 0.23 per cent of the total GNP of OPEC donors. In comparison, the proclaimed UN target for ODA to the LLDCs has been set at the lower level of 0.15 per cent of the donor's GNP. It may be added here that the DAC (industrialized) countries have, during the same period, given the equivalent of only

0.06 per cent of their GNP to the LLDCs.

The concentration of OPEC countries' assistance efforts on the world's poorest nations has naturally led to the result that their assistance has borne no relationship to the volume or cost of oil imported by the recipient countries. As is well known, more than seventy per cent of the Third World's oil imports are accounted for by eight developing countries, most of which are semi-industrialized. In fact the thirty-one LLDCs account for no more than four per cent of the oil imported by developing countries each year. Thus, if OPEC aid were tied to the cost of oil imports, the LLDCs would have received far less in aid from OPEC sources. In actual fact, this group of countries received in the period 1973 through 1979 about $4 billion in direct grants and soft loans from OPEC countries. This amount exceeded the incremental cost of their oil imports over the same period which is estimated at about $3.3 billion. This, it should be added, has taken place in spite of the fact that the volume of oil imports of the LLDCs increased by an annual average of five per cent in this period.

What has just been mentioned is by no means intended to suggest that enough has been done to help the LLDCs in their development efforts. On the contrary, greater assistance is called for in this area by all those who are in a position to extend it. It is intended only to underline two facts which until now have not, unfortunately, been clearly established in the public's mind:

The first is that the OPEC countries' assistance to the LLDCs represents in relative terms more than other donor groups have given and even exceeds by more than a hundred and fifty per cent the projected target for aid to the LLDCs established by the UN.

And the second is that OPEC aid efforts to the LLDCs as a group have surpassed in volume any additional cost they may have incurred as a result of the increase in oil prices, despite the steady rise of the volume of their oil imports.

As developing countries themselves, OPEC countries realize the extent of the needs to be met and the tremendous efforts which have yet to be exerted both by the LLDCs and their sources of external assistance. The liquidity which some of the OPEC countries have at present is not to be mistaken as a sign of added income, as it merely represents another form of their mineral wealth, which is fast being depleted. Yet they are using a generous part of it to assist other developing countries and will obviously continue to do so as long as they can afford it.

As far as is known, no international development institution has put as much emphasis on the LLDCs in its operations as the OPEC Fund. One hundred and twenty-two loans totalling US$490 million have so far been extended to these countries by the Fund representing forty-one per cent of its total lending. The Fund's grant programmes are also designed to benefit the poorest countries. We are happy to see the same philosophy prevailing in the other international institutions which receive significant financing from the Fund, such as IFAD (the International Fund for Agricultural Development).

The OPEC Fund's fifth programme of operations, currently under implementation, includes all the LLDCs on its priority list of recipient countries. So far this year, sixteen of these countries have received interest-free loans under this $1,350 million programme, with a few others scheduled to sign loan agreements this month. An invitation is extended to the Governments of the LLDCs which have not yet applied to the Fund for assistance this year to do so, and an assurance of the continued readiness of the Fund to participate in the financing of their development projects and programmes, especially those which fall within the Fund's priorities, i.e., energy and food production projects. As previously, the OPEC Fund will continue to exert maximum flexibility in dealing with the LLDCs, both in considering the types of financing to be extended and in devising the rules and procedures to be followed. It is a regrettable fact, however, that the LLDCs themselves do not always benefit from the resources made available to them, including those of the OPEC Fund.

The OPEC Fund offers to make grants to meet the total "directly contributed capital" to the projected Common Fund for Commodities to be contributed by thirty-five developing countries, including all the thirty-one LLDCs. Although this offer has been widely announced, a few LLDCs have contacted the Fund for this purpose and only one has to date (September 1981) concluded a grant agreement. In an attempt to accelerate the process of the implementation of the Agreement Establishing the Common Fund, an invitation is extended to the LLDCs which have signed that agreement to enter into grant agreements with the OPEC Fund whereby the latter undertakes to pay, as the agent of the receiving country, the share required from it in the directly contributed capital of the Common

Fund. In addition, the OPEC Fund will in due course pay more than US$46 million as a voluntary contribution to the Second Account of the Common Fund and will request that the bulk of this grant be used to benefit the poorer countries.

The following remarks, relevant to a discussion of the situation of the Least Developed Countries, should be taken merely as the views of the management of the OPEC Fund, derived from its own experience:

(i) We do not share the view, which seems to be gaining ground in certain Western circles at present, according to which, first, the poor nations are to be blamed for their poverty, and second the present international economic system allows for enough "social mobility" among nations. On the contrary, we believe that the developing countries which have managed to achieve some measure of prosperity under the present system did so in spite of the system, and not because of it.

(ii) However, we do agree that development starts at home and that while we call for a new international economic order we must ensure that new domestic economic orders are introduced whereby a greater discipline in the economic management of developing countries is coupled with a more equitable distribution of income and a more serious dedication to developmental objectives.

(iii) We also believe that the poorest countries of the world should not take their present population growth rates as an irreversible trend and should more clearly realize the tragic aspects of the demographic dimension, if left unchecked. This dimension should not be treated as merely a health problem, as is often the case in developing countries. It should receive the attention it deserves at the national level as a challenge of the highest political order.

(iv) Furthermore, we feel that the financial problems of developing countries differ in their causes and magnitudes and cannot therefore, be subject to uniform solutions. Most of the suggestions considered at present for easing the financial burdens of developing countries, such as greater access to capital markets, and the elimination of trade barriers in manufactures, may indeed be of little or no relevance, as far as the LLDCs are concerned. For these countries, we believe that it is necessary (a) to ensure a greater flow of external resources on the softest possible terms and (b) to ensure that such resources, together with the little domestic savings available, should be used in the most effective manner. To that end, the LLDCs are best advised not to fall prey to the vicious circle of international conferences issuing elaborate and often unrealistic plans of action. They would better concentrate on business-like discussions with interested sources of assistance on the ways and means of increasing the volume, effectiveness and complementarity of such assistance, taking into consideration that additional capital, though necessary, cannot alone solve complex development problems. Politically stable systems run by dedicated individuals and assisted by well-managed institutions have proven to be more important in the development process than the ready access to abundant funds and natural resources.

(v) The development process as experienced in the now developed countries, with its patterns of excessive consumption and its oil-based technologies, simply does not, in our view, suit present conditions in the LLDCs. It must give way to new development patterns which promote less wasteful consumption patterns and greater energy efficiency.

(vi) External sources of development assistance should realize the need for a special treatment of the LLDCs. This special treatment may best be reflected in (a) devising simpler procedures of lending to them, (b) giving greater attention to technical assistance, especially in project identification and preparation and in the process of institution-building, (c) providing assistance and close supervision in the execution of the assisted projects and (d) taking a more flexible attitude in meeting the recurrent cost and the local cost of development projects and programmes.

(vii) Last, but not least, we feel that, as they aspire to greater co-operation from external sources, the LLDCs should prove, through their own domestic action and the regional co-operation among them, that serious indigenous developmental efforts are being exerted and deserve to be supported. The greatest incentive to the donors is indeed to see the positive results of their assistance and its impact in helping the recipient countries achieve a greater measure of self-reliance.

CHAPTER 9

THE OPEC FUND – THE FIRST FIVE YEARS

First published in OPEC Review, *Vol. V, No. 3, Vienna, Austria, Autumn, 1981 then published with additional tables in English and French as an OPEC Fund Publication, Vienna, Austria, October 1981 and February 1982.*

INTRODUCTION

The performance of international development finance institutions is usually measured by such factors as the number of loans extended every year, the number of beneficiary countries, the ratio of disbursements to commitments, the ratio of administrative costs to disbursements, and the rate of growth of resources. On all these counts, the performance of the OPEC Fund for International Development (the Fund) establishes a new record. A comparison covering all multilateral aid agencies whose operations started about the same time as those of the Fund, confirms this conclusion. By the end of October 1981, the OPEC Fund concluded 266 loans and 50 grants. The loans benefited 79 countries, the loan's disbursements to commitments ratio reached fifty-five per cent, while administrative costs remained within the range of one per cent of annual disbursements.

The above-mentioned quantitative measures may not, however, present a definite way of judging the performance of an international develoment finance institution. The more indicative test is to be found perhaps in the extent to which an institution is fulfilling its respective objectives. Such a test would inevitably raise major issues as to the approaches and procedures followed by each institution; the target beneficiaries (countries, sectors and peoples), as well as the actual impact of the institution on the world scene. In the case of the

OPEC Fund, the objective was twofold: (i) to assist the development efforts of non-OPEC developing countries and (ii) to do this in such a manner as to strengthen the bond of solidarity between them and OPEC member countries, thus serving, to the extent possible, their common objective in establishing a more equitable world economic order.

APPROACHES AND PROCEDURES

Instead of copying the established practices, originally initiated by the World Bank and largely adopted by other international financing agencies, the Fund started its work with a fresh outlook. The Agreement Establishing the Fund reflected this attitude by defining the Fund's objective in broad terms enabling it to do all that its Board deemed necessary in assisting other developing countries. As a result, the Fund was the first international institution of its kind to combine balance of payments (BOP) support with project lending and to add to its direct assistance to governments the financing of other development agencies which play a particularly important role for the benefit of developing countries. By providing BOP support, the Fund was also able to ask each recipient country to deposit equivalent local counterpart funds to meet the local costs of development projects, thus solving a bottleneck created by the insistence of many existing agencies that they meet only the foreign costs of projects.

In addition, the Fund was the first institution to avoid duplicating the already extensive bureaucracies of existing agencies and to benefit, to the maximum, from the facilities of these agencies in support of the beneficiary countries. Furthermore, the Fund has demonstrated to the existing international agencies that the financing process could be completed in a much faster way than has hitherto been conceived. It has in fact initiated a dialogue with these agencies on the simplification of lending procedures, a process which has already yielded some positive changes in the approaches of many other agencies.

TARGET BENEFICIARIES

From the outset, the Fund based its activities on well-conceived lending programmes where the selection of beneficiaries, the types of loans and their amounts would be based on objective criteria established according to carefully studied data. In so doing, the Fund rejected the "first come, first served" approach which is likely to serve only the more advanced developing countries that need the Fund's assistance to a lesser extent than the poorer countries.

The Fund's Governing Board adopted the approach that its activities, though legally extendable to all developing countries (other than OPEC members), would be limited to the poorer countries and could only reach the high-income developing countries when the Fund's resources allowed for such an extension. This was particularly interesting in the case of the OPEC Fund, as the poorer countries happen to be marginal importers of oil, while the major oil-importers among the developing countries are those which, relatively speaking, are economically more advanced. As a result, the Fund's First Lending Programme was limited to the "Most Seriously Affected" (MSA) countries, as defined by the UN. The Fund has since adopted the approach that under each lending programme a list of "priority countries" will be established and will include all the "Least Developed Countries" (UN definition), all other MSA countries, and other low-income countries. The Fund's Board has, however, maintained a great degree of flexibility by authorizing lending operations in higher-income countries on a case-by-case basis, when the particular circumstances of the country justified such action. Thus, relatively high-income developing countries, such as Turkey and Jamaica, occasionally benefited from Fund's loans when they experienced severe financial difficulties.

The Fund's priorities were not only expressed in the choice of recipient countries but extended to the selection of priority sectors for its project loans. The Fund's two declared priority sectors, i.e., energy and food, have since been adopted as priority sectors by many other development lending agencies. It is particularly interesting to note that by giving top priority to the energy sector many loans are extended for the development of indigenous energy resources in the developing countries, thus emphasizing the fact that OPEC aid, far from being an instrument of export promotion, is altruistic in nature. The political objective of OPEC member countries in helping other developing countries achieve "energy independence" or lessen their dependence on energy imports was deemed more important than promoting oil-exports to these countries. The Fund's Board has also maintained the necessary flexibility by providing financial support to projects in other sectors when there were no projects ready for financing in the energy or food production sectors.

Within the above-mentioned country and sectoral priorities, the Fund placed special emphasis on benefiting, within each recipient country, the poorest segment of the population. It has thus applied its assistance to the electrification of rural areas, supplying water to deprived districts, land reclamation coupled with land reform, lines of credit to national development banks designed to benefit only small businesses, farmers and artisans, as well as other projects whose obvious beneficiaries are the poorer peoples of the recipient countries.

IMPACT ON THE WORLD SCENE

With its 265 direct loans reaching seventy-nine developing countries to date, and its grants to several UN Specialized Agencies, international agricultural research centres and other research and scientific institutions, the Fund has clearly made its presence felt as a recognized source of international development finance. Although the amount of each loan or grant was often small, the Fund's repeated performance (on average, one loan every week, with some countries having already received seven loans from the Fund) enabled it to develop close links with most developing countries and to generate a great measure of goodwill in the Third World.

More importantly, the Fund has enthusiastically pursued its conceived role, not merely as a development finance institution, but as a policy instrument for forging closer links between OPEC member countries and other developing nations, and for serving the developing countries as a whole in their struggle for the establishment of a more just international economic order. For instance, the Fund played an instrumental role in the establishment and evolution of the International Fund for Agricultural Development (IFAD). It also played an important role in the negotiations of the Agreement Establishing the Common Fund for Commodities and is presently providing financial support to enable this Fund to come into existence. It has already offered to pay the contributions to the Common Fund of thirty-five developing countries and declared its preparedness to provide, in due course, a sizeable grant to its "Second Window". In addition, the Fund was instrumental in the creation of the

"Centre for Research on the New International Economic Order" and is closely following the on-going dialogue on North-South relations and the role of OPEC member countries in respect thereof, as reflected in the Fund's publications, especially its "Occasional Papers" series. By acting collectively, through the Fund, in certain international fora, OPEC countries were obviously able to play a more effective role to the benefit of the Group of 77 as a whole.

In its attempt to give the OPEC aid efforts a fair reporting, the Fund held detailed discussions with OECD on its reporting system of OPEC aid flows. These discussions resulted in a noted improvement of the DAC reporting of Official Development Assistance from OPEC sources, as evidenced by their most recent publications. Meanwhile, the Fund arranged with the UNCTAD Secretariat the establishment of a UN reporting system on financial flows among developing countries, which proved to be more favourable to OPEC donors. The Fund also publishes papers in different languages analyzing OPEC aid efforts.

In all its activities, the Fund has maintained close co-operation and co-ordination with the bilateral and multilateral aid agencies of OPEC member countries. It is now active in joint and co-ordinated action with several of them including the co-financing of projects, mutual representation in international fora, joint research activities and co-ordinated information activities. Through such co-operation, the impact of the "OPEC aid phenomenon" as a whole is enhanced.

HIGHLIGHTS OF THE FUND'S OPERATIONS: MAGNITUDE
OF ASSISTANCE

Up to the end of October 1981, the Fund has concluded 266 loans consisting of 143 Balance of Payments Support Loans, 117 Project Loans and six Programme Loans. In addition, fifty grants were extended for technical assistance projects and other purposes. Out of the 266 loans, 126 have been totally disbursed and 103 are under active disbursement. The ratio between the disbursed amount and the total amount of all signed loans is fifty-five per cent. Disbursement of effective loans has reached sixty-five per cent.

One hundred and forty-six loans were allocated for Africa bringing total commitments to that region to US$578.06 million, seventy-nine loans were allocated for Asia, where the level of commitments reached US$564.02 million, and forty-one loans were allocated for Latin America where US$160.085 million was committed. In total, 143 loans were allocated for BOP support and 123 for project and programme financing.

One hundred and ten BOP support loans have been fully utilized, twenty-four are already half disbursed, and nine are to be declared effective shortly. Of the total amount of US$578.50 million committed for these purposes, US$308.05 million went to Africa, US$172.50 million to Asia and US$97.85 million to Caribbean and Central American countries. An equivalent of US$283.25 million in local counterpart funds has financed the local costs of 126 development projects in forty-nine countries. 26.6 per cent of this amount was committed to power projects; 16.11 per cent to the transport sector and 37.61 per cent to the agriculture sector.

Out of a total of US$701.3 million committed for project financing, US$378 million was allocated for Asia, US$251 million for Africa and US$62.2 million for Latin America. 45.2 per cent went to the energy sector, 14.2 per cent to agriculture, 19.0 per cent to transportation, 15.7 to industry and local development banks, and the rest was allocated for public utilities, communication and urban development. Sixteen project loans have been fully utilized, seventy-five are under active financing, and twenty-six are yet to be declared effective. US$32.5 million has been committed to programme loans.

An amount of US$29.4 million has been allocated for UNDP related projects covering agriculture, energy education (vocational training centres), research and public utilities (medical centres), and an additional US$13.4 million has been allocated for technical assistance projects in energy, agriculture and education under the auspices of other international agencies and centres. Moreover, US$1 million has been allocated for grants involving research and other intellectual activities which serve the Fund's objective. Almost one half of this amount has already been committed for specific purposes (fellowships, workshops, etc.).

US$435.50 million has been committed to IFAD's initial resources of which US$204.45 million has been paid in cash and US$147.89 million in promissory notes. Practically all IFAD's initial resources have been approved by that agency for specific loans and grants. Furthermore, a decision has been taken by the Fund in the replenishment of IFAD's resources in the amount of US$450 million, conditional on the contribution of US$650 million by industrialized countries.

US$110.72 million has been transferred to the Trust Fund administered by the IMF representing the profits accruing to seven OPEC members from the IMF gold sale. These amounts were in turn used through the IMF in concessional loans to developing countries experiencing special financial deficits.

US$83.56 million has been allocated to assist the projected Common Fund for Commodities sponsored by UNCTAD through a grant to its "Second Window" (US$46.4 million) and meeting the subscription of thirty-five developing countries (US$37.16 million) in its capital.

SOCIO-ECONOMIC IMPACT

The co-financing of a total of 3,300 MW generating capacity has been completed through forty energy projects undertaken since 1977. Hydro projects totalling about 610 m.m^3 of water reservoir capacity and other power projects allowing the creation and rehabilitation of 30,000 km of transmission lines have also been financed. Development of oil and gas fields in India and Bangladesh, co-financed by the Fund, will result in the production of 240,000 barrels a day of oil and 160 million cubic feet of gas per day.

Eighteen projects have been co-financed for providing irrigation facilities for 170,400 ha. of rural land and 470,000 tons of fertilizers. An estimated total of 30,000 ha. of land will thus be reforested and about seven million people and farm families will have been assisted.

Nineteen road projects have been co-financed for the construction, up-grading and improvement of about 26,000 km of roads serving an estimated population of thirteen million. Four railway projects have been co-financed for the rehabilitation of more than 400 km of railway and increasing the yearly tonnage of the systems by about 300,000 tons.

Four airport projects have been implemented and have considerably affected the economy of concerned developing countries especially in the commercial and tourism sector.

Ten lines of credit to national development banks enabled them to provide sub-loans to small and medium-scale enterprises in the manufacturing, agricultural and artisanal sectors.

CONCLUSIONS: SUCCESSES AND CONSTRAINTS

The positive achievements of the Fund are the natural result of a number of factors, including in particular:

(i) The continued support it receives from its member countries as evidenced by the repeated replenishment of its resources and the exemplary attitude of its members in using the Fund as a collective instrument of common policy rather than as an instrument of the national policy and interests of particular members.

(ii) The harmony and mutual confidence which has prevailed between the Fund's Board and its management and the fact that Board members are professionals with long experience and responsibility in the aid business in their respective countries.

(iii) The great network of relationships which the Fund has succeeded in establishing with existing aid agencies, both on the international level and on the national level of the member countries. Within this framework of co-operation the Fund has been able to benefit from the services of these agencies, thus achieving great economies in time and cost.

(iv) And last, but not least, the diligence and dedication of the Fund's carefully selected staff who, despite their extremely limited number, have managed to cope with the responsibilities of the task and carried out their jobs swiftly and efficiently.

The Fund's successes may, however, be adversely affected in future by the fact that it lacks a well-defined and predictable system for receiving additional resources. The timing and amount of each of the previous replenishments were decided on an *ad hoc* basis. Some members of the Fund suggested that this problem could be overcome by authorizing the Fund to borrow after changing its capital structure so as to endow it with callable capital, on the strength of which it could resort to borrowing. The same objective may also be served if the replenishments of the Fund's resources were effected at intervals which are known and agreed upon beforehand. Such an arrangement would not only help the Fund to properly plan its activities but would enable it to continue its operations on concessional terms.

As the Fund aspires to play a more instrumental role in the

development efforts of a large number of countries it realizes that it will have to face greater challenges in the future. A meaningful expansion of the Fund's involvement in the energy field alone would require a gradual strengthening of its capital resources and the building up of a strong institutional capacity in the identification, preparation and appraisal of energy development projects. It is strongly hoped that the positive factors which enabled the Fund to reach its present stage of growth, will enable it to meet the new challenges and to gain greater stature in future, to the satisfaction of both the countries which created it and the countries for whose benefit it was established.

PART II

ARAB EXTERNAL ASSISTANCE
AND INVESTMENT

CHAPTER 10

ARAB OIL POLICIES AND THE NEW INTERNATIONAL ECONOMIC ORDER

First published in Virginia Journal of International Law, *Volume 16, No. 2, Winter 1976, Charlottesville, Virginia, USA. At the time of writing, 1975, the Author was Legal Adviser to the Kuwait Fund for Economic Development.*

INTRODUCTION

The Programme of Action on the Establishment of a New International Economic Order issued by the UN General Assembly on 16 May 1974, specifically welcomed "the increasingly effective mobilization by the whole group of oil-exporting countries of their natural resources for the benefit of their economic development"[1]. Such a welcoming note may be viewed as an implicit tribute to the recent efforts of a small group of States, mainly the Arab oil-exporters, to change the basic structure of the world economic order and the interests underlying its governing rules. It is in this context that future historians of international law are likely to find the greatest contribution on the part of developing countries to the progressive development and wider acceptability of international law[2].

This article will consider the oil policies and practices of the Arab exporting countries. In spite of different ideological orientations, varying productive capacities, and disparities in the ability of their economies to absorb generated funds[3], these countries have managed to follow common policies on most issues related to oil. In fact, this achievement of a common ground may even result from the different characteristics of the economies of these countries[4]. For it is the nations with large populations and considerable development needs which tend to have either small oil reserves (Algeria) or large reserves but inadequate installed capacity (Iraq). They cannot, therefore, influence the world market if they opt for production or pricing policies which are not shared by the large producers. On the other hand, countries with massive oil reserves or large installed capacity (Saudi Arabia, Kuwait, Abu Dhabi, Libya and Qatar) are accumulating net liquid financial assets which deter them from adopting policies – such as full-scale production – that would be likely to undermine the interests of the smaller producers. Thus, the common interests of this group of nations have given rise to a cohesiveness that has proved to be valuable for all. As a result, the "effective mobilization" of oil, referred to in the above-mentioned resolution of the UN General Assembly, has been achieved by Arab oil-exporting states proceeding on identical or similar bases.

Common Arab oil policies have been identified, for the purpose of this study, by analyzing the actual practice and official pronouncements of Arab oil-exporting states in their individual capacities and as the leading members of the Organization of Petroleum Exporting Countries (OPEC)[5]. The recent "Solemn Declaration of Sovereigns and Heads of State of OPEC Member Countries,"[6] issued in Algiers on 6 March 1975, is particularly indicative of such policies as it sums up the points of agreement among all the States involved. These points cover five basic topics: production, pricing, aid, investment and conflict resolution. Policies in respect of each of these topics have a direct bearing on the new international economic order that is now emerging.

CONTINUITY OF SUPPLY

In spite of a popular contention to the contrary, the OPEC countries have never adopted co-ordinated programmes aimed at controlling prices through production cutbacks. Such a technique, if adopted, would probably support the technically inaccurate description of OPEC as a "cartel". But systematic production cutbacks have been resisted vehemently by Saudi Arabia, the major Arab oil-producer and the current market leader[7]. In fact, OPEC policy instruments have consistently been confined to fiscal and pricing measures[8]. The only instance of co-ordinated output restrictions by the Arab oil-exporters occurred during the period of October 1973-March 1974. And these restrictive measures were implemented outside the scope of OPEC and were meant to serve a specific political purpose completely unrelated to the price issue[9]. The price rises which followed these measures were thus to some extent "the consequence of the cutbacks rather than their objective"[10].

Nevertheless, the possibility of the adoption by OPEC members (including the Arab oil-exporters) of a programme to regulate production on a co-ordinated basis cannot be excluded. Such a course of action has already been advocated by many oil-producers as a defensive measure in the face of recent attempts by the consuming countries to bring down prices by dampening demand. It might have prevailed in the recent Algiers Summit Conference of OPEC members but for the opposition of Saudi Arabia[11]. Furthermore, the adoption of this course would not be inconsistent with customary international law, which contains no prohibition against monopolistic practices in international trade[12]. Many international commodity agreements authorize such practices, including production controls, without being described as contrary to *jus cogens* international law[13]. Far from ruling out such practices, the UN General Assembly's Declaration on the Establishment of a New International Economic Order and the related Programme of Action encourage the formation of "producers' associations" and support their activities[14]. The Charter of Economic Rights and Duties of States recently adopted by the UN General Assembly further confirms the right of all States "to associate in organizations of primary commodity producers" and requests all States "to respect that right by refraining from applying economic and political measures that would limit it"[15]. OPEC and like organizations are therefore envisaged as a legitimate feature of a new international economic order which would guarantee the effective protection of the interests of the producers of raw materials.

It is interesting to note, however, that even though the possibility exists that Arab oil-producers will adopt co-ordinated output restrictions in the future, the declared policy of these countries is to ensure a continuous and sufficient supply of oil to meet the essential requirements of the consuming countries. The Solemn Declaration of the Algiers Conference indicates, it is true, that such an uninterrupted supply will be subject to the abstention of the consuming countries from using "artificial barriers to distort the normal operation of the laws of demand and supply"[16]. But this safeguard clause, which understandably reserves for the suppliers the right to resort to defensive measures of retortion, is largely mitigated by a further provision in the Declaration to the effect that any co-ordination among producers should seek to maintain a "balance between oil production and the needs of the world market"[17].

In fact, the continued supply of oil has been officially regarded by Arab oil-exporting countries as an "international responsibility" of the highest moral order[18]. The moral obligation inherent in the supply of such an indispensable product to the industrialized world has frequently been recognized by Arab oil-producers and may thus be considered as part of their understanding of the "principle of co-operation" that is necessary to the international order[19]. It could be argued that the desire for amicable international relations allows the oil-exporters little choice other than to assume such a moral obligation[20]. For example, cuts in production merely to eliminate the emerging surplus of supply over demand in the world market have already been described by US officials as "an unfriendly act"[21]. In any event the Arab countries, with practically no assets other than the exhaustible oil resources and with a rather limited absorption capacity for depreciating oil income, are continuing a level of production far in excess of their financial needs[22]. The fulfilment of this "international" responsibility, however, has been subjected in actual practice to two types of limitations.

The Limitation on Supply for the Purpose of Conservation

It is impossible to overstate the need for conservation on the part of most Arab oil-producers. Their lopsided economies are almost totally dependent on one depletable, non-renewable resource. For these countries, the extraction of oil represents not merely the generation of disposable income but a basic change in form of the major national capital asset from crude oil, whose value is likely to appreciate when kept in the subsoil, to cash which is subject to continuous depreciation and devaluation. In addition, a substantial portion of this cash cannot be absorbed and utilized in the short run for the internal economic development of the oil-producers and thus has to remain captive in foreign lands. Libya was the first to recognize the need for production cutbacks for conservation purposes, early in 1968, and has repeatedly resorted to such measures since then[23]. The same practice has been followed by Kuwait since 1972[24], and its importance is now generally recognized by all Arab producers[25]. In fact, regulations for the conservation of oil resources were approved by OPEC as early as November 1968, but such regulations were not always easy to apply in the former pattern of relationships between governments and oil companies.

The Algiers Solemn Declaration has thus linked the recognition of "the vital role of oil supplies" to "the fundamental requirement" of the conservation of oil resources[26]. Such a linkage can hardly be questioned. No country could reasonably be asked to give absolute preference to the interests of other countries over its own economic welfare, especially when it is already willing to accept a measure of sacrifice for the benefit of others. Furthermore, the imposition of conservation measures is a question which falls readily within the domestic jurisdiction of sovereign states. Customary international law does not seek to outlaw such a practice, and treaties for trade liberalization, such as the General Agreement on Tariffs and Trade (GATT), often allow a general exception in favour of measures relating to the conservation of exhaustible natural resources[27]. The UN Declaration on the Establishment of a New International Economic Order also emphasizes the "need for all States to put an end to the waste of natural resources" as one of the principles on which the new order should be founded[28]. Fortunately, consuming countries have at long last come to share the concern for oil conservation, if only as a tactic to reduce demand in the hope of lowering prices. Official US sources have also come to admit, like many other Western spokesmen, that "unconstrained consumption of cheap oil is the principal cause of the present vulnerability of the industrial countries"[29].

The Limitation on Supply as an Act of Retortion in a War Situation

In October 1973, Arab oil-exporting States imposed an outright embargo on oil shipments to certain destinations and coupled it with across-the-board production cutbacks. Such exceptional measures were implemented during a war situation in which military personnel from Kuwait, Iraq, Saudi Arabia, and Algeria joined the Egyptian and Syrian armed forces in an attempt to put an end to the forcible Israeli occupation of Egyptian and Syrian territories. The objective of these measures was to discourage certain countries from violating their obligations of neutrality toward Arab belligerents and from continuing their encouragement of, or their acquiescence in, the illegal occupation and annexation of Arab territories. The measures were terminated shortly after the cessation of hostilities when the attitude of the embargoed countries showed a slightly favourable change[30].

The embargo and accompanying production cutbacks were in full conformity with customary international law. The use of export controls for political purposes is so widespread that no general rule of international custom could have developed to the contrary[31]. Bilateral treaty commitments, as well as the GATT prohibition against discriminatory trade restrictions, did not represent a legal barrier to the few Arab nations that were parties to such agreements. These treaty commitments generally contain an explicit exception in favour of national security interests which effectively limits the application of the *most-favoured nation* clause. Furthermore, a presumption in favour of such an exception and in favour of exemptions on grounds of international public policy obtains in these types of treaties even in the absence of an explicit clause[32]. On the other hand, the general prohibition against economic coercion contained in such instruments as the UN Declaration of the Principles of International Law Concerning Friendly Relations and Co-operation Among States cannot apply in a war situation to states seeking only to secure respect on the part of the affected countries for basic principles of international law[33]. International organizations have often authorized and even requested similar measures in situations involving far less acute violations of international law[34].

In applying the above measures, Arab oil-exporting states were merely following the steps of many other countries and were only exercising their recognized sovereign right to dispose of their natural resources in the manner which best suited their legitimate interests. Yet, while such coercive measures were in force, much emphasis was laid by Arab nations on the legitimacy of their objectives under international law and on their exhaustion of other means to achieve these objectives. Such behaviour on the part of the Arab oil-exporters does not in any way weaken the proposition that economic coercion may be characterized as illegal if applied in pursuance of an illegitimate or improper objective[35]. The Arab nations utilized coercive measures only as a last resort. In short, the numerous substantive and procedural limitations which characterized the Arab measures and distinguished them from acts of economic coercion practiced by some of the more developed countries certainly constitute a welcome addition to the legal principles surrounding the new international economic order. A careful reading of Arab oil policies suggests that further resort to such coercive measures could only occur within these limitations. And it certainly is to be hoped that all States will respect similar constraints in their use of export controls for political purposes.

FAIR PRICING

Fair Pricing and International Law

In the absence of a contrary treaty commitment, nothing in the present system of international law prevents a producing country from selling its primary products at whatever prices it chooses to fix. Indeed, the right of every country freely to dispose of its national wealth is an integral part of the universally acknowledged principle that a state possesses sovereignty over all of its natural resources[36]. Nevertheless, the inequalities which have traditionally characterized the world economic order prevented producers of primary commodities in past years from obtaining what they considered to be a fair price for their products. The power to influence prices generally remained in the hands of the primary possessors of capital and technology, i.e., the industrialized nations. Attempts made in the United Nations Conference on Trade and Development (UNCTAD)[37] and other fora to secure for primary commodities "stable, remunerative and equitable prices with a view to increasing earnings of developing countries"[38] were largely unsuccessful. As a result, the world economy continued to be distorted by the permanent transfer of real resources from developing to developed countries and the excessive consumption of scarce and non-renewable raw materials. The only commodity which now seems to be escaping the hold of that system is oil. In the wake of an acute world economic crisis, the oil-exporting nations have rekindled the hope of developing countries for a new and more equitable pattern of international trade.

The Arab oil-producers were rarely concerned with the price of crude oil before 1950, because their oil revenues were calculated until then on the basis of a fixed per ton royalty. Even when these producers adopted the profit-sharing principle in the 1950s, the size of their oil income was determined by a "posted price" which did not coincide with the actual "market price". In reality, the "posted price" and, to a great extent, the "market price" were determined by the trans-national oil companies which frequently acted – through complicated corporate devices – as both the sellers and the purchasers of crude oil. For reasons of their own, these companies kept the price of oil constant, and at times declining, for over twenty years. Meanwhile prices of other sources of energy, of refined oil products, and even of crude oil produced in developed countries followed the general world inflationary trend. During the period of constancy of the posted oil price (1950-1970), rising inflation rates caused a decrease in its real value of even greater proportions than in the cases of some other commodities. Even when a rise in the posted price of Arabian Gulf Oil was finally negotiated with the companies in 1971, it involved only a modest increase (33 cents per barrel) and allowed an annual adjustment for inflation (2.5 per cent) far below the actual prevailing rates[39]. Nevertheless, doubts were already being raised in the consuming countries as to "whether the producing countries could maintain the wide margin between oil prices and the real production costs without the international companies to serve as their tax collectors"[40].

The concept of a "fair price" admittedly raises thorny questions that may not be susceptible to objective answers. Since these questions are, by definition, a matter of equity, they can hardly be discussed on purely legal or economic grounds and they inevitably involve considerations of policy and ethics[41]. Nevertheless, with these limitations in mind, it may be possible to establish what is *not* an unfair price in the instance of oil. A price of a primary commodity should not be described as inordinate simply because it greatly exceeds the real costs of its production. The very fact of extracting a commodity like crude oil causes a real loss in the non-renewable capital wealth of the producing country that cannot be measured by the cost of the extraction process. Such cost may be an important factor in computing the return on the investment of the transnational oil companies, but it is obviously irrelevant in deciding what compensation is due to the producing country for the loss it sustains in its national wealth as a result of extraction. In addition, the unique importance of oil as the primary source of energy and as the basic raw material for about ten thousand derivatives in the petrochemical field cannot reasonably be ignored in determining its price.

It is also important to remember that a price is not unfair merely because it was not negotiated between producers and consumers. Although negotiation should provide the proper mechanism for reaching reasonable prices under free market conditions, such conditions did not exist with regard to oil when posted prices were fixed by the trans-national companies. As late as November 1973, the OPEC Conference, dismayed by the attitude of the companies, expressed its belief that "the pricing of petroleum, like the pricing of other internationally-traded manufactured goods, commodities and raw materials, should be market orientated"[42]. When agreement with the companies on a new market-based price could not be obtained by the oil-producers at that time, the subsequent posting for Saudi market crude was set at a price that was actually lower than market realizations[43]. Yet even a price which is higher than the ideal market level may not necessarily be unfair, especially if it aims at establishing an equitable relationship between prices of goods sold and bought[44]. Similarly, a charge may not be considered exorbitant merely because it is much higher than the former price of the same commodity. The new charge could be a just correction of a price that was previously too low, as indeed in the case of oil[45]. In fact, it has been widely argued that the former price of oil was the result of a pattern of exploitation which could equitably support, in the determination of the new price, an additional element of compensation for the prior unjust enrichment of the consuming countries[46]. In the final analysis the price of a given commodity could rightly be considered unfair because of the excessive hardships it creates for consumers, but this judgement must be made in the light of the relative sacrifices borne by the producers, their economic needs and their attempts to avoid adverse effects on the world economy.

Arab Oil Policy and Fair Pricing

This having been said, Arab oil policy with respect to the price issue becomes more clear in light of the following facts which, though uncontroverted, are generally ignored in the standard arguments advanced by the major consuming countries:

   (i) Despite unprecedented rises in the price of crude oil, this commodity is still the cheapest form of energy in the world market. In other words the price of substitute energy sources – which has been considered the natural ceiling to oil prices – is still far from being competitive.

   (ii) The oil price rise did not result merely from changes in supply; it was also prompted by important alterations in the prevailing conditions of demand. In particular, the increase in US demand for oil imports, which had remained within the range of eight per cent per annum during the period of 1962-1970, suddenly jumped by thirty per cent in 1973[47]. As already mentioned, the new forces of supply and demand prevailing at the end of 1973 easily could have justified higher prices than those fixed by the producing countries at the time.

(iii) The high increase in the level of prices during 1973-1974 was not a peculiarity of oil. Nor was oil the starting point in this inflationary trend. Before the oil crisis came the explosion of food prices which culminated in much greater rises in the prices of items such as sugar, cereals, rough rice and oil seeds. In June 1974, the Economic Commission Board of OPEC found that "the prices of seventeen primary commodities which accounted for a large share of member countries' imports, had increased, on the average, by more than 100 per cent during the last twelve months"[48]. On the other hand, it is now generally recognized that the increase in oil prices is only responsible for 2-3 per cent of the 1974 inflation rate in consumer prices which recently was estimated to be 14.5 per cent[49] in the countries of the Organization for Economic Co-operation and Development (OECD)[50].

(iv) Before the great increase in oil prices, decisions were made in the United States and Europe to devalue, revalue, or float various currencies, thus causing further reductions in the real value of oil payments received by the producing countries.

(v) Despite great increases in the price of crude oil, the price of refined petroleum products might well have remained unchanged if the major oil companies and the governments of the consuming countries had reduced their share of the profits arising out of the final product[51]. Instead, oil companies reaped an even greater portion of the net gain and realized enormous additional profits, without having to share any of the responsibilities which the oil-producers assumed as a result of their new wealth.

(vi) More than one-half of the oil import bill has never been paid in real terms by the consuming countries, due to limitations on the economic capacity of the oil producers to absorb immediately in real assets the full amount of their oil revenues[52]. The rest of these revenues are merely a credit, a paper transfer, which allows consumers additional time to strive for full payment in real resources (goods and services) in the future. Even then, the adverse effect on the balance of payments of the consuming countries will be redressed, at least in part, by the huge proceeds of their exports to the oil producers.

(vii) Part of the financial hardship suffered by the consuming countries in the aftermath of the increase in the oil price was due to over-stocking on their part. "By the summer of 1974 tankers were loading about three million barrels of oil every day, more than was being consumed at the other end of the journey, and it was becoming difficult to find anywhere to place these surplus stocks"[53].

(viii) Finally, oil is not a reproducible commodity. It is a fast wasting asset and, for many Arab producers, the only real asset they own. Thus, revenues accruing to producing countries from the exportation of oil should hardly be considered in the same manner as proceeds from the sale of agricultural or industrial products. Depreciating cash or paper claims are poor alternatives to a depleting real asset as important as oil. Indeed, the transformation of capital wealth from crude oil to cash may not be economically justified beyond certain limits, particularly for those Arab oil-producers who can spend the realized cash least quickly.

These facts taken as a whole should adequately explain the UN General Assembly's statement that the rise of crude oil prices was a "legitimate and perfectly justified action"[54]. It should be noted, however, that the whole price issue is still open to negotiation between producers and consumers, as indicated by the heads of state of all the OPEC countries[55]. Stabilization of the oil price remains the primary objective of these nations. But it must be maintained at a level that will ensure a just compensation for the producers while providing adequate incentive for the consumers to restrain their appetite for excessive consumption.

The Impact of Arab Oil Pricing Policy

Concern for the stabilization of oil prices had long been manifested by OPEC countries, unilaterally and as a group, even before the advent of the "energy crisis". Methods for obtaining this objective are presently under thorough study in OPEC quarters, but a general consensus already exists to the effect that the price of petroleum should be linked to certain objective criteria. Such criteria may include the price of manufactured goods, the price of certain raw materials and finished products, the rate of inflation, and the terms under which goods and technology are transferred into OPEC countries. Studies also are being conducted on the feasibility of using Special Drawing Rights (SDRs)[56] or a basket of currencies as the basic unit of account for the oil price instead of the US dollar (which might remain, for practical reasons, the unit of payment).

Should either or both of these changes (i.e., the linking of prices to objective criteria and the use of a less risky unit of account than the currency of one given State) be implemented, the oil-producing countries would achieve one of the basic objectives of the new international economic order. The UN General Assembly's Declaration in respect of that order specifically calls for a "just and equitable relationship between the prices of raw materials, primary products, manufactured and semi-manufactured goods exported by developing countries and the prices of raw materials, primary commodities, manufactures, capital goods and equipment imported by them"[57]. The related Programme of Action further emphasizes the need "to work for a link between the prices of exports of developing countries and the prices of their imports from developed countries"[58], and the need for "setting up general principles for pricing policy for exports of commodities of developing countries with a view to rectifying and achieving satisfactory terms of trade for them"[59]. Similar stress is laid on such a linkage in the resolutions of the recent Dakar Conference of Developing Countries on Raw Materials[60].

Apart from the question of linkages, the present pricing policy of the Arab oil-producers seems to be generally governed by three important factors, defined in the Algiers Solemn Declaration as follows: (1) "the imperatives of the conservation of petroleum, including its depletion and increasing scarcity in the future; (2) the value of oil in terms of its non-energy uses; and (3) the conditions of availability, utilization and cost of alternative sources of energy"[61].

If strictly applied these factors could lead, in real terms, to higher crude oil prices than those prevailing at the present time. But the oil producers, especially the country with the highest leverage in this matter (Saudi Arabia), seem to place greater emphasis on the stability and predictability of price than on its rise *per se*. Even Algeria, whose pressing economic needs may justify a keen interest in further price hikes, has expressed readiness to freeze the present charges and even to decrease them "provided, however, that the developed countries make a similar and simultaneous effort in return – with each contributing according to its means and responsibilities to the reorganization of the world economy and to the establishment of the stability required for development and prosperity"[62].

FOREIGN AID

Since the 1973-74 oil-price increases, the foreign aid performance of Arab oil-exporting countries has reached a level that is unprecedented in history. This phenomenon is not merely a consequence of sudden wealth; these Arab States have a combined population that is equivalent to seventeen per cent of that of the United States, yet the total oil revenues realized by these countries in 1974 amounted to less than five per cent of the US national income for the same year. Indeed, the average per capita income of the oil producers still lags far behind that of the United States, the European community, and Japan[63]. Nevertheless, the foreign aid performance of the Arab oil-exporters has become far superior to that of the Western nations. According to OECD's own tentative figures, as provided by its Development Assistance Committee (DAC)[64], OPEC members in 1974 disbursed 1.8 per cent of their GNP in foreign aid, as compared to 0.33 per cent in the case of DAC countries[65]. When this latter percentage is expanded to include the entire flow of resources from DAC countries to developing countries in relation to the GNP of the donors, it still remains within the 0.79 per cent figure[66], even though the aid target repeatedly requested by UNCTAD and accepted in principle by the DAC countries stands at 1.0 per cent of the GNP of the donor. Such a huge disparity between the foreign assistance record of the Arab States and that of the industrialized DAC countries is all the more striking in view of the difference in the nature of the monies distributed. For the Arab producers, as indicated above, are not really sharing their income with the less fortunate countries; in effect, they are giving away a substantial portion of their exhaustible and unrenewable capital[67].

Nor are cash commitments the only form of assistance which the Arab oil-exporters have extended to other developing countries. Low-interest deposits have quietly been placed with the central banks of some of the poor nations of the world to help them alleviate liquidity problems. Agreements on deferred payment terms for exported oil have been concluded with other countries of the Third World[68], despite the inherent financial risks of such deals. OPEC countries as a whole have decided "to promote the production of fertilizers with the aim of supplying such production under favourable terms and conditions, to the countries most affected by the economic crisis"[69]. Arab producers also are co-operating closely with the other developing countries in seeking more equitable and remunerative price levels for the exports of the latter[70].

The impact of the increase in the price of oil on the balance of payments of non-oil-exporting developing countries, taken as a whole, is serious. However, it is not as devastating or as unique as some Western reports have implied. Apart from the fact that the prices of some of the raw materials produced by these other developing countries have also risen, the estimated $10 billion cost differential between their consumption of petroleum products in 1973 and in 1974[71] is identical to the rise in the cost of their imports of manufactured goods from OECD countries between 1972 and the end of 1973[72]. At the same time, the amount of foreign support necessary to restore reasonable rates of growth in developing countries has been estimated at $3-4 billion per year (in 1974 prices) for the rest of this decade[73]. With these figures in mind, it should be recalled that total OPEC aid commitments exceeded $15 billion in 1974 dollars, of which more than $3.4 billion were actually disbursed according to UNCTAD reports[74]. It is thus significant that this Arab foreign aid was not a one-shot rescue arrangement. Institutions offering concessionary development financing are now operating in practically every Arab oil-exporting country[75], while new inter-Arab organizations have begun to provide assistance on a multilateral basis[76].

Theoretically, the application of differential oil-price levels in order to favour developing countries might have been more appropriate than granting assistance in the amounts indicated above. Such a method was suggested by Libya in early 1974[77], but was discarded by all other OPEC members for practical reasons. Not only would preferential pricing involve the drawing of invidious distinctions; it also would create the undesirable prospect of re-exportation to third parties at prices lower than those charged to such parties by the producers, the inevitable result being the establishment of a black market in oil. Furthermore, this method could invite rifts within OPEC and within the larger group of developing countries, while the administration and supervision of such a system might also require a costly and unwelcome interference in the affairs of the consumers.

Through the International Monetary Fund (IMF)[78] and through direct placements with the central banks of consuming countries, the Arab oil producers have also extended huge financial assistance to the *developed* countries. The purpose of this assistance has been to help redress the external imbalances of the economies of these countries during the period of adjustment necessary to their economic recovery. As will be seen shortly, such an objective also underlies the policies pursued by the Arab oil-producers in the investment of their net liquid assets. It is equally served, albeit indirectly, by Arab financial assistance to developing countries, the proceeds of which are frequently used in importing goods and services from the developed nations. Much truth could thus be found in the suggestion that the OECD Financial Support Fund[79], better known as the Safety Net Fund, could hardly have been established with its huge capital of 20 billion SDRs without such benevolent Arab policies[80].

From a legal point of view, the impressive aid record of Arab oil-exporting countries has two important implications. The first is that the conduct of these States contributes to the evolution of new legal rules in the sphere of international economic co-operation. For even though contemporary international law does not create a legal obligation upon richer States to provide assistance to the less fortunate countries, a moral obligation to this effect is gradually hardening into a binding international custom[81]. Present aid efforts of Arab oil-producing States are accelerating the establishment of this custom. It is particularly noteworthy that Arab donors have not only extended these huge amounts of aid, but in so doing have acted as though this were the normal, if not the necessary, course of action under the circumstances. Elements of the *opinio juris*, necessary in the conventional theory for completing the custom-making process, may thus be discerned in the oil-producers' behaviour even at this stage. More liberal jurists who find that the "juridical consciousness" manifested in the relations of some States could be adequate to transform usage into custom[82], may therefore find it plausible to argue, on account of recent Arab practices, that customary international law has already established an obligation of aid-giving in favour of poorer countries.

Moreover, Arab aid is creating a new pattern of international financial assistance, not only in that it is in no way designed to promote the economic interests of the donors, but also in some of its basic legal features. For example, loans of the Kuwait Fund for Arab Economic Development, though presenting a form of bilateral aid, are governed by the common legal principles of the lender *and* the borrower. Furthermore, the Solidarity Fund for Economic and Social Development of Non-Aligned Countries is to be established on the basis of equal voting, despite the expected disparities in the financial contributions of different members to its capital.

FOREIGN INVESTMENT

In view of the lopsided and vulnerable economies of Arab oil-exporting countries, the policies which these nations follow in investing their net liquid assets are likely to constitute a crucial factor in shaping their future. Their oil is being continually transformed into cash which, if not converted into permanent capital, will at best leave their future generations with nothing but depreciated paper claims. Therefore, the investment strategies of the Arab producers tend to pursue, despite differences in detail, two basic objectives: (a) the achieving of sound sources of investment for their liquid assets; and (b) the enlarging of their own economies' absorption capacity in order to facilitate investments capable of contributing to development[83].

The additional net liquid assets of OPEC countries, i.e., the difference between their revenues and the costs of their imports, reached an amount equivalent to about $60 billion in 1974. At least $40 billion of this amount was invested in the major Western countries[84]. A smaller surplus is expected to accrue in 1975, and according to official US sources "accumulations of 'oil surpluses' will effectively disappear before the end of the decade, and new investments will begin to decline before they reach a cumulative total of $200-250 billion"[85]. Such relatively modest figures fall far short of the estimates circulated in financial circles during the past two years[86]. At any rate, these figures are significant enough to justify the recent concern given this matter by both producers and consumers of oil.

For the oil-producers, the minimum requirement of investing in assets no less valuable than oil in the ground has proved to be a formidable task. Widespread fluctuations in currency exchange rates present anew the dangers of "pretended" repayments by the oil-consuming borrowers as a result of the continuous debasing of their respective currencies[87]. Erosion is also brought about by the spiralling prices of assets purchased by OPEC investors and by the inflated value of the money which they receive as earnings upon their investments[88]. But during this time in which oil revenues cannot be constructively absorbed in developing their economies, the Arab oil States are left with practically no choice but to make the best of the foreign investment opportunities open to them. In this respect, investment in the major oil-consuming countries remains attractive. These developed countries can readily absorb such funds, while the influx of capital into their economies will help redress the lack of equilibrium in their balance of payments and reduce the pressure on them to follow restrictive policies detrimental to the world economy as a whole[89]. Thus, the risks of economic instability and galloping inflation are not confined to the industrialized countries; the oil-producers, in their capacity as holders of large funds, have come to share a significant stake in the stability of the economies of industrialized countries and of the international monetary system at large.

The need for stabilization has made it imperative that institutional Arab investors avoid speculative operations and seek diversified long-term investments. Practical considerations may sometimes necessitate resorting to short-term deposits or short-term bonds until sound investment opportunities are identified, but this situation might have been less common if the oil-exporting countries had been better prepared to cope with the unexpected funds. In 1974, for instance, less than $1 billion out of the $11 billion of OPEC funds invested in the United States went into "permanent" investments such as stocks, long-term corporate bonds, or real estate[90]. The destabilizing effect of such a practice is actually controlled, however, by the generally responsible attitude shown by the investors in handling such deposits, as well as by the fact that, in the circumstances, even short-term deposits may be viewed as long-term if one considers them in the context of the western banking system as a whole.

At any rate, Arab oil-exporting countries seem to resent their confinement to the role of mere money lenders in the world financial markets. To maintain and increase the real value of their assets, they are aware that they must get involved in the capital formation process, especially through the creation of new productive capabilities[91]. They are particularly attracted to those Western industries which have strong links with their own economies or to the economies of the other developing countries of the Arab region. Bilateral co-operation between Arab investors and trans-national corporations is thus being promoted as a vehicle for pooling Arab funds with Western technology, to the mutual benefit of both parties. Triangular deals involving other developing countries which have sound investment potentials but are lacking in both liquidity and expertise are also in the making. The objective is to create joint ventures in which the Arab parties are not merely "exporters of raw materials, markets for industrial goods, or docile sources of finance"[92]. Such an attempt has far-reaching implications with regard to the very nature of the hitherto uneasy relationship between Western multi-nationals and the developing countries. Meaningful partnerships formed between Western sources of technology and expertise on the one hand, and Arab sources of funds on the other, possibly in co-operation with other developing countries offering sound investment opportunities, could present a new model of trans-national business ventures. If such a model were to develop, Arab oil-exporting countries would be promoting the objectives of the new international economic order in two of its most sensitive areas: transfer of technology[93] and regulation of the activities of trans-national corporations[94]. Such co-operation would certainly facilitate the avoidance of further disorder in the international monetary system, while the developed countries would be given the opportunity to restore the monetary stability necessary for safeguarding the value of the Arab exporters' financial assets.

Any consideration of Arab investment policies should not ignore the attitude of the Arab producers toward the foreign oil companies operating in their territories. Although all of the producers are now asserting control over these companies as a corollary to their sovereignty over their natural resources, they have followed different paths in doing so. Algeria, Iraq and Libya have resorted to outright nationalization of the assets of some of the companies operating in their respective territories. Such nationalizations have on occasion been described as "politically motivated" and "discriminatory"[95]. However, appropriate compensation was eventually agreed upon and paid to the affected companies. Such a practice may support the notion that a State is now free to resort to nationalization for whatever reasons it deems fit, even if they are politically coloured, so long as it pays appropriate remuneration. This broadly-defined notion, though inconsistent with the more restrictive doctrine prevailing in conventional Western literature[96], has been recently codified in the UN General Assembly's Charter of Economic Rights and Duties of States[97]. Other major Arab producers such as Saudi Arabia, Kuwait and the United Arab Emirates have conducted negotiated take-overs of a partial or total nature. In these cases, agreement on due compensation was reached between the parties (or is presently under discussion). None of the Arab take-overs of foreign oil companies, not even the Iraqi nationalization of US and Dutch interests during the war situation of October 1973, took the form of confiscation, declared or disguised. Since Arab oil-exporting countries are likely to hold large assets abroad for an extensive period of time, it is obviously in their interest to preserve the principle of compensation for expropriated properties as a key component of the new international economic order.

CONFLICT PREVENTION AND RESOLUTION

For reasons irrelevant to oil economics, the attempt by Arab oil-exporting countries to improve their terms of trade through legitimate measures falling within their domestic jurisdiction was depicted in the Western media as the major cause for the recent economic ills of the industrialized nations. Western politicians acquiesced, and at times openly participated, in the propagation of this accusation, using it as an excuse for their own poor performance. The fact remains, however, that the oil factor contributed only insignificantly to the high rates of inflation which plagued the economies of Western countries[98]. The OPEC states were thus right to reject "any allegation attributing to the price of petroleum, the responsibility for the present instability of the world economy"[99] and to condemn "threats, propaganda campaigns and other measures which have gone so far as to attribute to OPEC member countries the intention of undermining the economies of the developed countries"[100]. More importantly, OPEC members have met the attempt of industrialized countries to group against them with a conciliatory approach, affirming their support for "dialogue, co-operation and concerted action" to help solve "the difficulties experienced by other people which may affect world stability"[101].

In fact, this conciliatory attitude may be discerned even in the way that Arab oil-exporting countries handled their cutback and embargo measures during the Arab-Israeli hostilities of October 1973. First they imposed a modest five per cent cutback in production, for the explicit objective of ensuring the implementation of UN resolutions concerning the withdrawal of Israeli forces from Arab territories and the restoration of the lawful rights of the Palestinian people. No one disputes the legitimacy of such an objective and few would disagree with its necessity as a precondition to the establishment of a durable peace in the Middle East. When the initial cutbacks were met with increased American support to the Israeli war effort, an embargo was imposed on oil shipments to the United States, again with the declared intention of achieving the above-mentioned objective. However, the oil-producing states also promised to lift the embargo when the armed conflict subsided and steps were taken to begin implementation of a scheduled withdrawal of Israeli forces from Arab territories forcibly occupied since 1967. But even this reduced condition was later dropped, and the embargo was lifted on 18 March 1974, when the United States merely showed some interest in making efforts for the restoration of peace in the area[102].

Nevertheless, the flexible attitude of Arab oil-exporters should not be taken as a sign of their lack of determination. This flexibility is simply a result of their realistic assessment of the various political limitations on the means within their disposal. The Arab States would undoubtedly do everything in their power to defend themselves against military aggression. In the absence of this extreme state of affairs, they certainly would prefer to err on the side of world stability and prosperity. Indeed, it is their desire for stability and prosperity in a world in which they are highly dependent on others that prompts them to prefer dialogue over confrontation whenever the latter course can be avoided.

The desire of the Arab oil-exporters to enter into a dialogue with the main consuming countries was frequently expressed before the emergence of the energy "crisis". Even then, their objective was to link the oil price to the prices of manufactured goods in an attempt to control inflationary trends in both areas[103]. Western European countries, which receive eighty per cent of their petroleum supplies from Arab sources, were the first to react favourably to such a desire. As early as 4 October 1972, these countries had proposed a co-operation with the oil-producing states "going beyond the oil problem and constituting true economic and technical collaboration for the mutual interest"[104]. However, this proposal was not formally considered by the nine Common Market countries until their summit conference during the height of the crisis on 15 December 1974. There again they stressed the necessity of opening negotiations with the oil-producing countries "for the establishment of an overall regime covering extended co-operation for realizing the economic and industrial development of these countries, industrial investments and the supplying of member countries with energy at reasonable prices"[105].

The idea of discussing the oil problem within the framework of economic co-operation between producers and consumers was further developed in the thinking of the OPEC countries in two respects. The close link between the international monetary system, the international trading system, and investment flows necessitated a discussion of each of these subjects as an element of an interrelated whole, if meaningful agreement on effective steps to restore world economic stability was to be achieved[106]. Also, the growing solidarity between OPEC members and other developing countries prompted both to insist on extending the discussion to include all raw materials of developing countries – not just oil[107]. As a result, the proposal of the President of France for a worldwide conference on energy and related economic problems was welcomed by the OPEC nations on three conditions: (1) that the conference should address itself to the problems facing both the developed and the developing countries in an attempt to alleviate some of the major difficulties facing the world economy; (2) that the agenda of the conference should not be confined to an examination of energy problems, but should also consider the questions of raw materials of the developing countries, reform of the international monetary system, and international co-operation in favour of development; and (3) that all the nations affected by the problems dealt with should be equally and genuinely represented[108]. A preparatory meeting held in Paris in April 1975 was attended by ten delegations representing practically all groups concerned. The United States, Japan, and the EEC represented the industrialized countries; Algeria, Saudi Arabia, Iran and Venezuela represented OPEC countries; and Brazil, India and Zaire represented the non-oil producing, developing countries. This meeting was meant to prepare the agenda for a full-scale conference which was tentatively scheduled for July 1975. Unfortunately, no agreement was reached at the preparatory meeting as to the date or the agenda of that conference[109].

The position of the OPEC countries with regard to the proposed conference is clearly stated in the Algiers Solemn Declaration. They are willing to "negotiate the conditions for the stabilization of oil prices," to "ensure supplies that will meet the essential requirements of the economies of the developed countries", and to continue providing significant aid to developing countries. On the other hand, OPEC members want the developed states to "contribute to the progress and development of the developing countries through concrete action and in particular to achieve economic and monetary stability, giving due regard to the interests of the developing countries". A list of specific actions to be taken by developed countries in this respect is included in the Declaration as a prerequisite to the full implementation of the Programme of Action adopted by the UN General Assembly for the establishment of a new international economic order[110]. By adopting this balanced position toward the conference, OPEC countries assert themselves as the main sponsors of that new economic order which they hope to achieve through co-operation with all other states.

Such polycentric problems as the determination and stabilization of oil prices undoubtedly can be best solved through negotiation among all interested parties. Experience has shown, however, that negotiation is a useful mechanism for the resolution of conflict only to the extent that it provides the parties with a forum in which neither side can dictate its will on the other. Under the prevailing international economic order, this has hardly been the case in most negotiations between developed and developing countries. The failure of the Paris preparatory meeting may thus have pleased certain developed countries not yet willing to accept a fundamental change in their relationships with other nations. The US Government, in particular, had previously indicated that its strategy was to get the consuming countries to meet with the oil-producers only after the former countries had succeeded in transforming the market conditions for OPEC oil and in remedying the vulnerability of their economies[111]. This type of approach seeks to continue the old style of "negotiation" that has often proved, under the prevailing international economic order, to be inadequate for providing long-term solutions and at best capable only of forcing the continuation of unjust relationships.

CONCLUSION

Despite their obvious need for conserving a fast depleting asset, and their continued accumulation in its stead of depreciating liquid funds, Arab oil-exporting countries continue production at levels sufficient to meet all market requirements. Even when a war situation forced them to resort to the extreme measures of production cutbacks and boycotts, they applied these measures cautiously and lifted them before their legitimate objective was even near attainment. When the producing countries finally managed to exercise their right to fix the price of this precious and, in many cases, only source of national wealth, they set it at a level lower than prevailing market realizations. Once they started to accumulate net liquid assets, they embarked on a programme of aid whose relative size is unprecedented in history, donating in the first year alone amounts ranking in relation to their GNP ten to twenty times more than the annual official aid ever provided by developed countries. Their investment of the remaining funds was responsibly conducted, with the purpose of maintaining the purchasing power of such funds while helping developed countries in their efforts to restore stability to the international economic system. In the face of all the accusations and threats directed at them from sources whose interests are closely tied to the ailing international economis order[112], they expressed a readiness for dialogue, co-operation and concerted action.

The Arab oil-producers, along with other OPEC members, find in the present situation a unique opportunity to establish a new world economic order more just to developing countries. Their persistent attempts to seize this opportunity for the benefit of progressive change will continue. They have played a major role in the Sixth Special Session of the UN General Assembly, which issued the basic documents on the establishment of a new international economic order. They have also sponsored the cause of all developing countries in other fora between producers and consumers of raw materials. And they are aware that their success in introducing a new element of justice into international economic relations is likely to create a greater measure of economic and political stability in this troubled world.

None of the measures applied so far by Arab oil-exporting countries with respect to their oil is inconsistent with contemporary international law. Behind these measures, however, lies the strategic objective of establishing a new order to be governed by a more progressive international law that takes cognizance of the special needs of developing countries. Arab oil policies may thus be viewed as legitimate instruments of a long needed change in international relations – a change, one may add, that remained but a dream for developing countries until this new power came to be vested in the oil-producers.

CHAPTER 11

INTER-ARAB EQUITY
JOINT VENTURES

Based on a more detailed study distributed restrictively as UNCTAD Doc. TD/B/AC.19/R.5 (21 October 1975) and TD/AC.19/R.5/Add.1 (3 October 1975) which also appeared as a Kuwait Fund Publication in May 1976 (in Arabic and English).

INTRODUCTION

Three practical limitations restrict the scope of this analysis:

(i) Inter-Arab economic co-operation has mainly taken the form of lending operations from sources in Arab capital-exporting countries to public or private recipients in other Arab countries. The loans extended in these operations are currently estimated to account for more than eighty per cent of the flow of financial resources for investment purposes among Arab countries. Although the lender-debtor relationship might be loosely described as a contractual joint venture when it relates to co-operation in the financing of a specific project, such a relationship does not fall within the scope of this analysis. As indicated in its title, this study is confined to inter-Arab *equity* joint ventures, i.e., the association of two or more parties from different Arab States in order to undertake an economic project and to share in its risks and profits.

(ii) Arab equity joint ventures present, on the whole, a recent phenomenon. Despite repeated discussions among Arab economists and politicians since the early fifties on the relevance and importance of establishing such ventures for the strengthening of Arab economic integration, most of the present joint ventures have been established after 1973. As a result, no adequate analysis could be carried out at this point with respect to the operational policies of such ventures or the practical problems faced by them.

(iii) Among the limited number of such recent joint-ventures, many are banks or similar financial institutions. Such institutions follow on the whole a standard pattern and have little to offer in terms of operational experience in the productive fields.

As a result, this analysis is based in fact on the detailed study of a small number of companies of which most are still in their pre-operational stage. The first-hand experience of the author in the establishment of Arab joint ventures and of joint ventures between foreign companies or governments and host Arab governments has also been a primary source of many of the opinions and conclusions presented in this analysis.

FREQUENCY AND IMPORTANCE OF INTER-ARAB JOINT VENTURES

From the nationalist view-point of developing countries, it has traditionally been argued that the equity participation of foreign partners in local projects is not generally desirable, but should be encouraged only when a given project cannot be carried out properly on an exclusive national basis. Typical examples for the beneficial adoption of the international equity joint venture as a form of business organization are thus confined, in the standard argument, to situations such as the following: where the nature of the project necessitates its execution through a joint venture; where the cost of the venture can only be met by bringing in complementary financing from a foreign partner; where the implementation of the project is dependent on a degree of expertise (including managerial and marketing expertise) which cannot be obtained except through association with a foreign partner; and where such an association is an important means for the distribution of exceptionally high risks inherent in the project. Otherwise, a presumption seems to prevail in favour of the national equity ownership of projects. Consequently, preference in obtaining external financing for development projects is given, in principle, to borrowing from foreign sources (if it is to be obtained on reasonable terms) rather than to inviting their equity participation.

Such generalities do not readily apply however to inter-Arab joint ventures which are considered, in the prevailing climate of thought, to be important instruments for the achievement of the generally accepted ideal of Arab economic integration. The often-cited arguments against foreign direct investments in general are rarely quoted in the context of investments among Arab countries. On the contrary, some of these countries, such as Syria, Iraq and, to a lesser extent, Egypt, allow preferential treatment to investments originating in other Arab countries[1]. The latter investments, it should be noted, do not represent advanced economies or powerful foreign powers and thus rarely raise the traditional sensitivities associated with Western investments in developing countries. They may support, on the other hand, the desirable trend towards increasing the volume of inter-Arab trade and may eventually be instrumental in achieving a more rational use of productive factors in Arab countries through a better inter-Arab division of labour.

However, until the early seventies, inter-Arab equity joint ventures were virtually non-existent in spite of the long list of multilateral agreements signed under the auspices of the League of Arab States for the purpose of creating such ventures. The failure to implement significant steps in this direction up till that time may have resulted from the following factors in particular:

(i) The generally unfavourable investment climate (in its economic, political and psychological aspects) which prevailed in most of the Arab capital-importing states.

(ii) The lack of sophistication on the part of most investors in the Arab capital-exporting states to whom bank deposits and portfolio investments in Western countries presented a much easier outlet in comparison with direct investment in other Arab countries.

(iii) The lack of support from the investors' home governments, which were in many cases on uneasy political terms with other Arab governments.

(iv) The absence of institutions for the promotion of inter-Arab investments in both capital-importing and capital-exporting countries. Hence, the missing role of the active sponsor of joint projects and the catalyst in their implementation which identifies projects and facilitates the mutual choice of partners.

(v) The lack, at any rate, of large net liquid assets in the hands of Arab investors (public and private) in comparison with the amounts which started to accumulate on later dates.

The trend against investing surplus Arab funds in the Arab region began to be reversed, however, in the seventies especially after the Arab-Israeli war of October 1973 and the great increase in oil prices which followed that event. Such a change could easily be traced to four developments, in particular:

(i) The political relations between the major capital-exporting and capital-importing countries in the Arab region have greatly improved, allowing in the process a new direction in the outlook of countries of both groups towards inter-Arab economic co-operation.

(ii) The volume of net liquid assets accumulating in the Arab oil-exporting countries increased to an extent where new and complementary interests emerged between these countries and the other Arab countries which have a large absorptive capacity for profitable investments. It also became politically inevitable for the former countries to invest an increased portion of their assets in other related Arab countries.

(iii) Simultaneously, the investment climate in the whole Arab region underwent significant changes especially in countries like Egypt, the Sudan and Syria where the official hostile outlook towards private foreign investments was practically replaced by open encouragement to investments flowing from other Arab countries.

(iv) As a result of the above developments, new Arab Institutions (national and joint) were established for the promotion, protection and financing of inter-Arab investments and continue to give them additional support.

Certain sectors were first to benefit from this new trend. Joint ventures in the financial sector (development funds, investment companies, merchant banks, etc.) were formed as a first step towards co-operation in the implementation of specific projects to be identified through these institutions. Since January 1974 at least eighteen financial institutions with combined authorized capital of about $4 billion started operation as joint ventures among Arab countries or between some of them (as the leading partners) and other developing countries.

Another sector where immediate Arab joint action was possible is the petroleum industry. This did not occur merely as a result of the prominence of oil as the source of the new Arab wealth, hence the natural recipient of common attention, but was also due to the fact

that Arab co-operation in that sector had been already institutionalized through OAPEC. The latter organization has successfully sponsored four large joint ventures among its members, at least two of
which (the Arab Petroleum Investment Company and the Arab
Petroleum Services Company) are likely to promote further joint
ventures in the petroleum industry through the creation of affiliates
and subsidiaries in participation with national sources.

Along with the two above-mentioned sectors, which traditionally
have also been, though for different reasons, the main fields for joint
ventures between Arab parties and partners from developed countries, three other sectors are now receiving particular attention in
inter-Arab investment efforts. Maritime transport, especially in
countries like Egypt whose national fleet carries less then seven per
cent of its international trade, has attracted several multilateral ventures of which some involved non-Arab parties. Livestock
development, particularly attractive in countries like the Sudan and
Somalia, has also been a favourite sector for new ventures. The third
area of particular attraction is tourism and more generally, real estate
investments (especially in Egypt, Tunisia, Morocco, Sudan and
Syria). Concentration on these latter sectors may be justified by
certain common characteristics. They all meet established needs, call
for a minimum of pre-investment studies and do not require sophisticated technology for their implementation.

FACTORS EXPLAINING THE ESTABLISHMENT OF
INTER-ARAB JOINT VENTURES

The most general factor explaining the establishment of international joint ventures is obviously the fact that the resources and
interests between the parties to such ventures are complementary,
or, more accurately, that the parties are increasingly aware of that
fact. In the context of Arab states this factor is emphasized by the
following considerations:

(i) One of the basic contemporary divisions in the Arab region is
that which classifies its states into two groups: one accumulating large liquid assets in excess of its present absorptive capacity and the other suffering from acute shortages in financial
resources while having, in most cases, a greater absorptive
capacity than that of the first group. In this situation states in
the first group are seeking investment opportunities abroad

while those in the second group are offering such opportunities to outside financiers. The joint-venture formula presents itself in the circumstances as a happy solution, especially as stronger political ties continue to develop among the two groups and a better investment climate emerges in the Arab capital-importing countries.

(ii) Economies of scale may, in certain industries or projects, necessitate the adoption of the joint-venture formula for the implementation of Arab projects in need of a huge equity capital or an extensive market. National units in industries such as the petrochemical and the car industries have often proved to be economically not feasible without extensive governmental protection and support. Larger inter-Arab ventures in such fields could, on the other hand, acquire the necessary elements of economic viability on a purely commercial basis. Such large ventures could also aspire to deal with Western multi-nationals from a position of strength and may even eventually replace them in the region much more readily than the present national units could.

(iii) Through association with partners from oil-rich countries, local partners in Arab capital-importing countries, with foreign cash in hand, are likely to find more attentive ears in multi-national corporations whose involvement in the project as suppliers of technology and/or advanced management, and even as shareholders, could perhaps be secured in a shorter time and on better terms than otherwise. The interest of such multi-nationals to enter into trilateral joint ventures involving also capital-importing and capital-exporting Arab countries is obviously easier to excite than in the case where the Arab partners are offering only the investment opportunity or the cash.

(iv) The objective of Arab economic integration has proved to be unattainable through trade liberalization measures only, in view of the limited production capabilities of each Arab country and the competitive character of their products. Along with such measures, and perhaps prior to their full adoption, the volume and quality of the production of goods and services in each Arab country should therefore be such as to allow for meaningful trade among these countries. One means of achieving such changes in the pattern and scale of production capabilities in the region is the creation of joint ventures with greater resources than those available at present to national enterprises.

Besides these general factors, the establishment of Arab joint ventures is naturally influenced by the surrounding conditions in each case. Of particular importance is the method followed in the creation of each venture. Under the present institutional framework, these ventures could be classified in this respect into two broad categories:

Arab Ventures sponsored by inter-Arab Institutions

Sponsorship by Inter-Governmental Institutions

The factors explaining the establishment of an increasing number of ventures of this type (usually multilateral public enterprises) could be found in the objectives pursued by each sponsoring institution. Such an objective may be regional or sub-regional economic integration or more generally the strengthening of Arab economic cooperation, such as in the projects sponsored by the Council of Arab Economic Unity or by the League of Arab States, as well as those proposed by the Permanent Consultative Commission for the Arab Maghreb. The objective may relate, on the other hand, to the economic development of the Arab region as a whole or of a smaller or larger geographic area, as in the case of the projects sponsored by development finance institutions like the Arab Fund for Economic and Social Development and the Kuwait Fund for Arab Economic Development. Or else the objective may be the development of a certain productive sector in the economies of the countries concerned as in the case of the projects sponsored by OAPEC. In all such cases, the active role played by the sponsoring institutions is of great relevance in the identification of the project, the preparation of the studies and the legal documents related to it as well as in arranging for the prospective partners to form the venture and co-ordinating their conflicting interests in a manner satisfactory to all. Not all interested institutions have been equally successful in this respect, however. The Secretariat of the League of Arab States, which is not particularly suited to play that role, was naturally less successful than such business-like institutions as the development funds or OAPEC. Nor do these institutions share the same conception of their role as sponsors. Whereas the League Secretariat was content in most cases with a passive bureaucratic role (preparation of constituent legal documents), some other sponsoring institutions proved to be effective catalysts in the more challenging process of the actual formation of the venture. In all cases, however, the presence of a commonly accepted sponsor in the pre-investment stage was a decisive element in the developments which led to the establishment of the joint ventures concerned.

Sponsorship by Investment Companies

The establishment of a joint investment company to act as a holding company in the host country in charge of the formation of productive enterprises has also proved to be a successful mechanism for the creation of new private joint ventures. Investment companies of this type are now operating in Egypt and the Sudan in particular. Established as joint ventures with partners from the richer Arab states, they have succeeded in the creation of a number of other joint ventures with the participation of other foreign investors including their own shareholders and are expected to continue to play a useful role in this respect. Obviously, such investment companies do not confine their role to the pre-investment stage but do participate, as equity shareholders and/or suppliers of loan financing, in the ventures they help create and therefore, act as more effective catalysts in the establishment of new projects.

Ad hoc Arab joint ventures

These are the typical profit-motivated ventures in which the initiative is usually taken up by a certain investor (be it of a private or public character, in or outside the host country) or by an interested government. Owing to the lack of Arab investment promotion centres and of intermediary financial services' companies (with the exception of a few recent examples in Kuwait and Lebanon) the formation of such ventures is still a hectic process which depends to a large extent on personal relationships between prospective partners. Government agencies in charge of foreign investments in some Arab capital-importing countries (such as Egypt and Morocco) are aspiring to play a useful catalytic role in facilitating the establishment of this type of venture. The Arab Fund for Economic and Social Development and the Inter-Arab Investment Guarantee Corporation (which are both inter-governmental Arab ventures) also envisage a role for themselves in this field of activity. So far, however, the matter is left to the individual attempts of prospective partners acting in the absence of a sophisticated structure for capital formation at regional and national level.

The need of investors in the Arab capital-importing countries for foreign funds and for connections with business circles in the advanced countries often prompts them to seek association with investors from richer Arab states who may generally have better access to capital resources and more established business connections in the Western World. The latter investors are also giving increasing attention, albeit slowly, to this type of association, which continues to be encouraged by their home governments (both in their capacity as public authorities and as partners in investment companies) as well as by the host governments. Inter-Arab development finance institutions are also under a clear mandate in their constituent instruments to give priority in their operations to Arab joint ventures. Such positive factors are contributing at present to the process of joint-venture formation, despite the absence of organized business links between investment circles in the potential guest and host countries.

CHARACTERISTICS OF INTER-ARAB JOINT VENTURES

Existing Arab joint ventures cover a multitude of different arrangements of varying magnitude and scope. Generalizations about their operational characteristics could therefore be misleading. However, the following observations may be tentatively offered:

(i) Most Arab joint ventures have a clear governmental character as Arab governments quite often participate in them either directly or through local government-controlled corporations. Even when they are not partners, these governments exert a marked influence over such ventures. This governmental role may be ascribed to the following factors:

(a) many ventures have been sponsored by inter-governmental Arab organizations whose concern is naturally confined to the establishment of projects "among member states".

(b) the prominence of the public sector in the economies of most of the host countries.

(c) the leading role played by governments in most local investment companies in Arab capital-exporting countries.

(d) the absence of a large number of private entrepreneurs in the Arab region sufficiently sophisticated and large enough to consider long-term foreign operations through joint ventures with the private sector in Arab countries other than their own.

(e) the lack of an extensive capital formation structure on the regional level to provide small entrepreneurs in particular with ready access to the financing of their joint ventures and to facilitate the process of association among private investors from different Arab countries.

In most cases, member governments in the venture reserve for themselves the right to sell part of their share (usually not more than 49 per cent thereof) to their nationals. However, this right, which is sometimes granted subject to further limitations, has not been widely exercised by the governments concerned. The role of government as a direct promoter of joint ventures among private investors through its initial subscription in the venture's capital and the subsequent transfer of its shares to its nationals is, therefore, yet to be effectively performed.

(ii) As a result of the prevailing governmental character of Arab joint ventures, many of these, especially the multilateral examples have been established by virtue of international conventions and have taken the form of an international corporation not subject to the legal system of any particular state. The adoption of this particular form usually retards the pace of the effectiveness of the agreement establishing the venture. It could also cause a number of operational problems, as will be shown later.

(iii) As international corporations created by virtue of inter-State treaties, Arab ventures of this type often enjoy privileges and immunities beyond the normal business incentives accorded to foreign investments. Such extensive privileges, which resemble in some cases diplomatic immunities, are not confined to public utilities corporations or to ventures of the international organization type. They are even extended in a few cases to totally private companies such as the Alexandria

Navigation Company in Egypt. If such concessions are meant merely to deprive the host country from receiving unwarranted advantages from the presence of the seat of the enterprise on its territory and to free the enterprise from undesirable limitations in local laws, they have certainly exceeded their objective in many instances. Examples of such excessive privileges are to be found in particular in some of the Arab joint ventures recently established in Egypt where limitations of local law have been traditionally objectionable to foreign partners. Some joint commercial banks have been exempted for instance from the supervision of the Central Bank of Egypt as well as from the seizure of their assets and of the deposits of their clients even by virtue of court orders (e.g., the Arab International Bank). Some other inter-Arab ventures in Egypt are exempted from compliance with many provisions in the local labour laws, company laws, foreign exchange laws, etc.

(iv) In the ventures established by virtue of international conventions, disputes arising among partners or between any of them and the joint company are to be settled by arbitration, if not solved amicably. Jurisdiction of local courts is therefore limited to disputes between the joint company and third parties. This is not the case, however, in most bilateral ventures which usually have the nationality of the host country and are treated, in this respect, like the locally owned private companies.

(v) In almost all Arab joint ventures the contribution of the expatriate partner is confined to the supply of funds and to participation in the top management of the venture. This is an instance of the special situation of the Arab region where capital-exporting countries are not technologically advanced (in some instances even less so than the countries at the receiving end). The participation of expatriate partners is rarely reflected in the employment policy of the joint company. The dearth of professional talent and local labour in the oil-rich countries which are all net importers of manpower leaves the joint ventures established in other Arab countries almost wholly staffed by nationals of the host country.

Expatriate partners often try to offset this imbalance by insisting, on the strength of their share-participation, to reserve a leading role for themselves in management. (For instance most private companies established in Egypt and the Sudan in association with Kuwaiti partners have a Kuwaiti managing director). A poor choice in this respect may result in having the day-to-day decision-making power left in the hands of inexperienced management which can of course have disastrous consequences for the joint venture. In practice, however, this type of management relies heavily on foreign consultants and may opt for subcontracting the whole job to a management company in the initial period of operations. In any case, reliance on hired foreign expertise seems inevitable in most Arab ventures as advanced technology and expertise is usually lacking on the part of all partners. The sum of $1.8 billion has recently been estimated for the annual fees paid to foreign consulting firms in the Arab development market as a whole, including Arab joint-ventures[2]. This figure in itself draws attention to the importance of triangular joint ventures which involve partners from advanced countries as well. So far, however, the association of such foreign partners as third parties to inter-Arab ventures is limited mainly to banking institutions, as connections between financial circles in the Western countries and their counterparts in the Arab region are more firmly established than in the industrial or agricultural sectors.

(vi)   Many Arab joint ventures are based on the principle of equality among partners or at least among local and foreign partners. This is particularly the case in most OAPEC-sponsored ventures and in many bilateral projects. This practice is reflected in the composition of the governing boards of such ventures which often consist of an equal number of representatives of each partner or of a 50/50 participation between local and foreign partners. It should be noted, however, that the joint companies established through the participation of investment companies which are themselves joint ventures with the same expatriate partner allow a greater role for this partner in the control of the operating company even when such a company is based on an apparent 50/50 arrangement.

(vii) There seems to be little awareness on the part of Arab host countries of the possible uses of the concessions they grant to joint ventures as their share participation in the equity of such ventures. Whereas the mere licence to operate has been considered in other parts of the world as an important asset representing the share of the host government in the joint venture's capital, some inter-Arab projects established in the Sudan, Jordan and Egypt were granted important concessions merely to satisfy the expatriate partners' preconditions for entering the venture. Such concessions have often been granted without any other consideration or simply against royalties to be paid by the joint enterprise as a whole. The projected fisheries project for the exploitation of Lake Nasser through a joint company to be established between the Egyptian Government and Gulf International Co. of Kuwait may provide an example of such a practice. As the lack of cash on the part of the local partners is usually a serious constraint on the establishment of new Arab joint ventures, it is rather surprising that little use has been made of local participation in kind, especially in the form of governmental concessions and licences.

(viii) Present agreements for the establishment of Arab joint ventures as well as present investment laws in Arab host countries show little or no concern for the eventual complete naturalization of the venture through gradual withdrawal of the expatriate partners. The trend towards such an organized disinvestment through an agreed fade-out formula for the foreign partner, which is usually an important goal in ventures with investors from advanced countries, has not been emphasized in inter-Arab projects. This could be explained by the special relations between the countries involved and their common aspiration to regional economic integration. Disinvestment by expatriate partners in Arab joint ventures would thus occur only on purely business considerations and is left in most cases to the free will of the parties to the venture.

EVALUATION OF INTER-ARAB JOINT VENTURES

As most inter-Arab ventures are still in their formative stage or at best in their initial period of operation, it is obviously premature to pass final judgements on their operational policies or on their impact on Arab economic integration. Relevant experience, though limited, has however, yielded certain key indicators for the understanding of the present spread of inter-Arab joint ventures in the manner explained above. It also helps in discovering the elements of success or failure in each particular venture:

Decisive Factors of Success
In the Formation of the Venture

(i) The availability of a generally favourable political atmosphere among the states of the partners in the venture: The importance of this factor is explained by the prevailing governmental character of Arab ventures alluded to above as well as by the prominent role played by governments in the orientation of business in all Arab countries. It could also be explained by the exceptional risks borne by the expatriate partner in doing business in a country on bad terms with his own, especially when both countries belong to the rapidly changing developing world. The sensitivity of the establishment of inter-Arab joint ventures to political developments in the area has, in fact, been so great that it may be considered the single most important factor in the sudden rise in the number of Arab joint ventures in recent years.

(ii) The identification of a clear economic interest for all prospective partners in the implementation of the project: The lack of such a common interest has been a serious hindrance in the adoption of ventures which were suggested as pan-Arab multilateral projects but could perhaps have been adopted only in a more limited scope. While Arab States hesitated, for instance, in the implementation of a pan-Arab airlines project, North Yemen established its first airline as a joint venture with Egypt-Air. (This joint venture was terminated, however, when it proved to be economically detrimental to the Egyptian partner). One of the basic functions of the project's sponsor is therefore to identify the complementary interests between prospective partners and to help them in ascertaining the possible friction points and the practical ways in which they are to be resolved. This factor emphasizes the importance of working simultaneously on the establishment of regional, sub-regional and bilateral ventures depending on the range of complementary interests that could be identified between potential partners.

(iii) The presence of an interested sponsor for the project which follows a workable approach in presenting it to prospective partners and receives their serious consideration: The role of the "right sponsor", which quite often goes beyond that of a midwife to become an organic member of the joint venture, explains why certain ventures were stillborn under given circumstances but came to life later on when they received the attention of an active sponsor. The Arab Oil Tankers Company is a case at hand. The project, initiated in 1963 under the League of Arab States, could materialize only ten years later under the auspices of a better suited sponsor, OAPEC. The spread of joint Arab investment companies and Arab development funds in recent years could also mark an important step towards the creation of a growing number of inter-Arab ventures. The credibility of the sponsor in such cases is obviously enhanced by its potential role in the financing of the project, whether as a partner, lender or guarantor.

(iv) The availability of readily accessible channels for the mutual choice of partners: The process of such a choice has proved to be of crucial importance for the quick formation of the venture concerned especially when it is to be established between non-governmental entities, i.e., when it is not merely a matter for each government to nominate a local agency to participate on its behalf in the joint enterprise. At present the selection of prospective partners is all the more difficult due to the lack of adequate published data on Arab business concerns (unlike the case, for instance, when dealing with overseas multi-national corporations) as well as the lack of a developed financial market on the regional level.

(v) The undertaking of detailed pre-investment studies to prove the technical and economic viability of the venture: This type of study is lacking in most of the Arab ventures that have been agreed upon but did not enter into operation. In addition to their function in the definition and justification of the project involved, the studies in question play an important psychological role in generating serious consideration of the venture by prospective partners and could also be useful in securing financing for it from outside sources. Understandably, however, not all ventures require this kind of detailed study. It is, indeed, the ventures which require a minimum of studies and whose success depends basically on good management, such as financial and banking institutions, that figure prominently among the newly established Arab joint ventures.

(vi) The adoption of a workable form for the creation of the joint enterprise: The form of the "international public corporation" adopted for most Arab multilateral public ventures was certainly a delaying factor in their implementation. A corporation of this type could only be established by virtue of an international agreement subject to the ratification or acceptance of all member states in accordance with their constitutional requirements. It endows the joint corporation with privileges and immunities which usually liberate it from the provisions of any local law conflicting with its constituent instrument and require for their validity legislative action in all member states. Such time-consuming requirements are spared, when the venture is established as a national company under the laws of the host country. A company of this type could still enjoy a special status simply by the enactment of legislation to this effect in the host country only.

(vii) The proper drafting of constitutive legal documents: A defective agreement which fails to tackle the basic issues of concern to the partners, or conversely, attempts to protect against every contingency, falling, as a result, into a rigid and overly detailed coverage, could have a discouraging effect on the actual implementation of the project. A comparison between the ill-drafted agreements prepared under the auspices of the League of Arab States and the more sophisticated contracts prepared by OAPEC gives ample support to this conclusion. This point should not be over-stated, however, as in the context of Arab projects, lawyers usually pay a minor role in the decision-making process related to the creation of new Arab ventures. Some of the ventures presently in operation suffer from serious drafting shortcomings in their constitutive instruments which could reflect badly on their operations.

In the Operational Stage of the Venture

Experience of the few Arab joint ventures now in operation suggests that success in the formation of the venture does not automatically lead to its successful operation. The latter depends in particular on such factors as the following:

(i) The establishment of a management structure for the venture which takes due consideration of its trans-national character: This is particularly crucial for inter-governmental ventures especially the multilateral ventures which operate independently from a pre-established legal framework. The need for separation between ownership of the venture and its management is even more relevant in such ventures than in the typical public-sector national enterprise. Such a separation is not merely a safeguard for insulating the venture from political considerations but also helps in avoiding the conflicts inherent in any multi-national association. Constitutive instruments of multilateral Arab ventures are therefore right in tackling the details of the organization of each venture to ensure for its management as much independence from the partners' intervention as possible. The degree of governmental control and, when applicable, of the control of the sponsoring organization (such as in the OAPEC-sponsored projects) seems, however, to have exceeded, in some actual cases, the inevitable minimum. A bilateral venture involving a public entity in the host country may also raise delicate organizational questions. For this reason, domestic law on foreign investments in some Arab countries (e.g., Egypt) considers any joint venture with a public-sector local company as a private entity free from all rules applicable to the public sector in the host country.

On the other hand, legislation in many capital-importing Arab countries exempts approved joint ventures from the requirement of local majority ownership. In cases where the expatriate partner is a minority shareholder, the agreement establishing the venture seldom provides for special guarantees in favour of that partner in excess of local law requirements. Nor do the agreements establishing Arab ventures attempt, on the whole, to devise solutions for deadlocks in the decision-making process in the more common bilateral ventures based on a 50/50 ownership. Such a lacuna could of course create serious constraints on the project's management especially in the absence of a generally applicable domestic law. In the typical case, partners in such ventures are merely represented on an equal basis in the venture's board of directors where the chairman is chosen from among the representatives of one partner and the managing director from the representatives of the other.

(ii) The adoption of proper arrangements to facilitate the project's access to sources of finance: Partners from capital-importing Arab countries often request funding from expatriate partners through such devices as providing loan capital to the venture. In the recently agreed-upon Iranian-Egyptian Maritime Company, the Iranian Government is reported to have undertaken to grant the venture a subordinated loan many times its share capital of which 49 per cent is owned by the Egyptian partner. Unsuccessful attempts were also made by local partners to obtain from the prospective expatriate partners loans to finance part of the formers' contribution in the venture itself. The idea seems, however, to be gaining ground in negotiations on the establishment of some new inter-state Arab ventures. Understandably, such arrangements are exceptional owing to the opposition of expatriate partners, especially private investors, to their adoption.

A joint venture in need of loan financing may find itself in a worse position than that of a national venture, especially when borrowing from international development institutions which often insist on obtaining a governmental guarantee and may, at any rate, be reluctant to contract with an entity subject exclusively to an international legal regime. Although the host government may readily agree to provide the guarantee requested by the lending agency, its refusal to act as the sole guarantor of the venture is also understandable. The inter-state Arab Maritime Company reports, perhaps with some exaggeration, that the lack of governmental guarantees was the main reason for the failure of its attempt to receive financial assistance from the Arab Fund for Economic and Social Development. Some of the OAPEC-sponsored projects may, on the other hand, borrow on the strength of the collective or individual guarantee of their member states by virtue of explicit provisions to this effect in their constituent instruments. Under the circumstances, they could probably find it easier to obtain loans directly from their member countries.

(iii) The agreement on providing the venture with facilities necessary for its economic and financial viability, such as the basic infrastructure facilities, the supply of raw materials, the most suitable technology, access to local markets and access to research, when applicable: Of these obvious factors, agreement on marketing arrangements often raise delicate questions as to the extent of free access to the markets of the countries of the partners. A joint enterprise usually receives national treatment in the marketing of its products in the host country (unless of course it is meant to produce exclusively or mainly for export to foreign markets). It may be necessary, however, in certain instances to open the markets of all member countries to such products or to impose no restrictions on the venture's right to export. Imposing additional administrative barriers or tariff restrictions on the venture's access to local or foreign markets could easily put it at a disadvantage which may be economically disastrous.

A relevant issue is being raised at present by the Arab Maritime Petroleum Transport Co. which, having the nationality of all member states, feels entitled to the lifting privileges granted exclusively to the nationally-owned tankers companies in some states. In the two projected, Moroccan-Algerian Cement Co., and Tunisian-Algerian Cement Co., it was agreed, on the other hand, that the production of each company will be exclusively and equally purchased by its two partners on the basis of actual cost, the joint company being in such cases merely an operating agency of its shareholders. Marketing arrangements of this type may be more instrumental in the successful operation of the venture than the broad immunities granted at present to many multilateral Arab public ventures.

(iv) The choice of efficient management and staff capable of operating in a trans-national environment: The importance of this factor is self-evident. It is worth mentioning, however, in view of the special difficulties faced by most new Arab ventures in the recruitment of managerial and professional staff from member countries. Such difficulties are accentuated by two factors: most Arab countries, especially those exporting capital, suffer from serious shortages in well-trained manpower. Yet even where such manpower is available, it usually lacks the experience of working in an international business environment under a different orientation from that of local business. In many cases senior officers of the joint venture come from the higher echelons of the civil service of member states without any prior business background. As a result most Arab joint ventures are operating in a pattern not dissimilar to that followed by the exclusively national enterprises in the host countries and seldom aspire to wider perspectives commensurate with their trans-national character. The exclusive employment of local labour in the host country allows the venture, on the other hand, to avoid the frictions inherent in multi-national staffing which could otherwise cause several problems, especially in labour-intensive projects.

Impact on Arab Economic Integration

With a few exceptions, Arab joint ventures are being formed with little or no conscious concern for regional or sub-regional economic integration. In most cases the common objective of the partners in the venture does not go beyond the direct financial return expected by them. Although this in itself may be a guide to proper resource allocation within the region, the truth remains that, by and large, Arab joint ventures have not been carried out in implementation of a pre-existing comprehensive plan designed to facilitate Arab economic integration through a more rational division of labour on the Arab level. Nor are they tied to a regional scheme of trade preferences or to a general policy for the liberalization of the movement of factors of production in all or part of the Arab region. Such objectives are certainly sought by agencies like the Arab Council of Economic Unity and, to a lesser extent, OAPEC, in the joint ventures sponsored by them. They could also be traced in the trilateral ventures agreed upon, but hardly implemented, in the framework of the Union of Arab Republics (Egypt/Libya/Syria) as well as in some of the Arab bilateral ventures, especially those agreed upon between Egypt on the one hand, and Iraq or the Sudan on the other hand. The fact that such projects have not yet started operation emphasizes, however, the small impact which joint ventures as a whole have had on Arab economic integration.

This does not mean that the present spread of Arab joint ventures will not eventually have noticeable effects on the movement towards regional integration. Even though such joint ventures are primarily financial institutions whose short-term impact on Arab economic integration would be minimal, they should, in time, have a positive effect on the financing of productive inter-Arab projects and on the expansion of inter-Arab trade. The adoption of favourable national and regional policies in this respect would no doubt accelerate such a process.

STRENGTHENING AND STIMULATING THE ESTABLISHMENT OF INTER-ARAB JOINT VENTURES

The above analysis makes it clear that the establishment of an increasing number of Arab joint ventures and the strengthening of their role in Arab economic integration, depend on the adoption of further positive steps in the following areas in particular:

Sponsorship of New Ventures

Cutting across most of the cases and most of the issues that have been examined, one can easily discern, in greater or lesser degree, what may be described as a sponsorship problem in the establishment of Arab joint ventures. Reliance on the spontaneous initiative of interested parties is certainly inadequate in the absence of a developed financial market. On the other hand, many of the institutions which have assumed the responsibility of establishing inter-Arab projects lacked the financial resources to support their proposals and followed, in most cases, a bureaucratic and passive approach.

The relative success of such sectorial sponsors as OAPEC suggests a potentially useful role in this respect for the Arab Federation of Producers of Iron and Steel (Algiers), the Arab Food and Agriculture Organization (Khartoum), the Arab Centre for Industrial Development (Cairo) and the newly established Arab Federation of Fertilizer Producers (Kuwait). However, such organizations can only identify projects and, at best, carry out the preliminary pre-investment studies and present them to potentially interested parties. The fact that such organizations themselves have very limited resources and virtually no working relationship with Arab or other financial institutions greatly undermines the extent of their role as catalysts in the implementation of joint ventures. It is therefore their responsibility as it is the responsibility of Arab development finance institutions, both national and regional, to try to bridge that gap. The latter institutions, whose day-to-day operations have prevented them from taking the initiative in sponsoring new Arab projects, seem to have little confidence in the technical ability of other inter-Arab agencies to perform this task. Naturally, such ability could be improved through financial assistance from the funding institutions. The latter institutions may also employ their own consultants to do the technical work and subsequently propose the financial packaging for each project specifying, as an incentive, their own role in financing the project. The more business-like the sponsor's approach is, the greater the possibility for the actual formation of the venture.

Regional financial institutions such as the Arab Fund and the Inter-Arab Guarantee Corporation are bound by explicit provisions in their own statutes to give priority in their operations to inter-Arab joint ventures. The ceiling for the coverage offered by the latter corporation to investments in joint projects is also twice that which may be offered for unilateral investments. The Arab Bank for Economic Development in Africa is also requested by its constituent agreement to give preference to inter-African and Arab-African projects. All such regional institutions are still, however, in their initial stage of operations. There is practically no co-ordination among them, or between them and the national aid institutions in financing joint Arab projects. All such agencies could, therefore, independently, or better still, in a joint corporate effort, play a significant role in five important areas:

(a) The preparation and publication of the investment information needed for the planning and evaluation of Arab joint ventures, including information on existing joint ventures and those under discussion. Available data on these matters are still scarce.

(b) The creation of suitable fora and channels of communication to stimulate contacts between interested investors and among existing national ventures, both private and public, in co-operation, perhaps, with the Arab Federation of Chambers of Commerce and the national Chambers of Commerce in the main capital-exporting and capital-importing Arab countries.

(c) The identification of specific projects particularly suited for implementation through Arab joint ventures. This task could, of course, be carried out in co-operation with other specialized inter-Arab organizations.

(d) The presentation of the project to prospective partners after resolving conflicts of interest by means of an equitable distribution of cost and benefits.

(e) The financing of such ventures on such terms and conditions as to encourage participation by prospective partners who often need some inducement to accept the additional risks of a transnational project.

Arab financial institutions are the natural candidates for performing these tasks. To be able to perform them effectively, the present institutions will need, above all, to improve their technical capabilities beyond their present modest level. This would certainly be a more advisable course of action than the creation of new non-financial institutions designed specifically to promote inter-Arab joint ventures.

Form of the Venture

Arab joint ventures have so far been established in each of the following legal forms:

(a) The form of a partnership or company of a type recognized under the local law of one of the partners, or even of a third party. This ordinary local-law form is usually followed when all partners are private investors.

(b) The form of a national company with a special status recognized under the law of the host country by virtue of special legislation in respect of that particular venture, of a certain type of venture or of joint ventures in general.

(c) The form of a national company with a special status recognized by virtue of an international agreement between the states which are party, directly or indirectly, to the venture.

(d) The form of an international corporation proper created by virtue of an international convention as a non-national company not subject to any particular domestic law. In some instances such a company may even resemble an international organization in its internal structure.

The latter form was adopted, as mentioned above, in almost all multilateral Arab public ventures. It could be criticized, however, for the lengthy procedures required for the entry into force of the convention establishing the venture, which usually involve legislative action in every member state. It may also raise complicated legal issues with respect to the applicable rules in matters not provided for in the constitutive convention. Political considerations are more readily invoked in the creation of ventures of this form, both at the time of negotiation of the convention and at the time of its ratification in every member state.

It is preferable, therefore, to adopt for joint public ventures, whenever this is practical, the form of a national company established directly by the public agencies or corporations of interested states through the enactment, in the host country only, of legislation to be issued in accordance with the terms of the agreement between such partners. In such a case, the venture is likely to be formed in a much shorter period and will be subject to a previously known legal system while enjoying the special status provided in the agreement establishing the venture. Not being a treaty, such an agreement will not require ratification procedures in each of the countries of the partners for it to come into force. Such countries could also safeguard their interests in case of an unfavourable amendment of the law establishing the joint company, through appropriate clauses in the constitutive agreement concluded between them.

New forms for the establishment of Arab joint ventures could also be devised to meet growing business needs. One possible formula is the establishment of a system for the creation of "Arab Companies" on lines similar to those proposed for the "European Company". Such an Arab company would be formed by existing national companies or agencies in different Arab states and would have a recognized legal personality and the right of establishment in all such states. The establishment of such a company requires, however, the conclusion of a general inter-state convention on the legal regime of Arab Companies and on some form of international registration for them, for instance at the Council of Arab Economic Unity.

Another possible formula is that of a company established directly by the resolution of a competent regional organization subject to the exclusive control of that organization such as the companies which EURATOM is authorized to establish. In this instance an inter-Arab organization would have the power to create the company under its own system and to invite the participation of public and/or private investors from member countries in its share-capital. The organization itself may even participate in the company's capital. OAPEC and similar Arab organizations could not play such a role before their constitutions are amended to this effect.

The adoption of the above-mentioned new forms could eventually facilitate the establishment of inter-Arab ventures. It assumes, however, agreement by interested states on the detailed framework for the creation and operation of ventures of each type. Such an agreement, it should be added, may not be possible in the absence of a greater measure of inter-governmental economic co-operation in the Arab region than that available at present.

Financing of the Venture

The potential role of Arab financial institutions in the promotion of inter-Arab joint ventures has been outlined above. National invest-ment companies in capital-exporting countries are still, despite some recent encouraging signs, hesitant in playing an active role in this respect. With the exception of some Kuwaiti companies such as Gulf International, KFTCIC, AFARCO, KIC and the Real Estate Investment Group, the bulk of Arab investment companies are still content with the underwriting of bond issues and similar brokerage activities with little concern for the more challenging task of direct investment in Arab and other developing countries through venture capital operations and the like. Such companies remain, however, the best candidates for playing an important catalytic role in the formation of new private joint ventures without risking, in the process, too much capital of their own. Their contribution is particu-larly needed in arranging the financial packaging suitable for such ventures. The constraints on expanding their role in this respect are primarily due to their limited experience and to the greater risks involved in such operations compared with their present activities. Such constraints could be gradually alleviated, however, through developing strong working relationships with agencies such as the Inter-Arab Investment Guarantee Corporation and the several development finance institutions in the Arab region.

Regional development finance institutions have expressed theoretical preference in financing Arab joint ventures, but, as previ-ously mentioned, have done little to achieve this end. In its relatively long experience, the Kuwait Fund was an active sponsor in the formation of one multilateral Arab venture, the Investment Guaran-tee Corporation, and, to some extent, one bilateral Kuwaiti-Sudanese venture. It also played a major role in drafting the con-stituent documents of the Arab Bank for Economic Development in Africa and the Solidarity Fund for Economic and Social Development in Non-Aligned Countries. The Arab Fund is still, on the other hand, in the process of providing its first loan to a joint venture, the Algerian-Moroccan Cement Company. It is also working, at present, on the creation of an inter-Arab organization for agricultural development in the Sudan. The Abu-Dhabi Fund, which is explicitly authorized to go into equity participation, has recently participated in the equity of a tourism company in Tunisia and is also a shareholder in one of the Arab-European banks. Such has been the role of Arab external development finance institutions with respect to Arab joint ventures.

A much greater role could certainly be assumed by such institutions in the financing of inter-Arab ventures both through loan financing and equity participation. To facilitate their lending operations they could enter into prior arrangements with the governments concerned to secure the guarantee of such governments of the loans provided to joint ventures whenever such a guarantee is a necessary requirement for extending the loan. A broad interpretation of the constituent instruments of such institutions could also enable them to include in their operations participation in the equity of Arab joint ventures. Such a participation could, at any rate, be one form of the investment of a portion, albeit small, of their liquid assets. The Islamic Development Bank, which would be involved mostly in equity participation as it is barred from receiving interest on loans, should also be particularly instrumental in promoting joint ventures among its member countries.

The creation of new financial institutions exclusively for the financing of Arab joint ventures may not be called for in view of the present proliferation of Arab financial institutions. Present institutions could be encouraged, however, to establish special funds for joint venture operations especially as many of them are already required, by virtue of their constituent instruments, to give priority to the financing of such ventures.

Legal Framework

Constituent instruments of joint ventures should be carefully drafted to reflect with accuracy the intended relationship between the contracting parties and the legal status of the enterprise. It does not follow, however, that an attempt should be made at this stage to elaborate a general model form of the constituent instrument of Arab joint ventures. The particular features of such ventures can vary greatly from case to case while proper drafting should suit the particularities of each instance. However, it will certainly be useful for future draftsmen to have beforehand a comprehensive list of the issues that should be tackled in each particular field where the interests and operational requirements of the parties establishing the venture may be similar. Different lists could therefore be prepared for sectors such as maritime and air transport, fisheries, real estate development, industrial projects etc.[3]. Model forms could even be developed for the constituent agreements of joint ventures in each of these sectors[4]. At present, no such standardization is followed in the Arab region, except for routine reasons in the agreements prepared by the same sponsoring agency. Some Arab countries, like Egypt, require foreign investors, as a general rule, to enter into joint ventures with local investors in accordance with a model prepared by the government. In the case of Egypt this text is quite similar to that applicable to local shareholding companies and fails to take cognizance of the peculiarities of each type of venture.

A convention for the treatment of inter-Arab investments is, on the other hand, already effective among the Arab country members of the Council of Arab Economic Unity and goes as far as banning all forms of expropriation and nationalization. Bilateral treaties abound also in this respect, while most local investment codes in capital-importing Arab countries provide adequate guarantees and exemptions to foreign investments especially those originating in other Arab countries. As a result, a new international agreement on the treatment of imported Arab capital is not particularly wanting. Further steps could be taken, however, in extending additional incentives to inter-Arab ventures especially those which help Arab economic integration. Such incentives may realistically be adopted in national legislation within a general and flexible framework to be agreed upon at regional or sub-regional level. Arab governments may thus agree on giving Arab joint ventures the same treatment as local investments, along lines similar to those contained in decision 46 of the Andean Group. Furthermore, they may grant such ventures preferential treatment under their laws in those areas where such treatment is justified. A regional agreement on the legal treatment of joint ventures, especially in terms of taxation, labour regulations and management structure, could provide a useful system to many of the Arab public joint ventures, which operate at present in a legal vacuum outside the provisions of their constituent instruments. The absence of such an agreement should not, however, be considered a serious limitation on the spread of Arab joint ventures.

Management Training in Arab Capital-Exporting countries

As holders of huge net liquid assets, oil-exporting Arab countries are increasingly involved in investments abroad. A major constraint on expanding their direct investment operations, as against lending operations, is the lack of adequate indigenous management to cope with such an extensive task. This is also a serious limitation on the success of existing inter-Arab ventures and indeed of some of the local ventures as well. There is therefore a basic need to develop in these countries a sophisticated class of business managers who could be responsible for the administration of their investments abroad, which are likely to account in future for a great part of their national income. The availability of an increased number of qualified and experienced personnel is bound to affect the investment decisions of such countries and to encourage their involvement in direct investments abroad. The implementation of ambitious business management programmes for the training of economists, engineers and lawyers in these Arab countries seems, therefore, to be a decisive factor in the expansion and success of joint ventures between them and other countries in the area.

Co-ordinated National Policies

Agreement between states on the establishment of a particular joint venture whose cost and benefits could more or less be ascertained in advance, is certainly a much easier task than their agreement on politically loaded measures such as joint trade policies or co-ordinated economic plans. It is not realistic, therefore, to tie the establishment of new Arab joint ventures to the agreement of Arab States on joint or co-ordinated trade and planning policies. Each country could, however, develop its national trade policy as well as its policy towards foreign investments in such a manner as to favour the establishment on its territory, of joint ventures in the fields where it feels that it has some economic advantage. Institutions like the Council of Arab Economic Unity could work on the establishment of links between the measures adopted in such national policies and the regional trade preferences scheme it is supervising at present. However, only minor results can realistically be expected from such endeavours at present. The Council may, nevertheless, play an important role in advising member governments of the projects which are likely to serve the objective of economic integration and deserve, as a result, special attention in their national policies and legislation. Projects which increase the productive capabilities of Arab countries, which facilitate the means of transportation and communication among them, and which diversify their products and improve their quality, provide themselves with the principal, most practical means of expanding inter-Arab trade.

CHAPTER 12

ARAB POTASH COMPANY:
PROJECT DEVELOPMENT
(ANNEX TO CHAPTER 11)

Also distributed as part of UNCTAD document TD/B/AC.19/R.5 and appeared, revised, as a chapter in International Business in the Middle East, *Kapoor, Ed., Westview Press, Boulder, Colorado, USA, 1979.*

At the time of writing this case, Dr Shihata was senior legal adviser of the Kuwait Fund for Arab Economic Development. The case study was part of a larger report by Dr Shihata to the UNCTAD secretariat and was distributed on 21 October 1975, as UN Document TD/B/AC.19/R.5.

The views expressed are those of the author and do not necessarily reflect those of the UNCTAD secretariat or the OPEC Fund. The terminology is that of the author. The designations employed and the presentation of the material in this document do not imply the expression of any opinion whatsoever on the part of the secretariat concerning the legal status of any country, territory, city or areas or of its authorities, or concerning the delimitation of its frontiers or boundaries.

This case describes efforts to establish an inter-Arab joint venture involving the participation of public international organizations and international companies. Several characteristics of such ventures are highlighted.

The Arab Potash Company (APC) is the first multilateral Arab economic venture ever to be conceived and, until 1974, the only such venture to be realized among Arab governments in the industrial field. The agreement establishing APC was prepared under the auspices of the League of Arab States. This regional organization later acted, with little success, as the sponsor of many other multilateral economic ventures. Its sponsorship of the project in its early stages had an effect on some of the later developments.

The founding partners in this venture included six Arab states and one private commercial bank. In a later development, majority participation was vested in private investors of different Arab nationalities, thus turning APC from a public international enterprise into a mixed economy joint venture.

Western technology was sought in the implementation of the venture through several consulting, management, and sales agreements. Equity participation of Western partners was also sought and almost realized at one point. It may still materialize in the eventual implementation of the investment. International as well as foreign national lending agencies have been heavily involved in the several attempts actually to implement the project.

Although APC failed for a long time to realize the initial expectation, its experience in arranging the complicated technical and financial details may serve as a useful example for future action in this and other ventures.

It is important to consider the following questions in reading the case:

(i) What have been the implicit and explicit issues of negotiation between the shareholders of APC and the management of APC and international companies whose affiliation with the project has been sought?

(ii) In what ways and why have the issues of negotiation changed over time for the host country (Jordan), the Arab shareholders, public international agencies, and private international companies?

(iii) What are the requirements for acting as a catalyst in effectively promoting a project such as APC?

(iv) What are the essential conditions for establishing successful multi-party projects such as APC?

(v) What role should the international company play in such ventures?

Interest in the exploitation of the mineral resources of the Dead Sea was initiated by the government of Jordan in the early 1950s. As a first step, the government entered into agreement with an American concern, Chemical Construction Corporation of New York, for the study of the feasibility of establishing a potash plant on the north shore of the Dead Sea in the old site of the Palestine Potash Company. The study submitted in 1954 recommended the implementation of a project for the production of 70,000 tons of potash per year if positive results were yielded by a pilot plant recommended by the study. A number of Dutch experts were also consulted at that time on the technical aspects of the civil works of the project.

On the basis of these studies the government of Jordan sought the participation of other Arab countries in the financing of the project. The matter was discussed in the Economic Council of the League of Arab States, which approved in January 1956 a draft agreement establishing the Arab Potash Company Limited. On 21 June 1956, this agreement was signed by Jordan, Saudi Arabia, Iraq, Egypt, Syria and Lebanon, as well as by the Arab Bank, a Jordanian private commercial bank. APC's authorized capital was fixed at Jordanian dinars (JD) 4.5 million (then equivalent to $12.6 million), of which JD1 million was initially subscribed as founders' shares. A subsequent issue of shares in 1961-62 was subscribed by Kuwait, Qatar, and a number of private investors of different Arab nationalities, whose participation exceeded that of the member governments. As a result, the subscribed and paid-up share capital amounted to about JD3.2 million, distributed as follows:

Governments	Value JD
Jordan	500,000
Iraq	125,000
Kuwait	125,000
Saudi Arabia	125,000
Egypt	125,000
Lebanon	62,500
Syria	62,500
Qatar	50,000
	1,175,000
Private	2,029,000
	(paid 2,016,011)
Unsubscribed	1,296,000
TOTAL	4,500,000

The agreement establishing the company provided that APC's shares, which remained unsubscribed after the public call to subscription, would be covered by the then projected Inter-Arab Financial Corporation. In the event that this latter corporation was not established (as was indeed the case), subscription would be made by the founder governments "according to the percentage of their contribution to the budget of the Arab League". This strange requirement has been ignored, however.

Although the agreement did not specify the nationality of the company, it was clear that the corporation would be established as a Jordanian shareholding company to be registered in Amman. No special privileges or immunities were conferred on the company by virtue of its constituent agreement except for its reference to a concession for the exploitation of the Dead Sea minerals, which the company was to acquire by agreement, subject to ratification by law, with the Jordan government. This concession was later granted for one hundred years as of 18 February 1958.

The first board of the company was to consist of a representative of each participating government unless its subscription reached JD0.5 million or more, in which case it was entitled to two representatives on the board. Representatives of private shareholders were also to be included on the board in a number proportionate to their participation in the subscribed capital. After the large subscription by private investors in 1962 was completed, APC's Articles of Association were amended to provide for the composition of the board of seven members, two to be nominated by the government of Jordan and the rest to be elected by the private shareholders, thus leaving all other Arab governments without representation in the board. This amendment, which was obviously made without the approval of the other participating governments, was justified at the time by the fact that such governments were previously represented by their ambassadors to Amman, who contributed little to the board's activities. The amended articles provided, however, that an Arab government may be represented on the board only when it subscribed at least JD250,000 in the company's capital – a requirement that has not been met by any member government other than Jordan. The amendment has thus emphasized both the private and the domestic character of the company and has led, in fact, to lessening the role of other Arab states in the developments related to the project.

CHARACTERISTICS OF THE VENTURE

From its inception, APC has commissioned a number of feasibility studies, operated a small pilot plant on the Dead Sea, and made numerous contacts with various foreign agencies and industrial companies regarding the financing of the project. In 1961 Western Knapp Engineering Company of Los Angeles was commissioned as consultant, and in 1962 it completed a comprehensive feasibility report for a 250,000-tons-per-year (tpy) plant, initially projected at an estimated cost of $36 million excluding the road to the port of Aqaba. (The plant was originally envisaged to have a 70,000-tpy capacity.) The Knapp report was the basis for applications for financial assistance submitted in 1962 by the government of Jordan to the International Development Association and the US Agency for International Development (AID), and was to be used in discussions with potential foreign partners. However, a project based on that report was found unattractive to potential financiers. At the World Bank's request, a new feasibility study was completed by Knapp in July 1964. The revised total cost estimate for the plant was increased to $45 million, which rendered it economically unfeasible for the project to produce only 250,000 tons annually. Discussions with potential foreign partners, the most serious with Dow Chemical, produced no firm agreement or commitment to invest. Meanwhile an offer made in 1963 by Arthur Mekky Corporation (the parent of Knapp) to implement the project and provide management and sales services to it could not be accepted by APC and the Jordanian government.

US AID's continued interest in the project led it, with the World Bank's and APC's concurrence, to entrust Jacobs Engineering Company of California with the reappraisal of Knapp's proposals. The Jacobs report submitted in March 1965 was considered by both the bank and AID to provide a more sound basis for project implementation, although it recommended a plant of twice the capacity envisaged by Knapp. The report concluded that a project to produce initially 500,000 tons of potash was feasible at an estimated capital cost of $60 million, provided that first-class management and marketing could be made available and that financing on appropriate terms was arranged. On the basis of that report, the World Bank gave its approval in principle of a loan of $30 million for the project. Shortly afterwards, AID approved a commitment of $15 million. It was assumed by both agencies that the remaining $15 million would be met by APC's equity after doubling it, and by the inclusion of a foreign partner who would also assume responsibility for the management and operation of the project and provide appropriate assurances for marketing the output, primarily outside the Arab region. It was also assumed that the government of Jordan, which was acting throughout as the sole sponsor and guarantor of the project, would meet the cost of a suitable road to Aqaba and a township on the site and would assume any additional finance in case of cost overruns. The Kuwait Fund for Arab Economic Development, whose interest in the project was sought in late 1965 by the Jordanian government and the World Bank, offered its good offices in interesting private Arab investors to participate in APC's equity.

Subsequently, the World Bank took an active role in the selection of the foreign partner in APC. Discussions held with ten interested multi-national companies resulted in the selection of International Minerals and Chemicals (IMC) of Skokie, Illinois, then accounting for about 30 per cent of US and Canadian potash capacity. Negotiations between APC and IMC started in the fall of 1965 and led to the signature of a Memorandum of Understanding in December 1965, which was to be followed by more detailed agreements. According to the memorandum, IMC was to participate in the equity capital of APC by taking 50 per cent of the shares after recapitalization of the company at $15 million (not including $2 million of past expenses on the pilot plant and the Knapp report, which, it was agreed, would be written off). IMC was also to have full control over the management of APC and the marketing of its products.

Later in 1966, IMC withdrew its offer, due in part to the rejection by the Jordan government of IMC's proposal to enter into another contract with the Jordan Phosphate Mines Company for the sale of phosphates. Other reasons for the withdrawal were (1) the failure of IMC to break the hold of the Franco-German cartel for the sale of potash in Europe and (2) IMC's fears of an oversupply of potash in the 1970s. As a result, APC had to look again for a new foreign partner. With the assistance of International Finance Corporation, who learned of the project through the World Bank, many multi-national companies were contacted. Of these, four showed interest, especially W. R. Grace & Co. Meanwhile, Jacobs and its subconsultants for civil works, Alexandre Gibbs of London, continued technical work on the project. Some of the companies contacted for equity participation raised from the outset the possibility of planning for a plant capacity of one million tons, and Jacobs was asked to study the economies that such a capacity would be likely to achieve.

Results of the Jacobs reappraisal confirmed the soundness of a project with an increased capacity of 1,000,000 tpy. Capital requirements would be $100 million. Renewed discussion among potential financiers (World Bank, IFC, AID, and Kuwait Fund) resulted in a common understanding on a new financial plan, whereby 25 per cent of the newly estimated cost would be met by equity and 75 per cent by debt to be provided in equal amounts by the World Bank, AID, and the Kuwait Fund. The $25 million equity was also to be covered on the basis of 51 per cent by Arab shareholders (APC), 14 per cent by IFC, and 35 per cent by a foreign partner to be entrusted with management and marketing. In a January 1967 meeting of these financing agencies – the government of Jordan, APC and W. R. Grace and Company – it was agreed that a new corporation, to be called Jordan Arab Potash (JAP), would be formed by APC under the laws of Jordan to carry out the project. APC would thus continue in existence holding only 51 per cent of the capital stock and junior subordinated debt of JAP, and would transfer to JAP the concession agreement to the extent necessary for the operation of the project. The rest of JAP's equity would be held by IFC (14 per cent) and by a joint company to be formed by Grace and a partner (35 per cent). The government of Jordan would have a representation in the board of JAP along with the three shareholders. The joint company (Grace and its partner) would also enter with JAP into a management and operating agreement as well as an exclusive marketing agreement. The originally envisaged inter-Arab joint venture was thus to be turned into a Jordanian/American venture with very little trace of joint Arab action. Details of these arrangements were later negotiated, leading to the preparation of a draft new concession law, draft management, and marketing agreements, draft loan agreements between each of the lending agencies and JAP, and draft guarantee agreements between them and the Jordanian government. The meticulous efforts involved in the process proved, however, to be futile. The final negotiations held in Washington in early June 1967 were terminated on 3 June at the request of W. R. Grace because of political developments then prevailing in the Middle East. Two days later war erupted. One of the minor and less known effects of the Arab-Israeli war was the shelving of the potash project for many years to come.

Shortly after the war subsided, the World Bank proposed a new "emergency plan" for the project, whereby financing and execution would initially be limited to a pilot programme, including studies and trial tests, leaving further steps for discussion in light of the results of this preliminary phase. It was estimated that the pilot programme would cost $6 million and last for eighteen months. JAP would still be formed, but with a much smaller capitalization. The government of Jordan and APC would each contribute $1.25 million, with APC being required to put up only $250,000, as the rest of its contribution was to be accepted in kind (the estimated value of the previous studies financed by it). Complementary financing would be met through loans from the World Bank ($1.5 million) and the United States government ($3 million). Although this plan was approved by the Jordan cabinet in April 1968, and a new American concern, Tenneco, was being considered as a potential replacement for W. R. Grace, no action was followed in either direction.

In June 1969, the government of Jordan requested APC to return to its private shareholders the nominal value of their shares up to a maximum of 200 shares per shareholder. This step was complemented in March 1972 by APC's decision to return the nominal value of the shares to the remaining private shareholder, thus reducing drastically APC's subscribed capital. The authorized capital remained unchanged, however.

The Arab governments that had remained "sleeping partners" in APC since their exclusion from its board of directors in 1962 came to express new interest in the project late in 1973. On the recommendation of the government of Iraq, APC convened a meeting of representatives of these governments to discuss with its board members ways of resurrecting the potash project. The meeting, in which each side was blamed for ignoring the other during past developments, recommended that APC apply to the Arab Fund for Economic and Social Development, a regional inter-Arab organization in operation since 1972, for help in the financing of the project. It also requested APC to resort to the financially able Arab governments to increase their equity participation in APC and to contact the governments of potash-consuming countries and interested foreign companies to determine their participation in its activities. The representatives of the Arab governments comprised a group of shareholders not represented in the board of the company but holding majority participation. As such, their legal authority was questionable. Nonetheless, their recommendations were officially adopted by APC's board. An application for financing was presented to the Arab Fund in 1973 and contacts were renewed in the same year with both the Kuwait Fund and the World Bank. Jacobs was also asked to look into the possibility of updating its study of the feasibility of the project.

Late in 1974, APC started a new phase of the project by the preparation of up-to-date feasibility studies and the construction of a trial dam and dykes in the Dead Sea to help in the technical evaluation of the project. This phase was estimated to cost $10 million. The US AID provided a loan for this purpose of $6 million, and the World Bank $1 million, while the remaining $3 million was met by the government of Jordan. The financing of the actual implementation of the project was to be discussed with the World Bank, AID, and Arab sources of the development finance in the light of the results of this preliminary phase.

The pilot project was carried out during 1976 and 1977 with the assistance of consultants Jacobs and Alexandre Gibb. Based on the results of the pilot project, a preliminary feasibility report was issued by the consultants in 1976, and a final report in 1978 indicated that a full-scale project for the production of one million to two million tons of potash was viable.

The project, as currently envisaged, will be owned and operated by APC, which is now owned 51 per cent by the Jordanian government, 25 per cent by the Arab Mining Company (itself owned principally by four Arab governments), possibly 10 per cent each by the Arab Investment Company (an inter-governmental Arab venture) and the Islamic Development Bank, and the remaining 4 per cent by various Arab governments and private investors. APC's shareholders will contribute $170 million equivalent in equity, representing 40 per cent of the estimated total project financing requirements of $422 million. The government of Jordan has invited concessionary financing proposals from a number of multilateral, bilateral, and regional financing institutions, including the World Bank, the US AID, the Kuwait Fund for Arab Economic Development, the Arab Fund for Economic and Social Development, and the OPEC Fund. These institutions have all given their agreement, at least in principle, to provide a share of the long-term debt financing required. This new financial plan is now expected to be finalized before the end of 1978.

EVALUATION

Despite the subscription of a number of governments and private investors of different Arab countries to APC's capital, APC has acted and has been treated as a national Jordanian company. Member Arab governments were initially represented in APC's board, but since 1962 have been practically isolated from the company's activities and have acted as sleeping partners. The company's management and personnel have also been exclusively Jordanian. As a result, it is difficult to evaluate APC, the oldest inter-Arab company, as a joint Arab venture. The participation of different Arab governments in the company's capital may have provided an additional incentive for the different lending agencies which showed interest in financing its activities. Other than this, however, the company has been operating as a local company subject to the strict supervision of the government of Jordan.

The role of the government in this instance was certainly greater than its role vis-à-vis other private shareholding companies. This may have been due in part to the multi-national nature of APC's capital composition, but it can more plausibly be traced to other factors. For a long time the company became a symbol of failure (especially when compared to another potash project implemented by Israel on the other side of the Dead Sea), and has since become an issue in international Jordanian politics. The keen interest of the government in APC's future has benefited the company to the extent that the former was prepared to provide alone all the financial guarantees required by foreign lenders and to finance the required infrastructure, despite the fact that it was only a minority shareholder in a joint venture.

The difficulties met by APC may be attributed to many factors. The company was formed before the technical and economic feasibility of the project was established beyond doubt. Originally conceived to produce 70,000 tons of potash, APC was soon advised to plan for a production capacity of 250,000 tons, then 500,000, and finally 1,200,000. The "initial" stage for completion of studies and trial tests was undertaken only after more than twenty years of development, while the size of the project and its financial needs remained uncertain. APC management has, on the other hand, played a minor role in its affairs, which were taken up on the whole by the government of Jordan, a minority shareholder. An important major factor (the Arab-Israeli War) also hindered implementation of the project in 1967. None of these difficulties could be blamed, however, on the inter-Arab nature of the venture. On the contrary, if other Arab partners had played a more active role in the venture, especially for meeting additional financial requirements, some of these difficulties could perhaps have been avoided, as the most recent developments have amply proved.

CHAPTER 13

ARAB INVESTMENT GUARANTEE CORPORATION – A REGIONAL INVESTMENT GUARANTEE CORPORATION

First published in Journal of World Trade Law, *Vol. 6, No. 2, March, April 1972. An expanded version was published in Arabic by the Kuwait Fund in January 1974. At the time of writing the Author was Associate Professor of International Law, Ain-Shams University in Cairo. He had earlier participated in drafting the Agreement Establishing the Arab Investment Guarantee Corporation.*

INTRODUCTION

As a much needed source of such basic elements in the development process as capital, skills and technology, private foreign investments still present an important potential for developing countries. Objections to this assumption[1], though not uncommon, are not generally shared by most present-day governments in the developing world. Many of these governments are now entering into an increasing number of bilateral treaties[2] and are promulgating new laws[3] for the protection and encouragement of foreign investments. Such measures, undoubtedly relevant in stimulating the inflow of needed foreign capital, have remained, however, short of attaining their objective. In particular, they did not generate the desired feeling of security among foreign investors against increasing non-commercial risks, since their possible violation by host countries remained a menacing potentiality. The idea of providing the foreign investor with a financial guarantee to be readily received from an outside source in case of losses due to measures of the host government or other political risks, emerged therefore as the practical solution for the confidence gap between foreign investments and countries in need of them[4]. It was first suggested and implemented by the capital-exporting, developed countries themselves. The US took the lead in 1948[5], to be followed by almost all other industrial countries outside the Eastern Bloc.

National investment guarantee programmes, though often adopted as measures of export promotion, have figured in many instances as part of the aid programmes to host countries[6]. The success of these national schemes and the growing awareness of developing countries of their need for a greater flow of foreign capital have prompted many attempts for the realization on a multi-national level of an investment guarantee programme[7]. The projected International Investment Insurance Agency sponsored by the World Bank is perhaps the most important available example[8]. But the chances of the actual application of this particular project in the near future are still doubtful. The major capital-exporting countries which are assumed to bear the financial burden of the suggested insurance already have their successful national programmes, and consequently seem to be under no overwhelming pressure to favour the multi-national approach. There are two other important examples for the realization of a multi-national guarantee programme, though only on a regional level. The *Fonds d'Entraide et de Garantie des Emprunts* has already been established in West Africa and provides guarantees for specific foreign loans[9]. A much more ambitious scheme is now envisaged for Arab countries in the projected "Arab Corporation for Investment Guarantee"[10].

Viewed as one group, Arab countries present an ideal field for a regional application of an investment guarantee programme. Although they are all underdeveloped in varying degrees, not all of these countries fall under the typical description of "have-not nations". In fact, countries like Kuwait, Libya and Abu-Dhabi rate among the world's richest *per capita* and accumulate capital surplus beyond the present absorption capacity of their economies. Most other Arab countries remain, however, in dire need of new investments. Instead of the outflow of surplus capital from the rich Arab countries to their neighbouring countries, most of this capital has been invested in the more advanced Western economies. This is likely to be due mainly to the rather unstable investment climate in the poorer Arab countries which adopt, on the whole, a somewhat suspicious outlook towards private and foreign investments. There is, however, a general recognition of the important role Arab capital can play in financing the development of these countries. It is also clear that whatever reservations such countries may have against foreign investments, they can hardly be justified in the case of investments coming from the richer, but much smaller, Arab states.

Little effort has been made, however, to alleviate the fears of Arab investors from political risks in other Arab countries. On their part, the home governments of potential investors have not adopted national guarantee programmes, since they apparently do not share the motives which prompted the adoption of such programmes in the advanced industrial countries. Receiving countries, on the other hand, have done little to encourage other Arab investors and have even behaved in some instances as though they were hostile to the reception of their capital[11]. A multi-national treaty signed in 1953 between six Arab states for the facilitation of capital movement among their territories had almost no effect on this gloomy atmosphere[12]. Bilateral treaties for the protection of Arab capital remained exceptional and vague[13]. Thus, short of an adequate legal protection on the domestic as well as the international levels, and without financial guarantees from their home governments, Arab investors simply opted for the seemingly less profitable but more stable markets of the West. In such a situation, an Inter-Arab investment guarantee corporation may clearly bring forth a positive influence. By providing potential Arab investors with guarantees against such non-commercial risks as would meet their investments in other Arab countries, the Corporation would be alleviating the major obstacle facing these investors at present. Moreover, it would achieve this important objective without adversely affecting the "economic sovereignty" of the receiving Arab states.

The proposal for establishing an Arab Investment Guarantee Corporation was first made in the Arab Industrial Development Conference held in Kuwait in March 1966. (This was the time when the World Bank had just started a discussion on the "basic issues" involved in creating a multi-national investment insurance agency.) The idea was well received in the Conference, which requested the government of Kuwait to arrange for a meeting of Arab financial experts to study its implications. Kuwait conferred this task on the Kuwait Fund for Arab Economic Development, the major vehicle for providing Kuwaiti economic aid to other Arab countries. The Fund, while welcoming this opportunity for playing a new role in improving the investment climate in Arab countries, first took the view that the question of financial guarantees could not be tackled in isolation from other substantive and procedural safeguards. As a result it issued a report comprising an outline of suggested agreements on three subjects: (1) an Inter-Arab investment code, (2) a regional machinery for the settlement of Inter-Arab investment disputes, and (3) an Arab investment guarantee programme[14]. This seemingly ambitious report was approved by the First Meeting of Arab Financial Experts (Kuwait, November 1967) which in turn asked the Fund to prepare the proposed agreements for consideration before another meeting. Here, an interesting development evolved in the Fund's approach. Faced with the task of actual drafting, it soon realized the virtues of the implementation of its comprehensive plan in stages. For logical and practical reasons the investment guarantee programme figured again, among the three suggested goals, as the one deserving immediate concern. As a result, a draft convention for the creation of the Arab Corporation for Investment Guarantee finally came out in November 1968 and was later discussed in March 1970 by the Second Meeting of Arab Financial Experts. This meeting was attended by delegates from eleven Arab countries and by observers from interested international organizations along with some representatives of potential investors. It succeeded in approving a modified version of the Fund's draft. This was again approved, in August 1970, by the Council of Arab Economic Unity whose membership includes Egypt, Syria, Iraq, Kuwait, Jordan, Sudan and Yemen. On 27 May 1971, the convention was signed in Kuwait by Jordan, Kuwait, Sudan, Syria and Egypt. Fourteen other Arab countries subsequently signed the convention which entered into force in 1974.

The projected Corporation was envisaged as a multi-national public enterprise created by Arab states without distinction between the capital-importing and the capital-exporting among them. A contracting party may choose to be a member of the Corporation or may designate for this purpose one of its public agencies. Members subscribe in the share capital of the Corporation and are liable only to the extent of the value of their shares. The Corporation issues guarantees for Arab investments against one or more of three specified types of non-commercial risks. Should any of these risks materialize, the Corporation would be under the duty to cover the losses sustained by the guaranteed investor. For this purpose, it would draw on its own capital and reserves, and also, to the extent possible, on the premiums paid by investors. All parties would accept the succession of the Corporation to the claims of the investor indemnified by it.

This rather simple structure designed by the convention establishing the Arab Investment Guarantee Corporation involves, however, some interesting details as evidenced by the following analysis.

INSTITUTIONAL AND FINANCIAL STRUCTURE OF THE CORPORATION

The structure of a multi-national public enterprise in charge of an investment guarantee programme could in practice follow one of at least three possible patterns[15]. These patterns are: (1) an independent public corporation endowed with a share capital of its own and with the authority to conclude contracts of guaranty on its own behalf while bearing itself the financial risk of such guarantees, (2) a public agency which conducts its guarantee operations as the agent of, and for the account of, its members without engaging its own liability, and (3) a branch or even a department of an existing organism whose general objectives allow it to undertake such operations (such as an international development bank or an investment promotion agency). The drafters of the proposed Arab Corporation chose the first pattern basically for the following reasons.

An Arab investment guarantee corporation operating only on behalf of its member governments (i.e., as an agent, pure and simple) may not easily acquire, in the prevailing circumstances, the much needed confidence of its potential clients. These clients look, above all, for a direct and ready method of compensating their non-commercial losses. If the agency relies on the creditworthiness of its members while these do not inspire investors with enough confidence in their ability to pay and their efficiency, the project would be lacking an important element of success. This explains why the second pattern has in fact been adopted only in projects limiting the financing of losses to developed capital-exporting members, such as in the case of the International Investment Insurance Agency proposed by the World Bank. No such assumption obtains, however, in the Arab project where in actual terms the participation of all members in loss-financing is required. Most of those members, it is recalled, suffer from chronic deficits in their balance of payments and from acute shortages in foreign reserves. There should be little doubt therefore that the setting up of a financially independent corporation based on a subscription financing system presents the more suitable pattern for achieving the purposes of this project. The third pattern was not in fact considered if only because of the absence of another inter-Arab corporation to sponsor a programme of this kind.

The Arab Corporation will thus be created with an open-end share capital amounting initially to 10 million Kuwaiti Dinars ($28m.) divided into 10,000 nominal shares. One-half of the value of each share is to be paid in five equal annual instalments while the balance remains subject to call. All capital must be paid in Kuwaiti Dinars at their present official gold parity or in equivalent freely convertible currencies. A State suffering from an exceptional balance of payments crisis may, however, pay part of the callable capital, not exceeding 25 per cent of the requested amount, in its local currency. Such a payment can only be authorized by the special permission of the Council and subject to the undertaking of the paying member to repurchase the same by transferable currencies as soon as circumstances permit. In view of the ambitious objectives of the Corporation, the initial capital of KD10 million is undoubtedly small. It was decided upon, however, to facilitate the actual implementation of the project, with the generally expressed hope that the initial success of the Corporation would ordinarily lead to an appropriate capital increase.

There is much to be said in favour of the subscription financing system where every member of the corporation is also a shareholder, while it relies mainly on its own capital to meet its obligations. One obvious advantage is that there will be no need here to draw the distinction, maintained in many other projects, between capital-importing and capital-exporting countries in the process of loss financing. This distinction, often difficult to apply, becomes necessary when overwhelming reasons require that only one of the two groups assume the financial burden of the programme. To be sure, there are no such reasons for this discrimination in the Arab project. The richer Arab countries seem to have no particular economic interest in encouraging their nationals to invest in the territories of their less fortunate neighbours. This is obviously unlike the case of developed industrialized countries which may secure special economic advantages from the encouragement of their nationals to invest in the less developed areas, advantages such as increasing the volume of their exports or gaining a foothold in the sources of raw materials. Participation of the capital-importing countries in the financing of the project helps, on the other hand, to make them financially interested in avoiding the events which give rise to losses guaranteed by the Corporation. However, in order that the requirement of their participation may not prove self-defeating, it should not be effected in such a manner as to discourage the subscription of these countries in the project altogether. This could perhaps be ensured by applying the criterion of ability to pay in establishing the percentage of capitalization to be subscribed by each member. Such a criterion is actually ignored in the Arab project which requires only a minimum contribution from each member (5 per cent of capital). Yet, some equilibrium is likely to prevail in fact. All capital-importing Arab countries which have so far signed the convention have limited their declared subscription to the bare minimum. As a result the project will not be implemented unless richer members subscribe in larger percentages and thus bear a greater share of the risks involved.

The adoption of a subscription financing system usually leads to a voting structure which ties the number of votes of each member to the amount of his subscription in the share capital. This is ensured in the Arab project by the formula allowing each member a number of votes (500) in respect of the minimum shares held in the capital, plus an additional quantity based upon the number of additional shares held in excess of such a minimum (one vote for every two shares).

On the other hand, the convention does not adopt the standard institutional structure distributing administrative powers between a general assembly and a board of directors. Having regard to the limited number of potential members, it sets up one organ (the Council) to act simultaneously as the general assembly and the executive board. To offset possible disadvantages of this solution, the convention provides for large powers for the director-general and establishes a permanent supervisory committee over the Corporation's Management. The Council is composed of one representative of each member and exercises all powers not explicitly granted to the director-general and the supervisory committee. It is endowed in particular with the power of interpretation and modification of the constituent convention. This latter power ensures for the Corporation both independence and flexibility, elements proved by practice to be of special importance for the sound functioning of international economic agencies. With the exception of certain prescribed decisions which must be passed by a special majority of two-thirds, all other decisions of the Council are taken by the simple majority of the required quorum (three-quarters of the total votes, or, if this quorum does not obtain, two-thirds of the total votes at a subsequent meeting). The setting up of a supervisory committee is not a typical procedure in international agencies of this kind. It is justified, however, both by the fact that the Council, unlike an executive board, convenes only at long intervals (once every six months) and by the wide range of powers accorded to the director-general. This committee serves therefore as an eye for the Council over the management of the Corporation. It may also tender advice to the director-general, but should not interfere in the day-to-day operations. The Council chooses the committee's three members according to a special procedure. Two of them are chosen from candidates nominated by the members of the Corporation and the third from candidates nominated by the Union of Arab Chambers of Commerce. The participation of the latter body in this process is obviously meant to familiarize the potential clients of the programme with the Corporation's work.

SCOPE OF GUARANTEES PROVIDED BY THE CORPORATION

The scope of the guarantee offered by the proposed Corporation is limited in many respects. Risk coverage is confined to three designated types. Eligible investments, though widely defined, must belong to contracting parties or their nationals and must be carried out in the territory of a contracting party. Coverage may extend to the whole loss, but the Corporation may not exceed a certain ceiling in all its operations and must maintain some equilibrium in the distribution of these operations among different host countries.

Risk Coverage

Despite a general agreement in the different proposals for the creation of a multi-national investment guarantee programme to limit coverage to the so-called "non-commercial risks", there is a wide range of differences in the approach of each proposal in defining such risks. While broad definitions are likely to secure the advantages of flexibility, they usually threaten the element of predictability, most important to the inquiring investor. Bearing this in mind, the drafters of the Arab convention adopted an intermediate course. Each insurable risk is defined in the convention in a rather broad language followed by appropriate examples, while it is categorically emphasized that more specific terms must be used in the contracts of guaranty. The Corporation is thus authorized to provide guarantees against all or part of a loss resulting from one or more of the following types of risk:

(i) Measures of the public authorities of the host country, whether taken directly or through an intermediary, which deprive the investor of substantial rights over his investment. Such measures include, but are not limited to, expropriation, nationalization, confiscation, seizure and sequestration. They also include the deprivation of a creditor from collecting or disposing of his credit as well as moratoria imposed on foreign debts for unreasonable periods.

(ii) New measures (i.e., subsequent to the conclusion of the guaranty contract) taken, directly or indirectly, by the public authorities of the host country which substantially limit the investor's ability to transfer abroad the principal, the income or the depreciation allowances of his investment. This also includes the adoption in the host country of obviously discriminatory rates of exchange on transfers and the unreasonable delays in granting transfer permits. They do not include, however, the risk of devaluation or depreciation of currency.

(iii) Any military act or civil disturbance, including revolution, rebellion, insurrection and general mob violence, which *directly* affects the material assets of the investor.

These three types of risk, respectively termed in standard writings the "political risk", the "transfer risk" and the "war risk", are also covered in most investment guarantee projects. But the Arab convention mentions them in exclusive terms, not by way of example. Blanket statements such as "similar risks" or "other non-commercial risks" which are generally used in some of the other projects have no equivalent here[16]. Moreover, this convention adds three requirements, all negative in character, which further limit the scope of insurable risks. First the risk must be such as could not be insured through normal commercial channels at reasonable rates. Secondly, the investor must not have agreed to, or have directly been responsible for, the risk involved. And thirdly, the insurable risk cannot be merely a normal non-discriminatory measure taken by the host government in the course of its regulation of economic activities in its territory.

Though obviously justified, the last of the above-mentioned requirements may raise immense difficulties in practice. For it is a thin line indeed that separates such "normal measures" from the less justifiable ones which may amount to a creeping expropriation. To solve this problem, a more definite criterion will probably have to be developed by the Corporation in the course of drawing up contracts in order to ensure for each client some certain knowledge of the limits of his coverage. In a few national programmes payment of the guaranteed amount is sometimes based on the illegitimacy of the measure insured against, i.e., its violation of accepted standards of domestic or international law. But this is a criterion which may better be avoided by the Corporation, as the latter standards are often too diverse and uncertain to serve as useful guidelines in this respect. Insistence on the application of such standards is even likely to produce adverse effects. It will unduly involve the Corporation in the sensitive task of proscribing the conduct of host governments and may also delay indemnification of the aggrieved investor until the governmental measure involved is proved illegitimate. Obviously the first of these effects can hardly be tolerated by member governments while the second may not be readily accepted by investors. The Corporation should rather be able to provide guarantees against any form of actual "taking of property"[17], with the exception of confiscation ordered by a court of law after a fair trial. The description given by the government of the host country to its own measures should not in principle bear relevance in this respect.

Nationality of Investor

The Corporation's guarantee is limited to investments in contracting countries represented by assets which belong to other contracting countries or to their nationals. A broader view allowing the Corporation to cover, in exceptional cases, other foreign investments was suggested in the draft prepared by the Kuwait Fund but was later rejected by the Conference of Arab Financial Experts. The more restrictive attitude adopted in the final draft is generally justified by the contention that the project should serve only the economies which participated in its financing. This contention fails, however, to consider the wider interests of the receiving states, and may hide in fact reservations towards non-Arab investments based on non-economic factors.

The convention maintains, however, a distinction in the matter of nationality between individual investors and corporate bodies. Whereas the former must be "nationals of the contracting countries"[18], the latter may simply be corporate persons whose shares are substantially owned by one of the contracting countries or their nationals and which have their seat (siège social) in one of these countries. This obviously means that an eligible corporate investor must be under the substantial control of nationals of the contracting states, but it does not mean necessarily that it must have the nationality of a contracting party. A corporation owned by nationals of one member state and having its seat in the territory of another member might nevertheless enjoy the nationality of a non-member, e.g., because it has its main business in that latter state. The distinction maintained in the convention equally serves the important purpose of allowing the guarantee of joint Arab enterprises between member states or their nationals. For such enterprises, it is to be noted, may not acquire any nationality or may be endowed with a more convenient nationality than those of their members[19].

The condition of nationality must obtain both on the conclusion of the guaranty contract and at the time of claiming indemnification of the guaranteed loss. In case the investor has two or more nationalities, the nationality of a contracting party would prevail over that of a third state, and the nationality of the receiving state would prevail over that of any other party. In all cases the Corporation cannot provide insurance to a national of the host country. If this latter limitation is justified by the purpose of the Corporation (encouragement of *foreign* investment), it probably has exceeded its objective. An investment may be foreign in economic terms, i.e., represented by additional assets transferred from abroad to the economy of the receiving state, even though its owner is a national of that receiving state. By limiting the condition of foreignness to the "investment" rather than the "investor", the convention could thus have encouraged the return, under the Corporation's guarantee, of the large amounts of capital which had previously fled the Arab countries to more stable markets abroad. It is regrettable therefore that this objective, secured in the earlier Kuwait Fund draft, was sacrificed in the final version of the convention on some shaky political grounds.

Nothing in the convention requires, on the other hand, that the guaranteed investment originates in a capital-exporting country or materializes in a capital-importing one. The explanatory note attached to the convention goes further to state that "it may be useful in the present Arab circumstances to encourage the transfer of capital and know-how in every direction and not merely in one". This is an assertion to which the Corporation may, we hope, take exception. For it is generally assumed, and quite reasonably so, that the basic function of the projected Corporation will be to help encourage the flow of surplus capital from the rich Arab countries to their less fortunate neighbours, not *vice versa*.

Eligible Investments

Almost all types of investment are eligible for guarantee under the proposed Arab programme. Only loans must exceed at least a three-year maturity, unless the Council authorizes the Corporation to waive this limitation. Management policy may, of course, be more restrictive and, taking into consideration the developmental role of the programme, special importance may appropriately be attached to the long-term character of eligible investments. The convention tacitly suggests this course by referring the Corporation, in determining eligible investments, to the IMF guidelines related to the definition of long-term credits and debits in balance of payments statistics.

Pre-existing investments cannot be guaranteed, however, as "only new investments whose execution follows the conclusion of the insurance contract" are eligible. There is no reference in the convention in this respect to the "waiver letter" procedure adopted in some of the national programmes to mitigate the negative effects of this requirement. In this latter procedure an investment may be regarded as new if it is carried out after the issue, by the insuring agency, of a letter waiving the above requirement and authorizing the investor to proceed with his investment before the contract of guaranty is finally made. In such a manner, the investor will not have to wait for the final conclusion of the contract and keep his capital tied up or lose competition opportunities in the meanwhile. Practical considerations may require that a similar procedure be followed in the Arab programme. Reinvestment of earnings from existing investments is considered, on the other hand, as a new investment and therefore eligible. No statutory limitation is provided for in this regard, but the Corporation may be well justified in confining its coverage to earnings which are freely transferable at the time of reinvestment or at least to those distributed as dividends.

Apart from its newness, an eligible investment must be approved by the host country, both for execution in its territory and for the purpose of guarantee against the designated risks. Taking into consideration the bureaucracies of Arab governments, this double approval may prove to be a cumbersome and lengthy procedure that could put off an investor from ever trying. The Corporation should therefore be able to work out some formula with the appropriate authorities of host governments so as to simplify this procedure. For instance, the Corporation may assume that approval is granted if it is not declined within a fixed period of time. It may also request some governmental department in the host country to pursue the matter on its behalf or even to finalize such a procedure before the application is submitted to the Corporation.

Investments need not, on the other hand, be privately owned in order to be eligible for guarantee. The convention categorically authorizes coverage of "private investments as well as other mixed and public investments operating on commercial basis". This is a unique approach, not adopted in any of the other investment guarantee projects and proposals (with the partial exception of one individual proposal, Mr Pontzen's, which suggests that private as well as public "loans" may be eligible)[20]. Yet, it is a reasoned approach under the circumstances. On the one hand it is not always true that only private investments need the protection offered by the Corporation. Public foreign investments are at times more amenable to political risks particularly when relations between the governments concerned reach a dangerous break. The very experience of some of the Arab countries supports this point. It is immaterial, on the other hand, for some risks, such as military actions and the like, whether the investment is public or private since both may be equally exposed to the ensuing damages. Covering mixed investments without limitation while excluding public investments may also lead to absurd results. For what is the real difference in this respect between a wholly government-owned enterprise and one that is only substantially owned by the government? Finally, and more importantly, many of the Arab countries have a public sector type of economy and would therefore be discriminated against if only private or mixed investments were admitted for guarantee.

No further eligibility requirements are stipulated in the convention; only some directives give priority to certain types of investment. Priority may thus be given to investments which promote inter-Arab economic co-operation and, in particular joint Arab ventures; to investments considered by the Corporation as instrumental in strengthening the productive capabilities of the receiving country; and to investments which may not be carried out without the Corporation's guarantee. The order of these priorities is not conclusive, however. Furthermore, the convention does not seem to create a legal duty on the Corporation to respect such priorities in the course of drawing up each guarantee contract. They should only be generally reflected in its operational policy.

Other Limitations

Four general limitations lay down the general framework of the Corporation's coverage of insurable risks. These limitations are: first, the compensation paid to the guaranteed investor should not exceed the lesser of two amounts; the losses actually sustained or the agreed amount of guarantee. This follows from the nature of the guaranty contract as a contract of indemnity. Secondly, the Corporation's Council must set the maximum limit for the total value of all insurance operations provided that it does not exceed at any given moment five times the Corporation's capital and reserves. This rather high ceiling was devised in the conference which fixed the initial capital of the Corporation at KD10 million, so as to offset the limitation imposed by this modest capital. But this is obviously an ill-devised solution, for the Corporation cannot in fact issue guarantees equalling five times its capital and reserves if it has no other source to rely on in meeting its obligations. A more plausible financial structure would have probably required a lower ceiling for the guarantee operations in proportion to capital, and a bigger declared capital with perhaps a smaller percentage of its paid-in portion. Thirdly, the amount of guarantee in any one single operation must not exceed 10 per cent of capital and reserves, or 20 per cent if the investment is an inter-Arab joint venture. Finally, the Council must ascertain that guarantee operations are distributed among contracting parties. This is obviously meant to diversify the directions of investible funds in order to maintain some geographic equilibrium in the flow of inter-Arab investments, as well as to avoid excessive exposure of guaranteed investments.

Premiums and Charges

The Corporation is authorized to receive fees for examining the investors' applications and premiums for coverage of each type of risk. Such fees and premiums are not meant, however, to finance fully the Corporation's costs. For, despite misleading appearances and language, the Corporation does not sell here insurance in the technical sense, as its operations do not involve the distribution of risk among guaranteed investors[21]. Furthermore, non-commercial risks cannot be readily calculated on an actuarial basis and as a result, are not technically insurable. Premiums designed to finance losses resulting from such risks would have to be arbitrary and at any rate too high to serve the purpose of the Corporation. On the other hand, the Corporation, like all other investment guarantee agencies, is not envisaged as a co-operative institution among potential investors. Rather, it is meant to encourage the flow of inter-Arab investments by placing the cost of non-commercial risks which may face them mainly upon member states, not on the investors themselves. Charges and premiums are thus required, as the convention explicitly suggests, for the more modest purpose of "meeting administrative expenses of the Corporation and, to the extent feasible, providing suitable reserves". They also ensure the seriousness of applications so that the Corporation's limited resources may be allocated to the investments which need them most.

The text of the convention is clear in permitting a differentiated premium for each type of risk. It prohibits, however, discrimination among contracting parties in the premiums required from investors in the territory of each. Such a discrimination might be defended as a deterrent against bad policies in host countries and an incentive for better ones. Yet, bearing in mind the anticipated low rates of premiums, they could hardly play this role effectively. Even if they did, they would be discouraging investments in the more risky countries where guarantees are certainly more needed. Discrimination would also involve the Corporation in the embarrassing and uncalled-for situation of adopting prejudged views about investment climates in the different member countries, branding some of them as more risky than others. It is wise policy therefore that the convention interdicts this type of discrimination.

To further encourage potential investors to seek the Corporation's guaranty, the convention authorizes it to enter into special agreements with host countries in which the latter may undertake to share in the cost of, or even to pay fully, such charges and premiums as may be required from investors in their territories. This is the only gesture in the convention suggesting the underlying assumption that the guarantee programme serves the interests of host countries more than those of the capital-exporting members.

SETTLEMENT OF DISPUTES AND RELATED PROCEDURAL MATTERS

Time of Presentation of the Investor's Claim for Compensation

The moment at which a contracting investor becomes entitled to claim compensation from the Corporation is not categorically spelled out in the convention. Theoretically this may be one of many possible moments beginning with the date of the realization of the particular risk covered by the contract until the inexecution by the host country of such arbitral award or judicial decision as the investor may finally obtain against it. The ideal moment should, however, be one that is not so early as to expose the Corporation to premature claims nor delayed to the point of diminishing the value of the Corporation's guarantee. In the absence of a contractual provision determining such a moment, it may be safely assumed that the investor can legitimately present his claim to the Corporation as of the date of definitely sustaining the guaranteed loss. The question remains, however, as to determining this particular date. The Corporation should not defeat its purpose by requesting the investor to exhaust first every conceivable means of redress. If it does, it will be unduly restricting the scope of its guarantee to the one risk of the failure of the host government to arbitrate, including its non-compliance with unfavourable decisions. Yet, on the other hand, the Corporation could be reasonably expected to require the aggrieved investor to exert a minimum effort by using such remedies as may be readily available to him in the host country. The extent of these remedies varies, however, from one case to the other. The Corporation should therefore be careful to avoid possible disputes over this matter by specifying the required measures in the most precise terms in each contract of guaranty[22].

Subrogation

Contracting states accept, by virtue of an explicit provision in the convention, the transfer to the Corporation of the rights and claims of the investor whom it indemnifies or agrees to indemnify. The particulars of such a subrogation, no doubt subject to differences in national legal systems, are to be covered by individual contracts of guaranty. An important question arises, however, in relation to the rights of the Corporation over the assets to which it may be subrogated. In particular, would the immunities accorded by the convention to the Corporation's property extend to such assets? And must the Corporation exhaust all local remedies previously available to the investor before it resorts to international methods of settlement of disputes with host countries? Unfortunately, the text of the convention provides only partial answers to these questions. It is explicitly provided, for instance, that funds accruing to the Corporation as successor to investors will not enjoy immunity from exchange restrictions merely by virtue of its subrogation to them. But the convention mentions in general terms that host countries will accord the Corporation suitable facilities to enable it to benefit from the rights to which it may be subrogated. This may prove to be a particularly useful provision, especially as the Corporation could eventually receive from host countries large sums of local currencies which it may not otherwise be able to use in pursuing its purposes.

No mention is made, on the other hand, of the requirement of exhaustion of local remedies by the Corporation. The convention and its annex specify, as will shortly be seen, direct methods for the settlement of disputes between the Corporation and member states. It may thus be reasonably argued that, by agreeing to these methods of settlement, host countries waived the requirement of exhaustion of local remedies as applied to the Corporation in its capacity as subrogee to investors indemnified by it.

Jurisdiction

Four possible jurisdictions are designed in the convention for hearing and deciding future disputes, depending on the subject-matter of each dispute, and the identity of the parties to it. A dispute may thus be settled either directly by the Council of the Corporation, or in accordance with a special procedure elaborated in an annex to the convention, or by a method to be specified in each contract of guaranty, or through a competent domestic court, according to the following details:

(i) Disputes between members of the Corporation (or contracting states, if they are not members) either among themselves, or between them and the Corporation, with respect to the interpretation or application of the convention are to be settled by the Corporation's own Council. This is a rather common procedure in international economic agencies (although it has not been adopted in the World Bank's draft convention on the International Investment Guarantee Agency)[23]. Lest this procedure should violate the rule *omni judex in re sua*, an important exception is provided for in the convention. Disputes between the Corporation and a former member or a state which has withdrawn from the convention are not to be settled by the Council, but only in accordance with the procedure provided for in the annex.

(ii) All other disputes between contracting parties or other members on the one hand, and the Corporation on the other, especially those related to investments guaranteed under the convention, are also to be settled in accordance with the procedure elaborated in the annex. Due respect must be given, however, to the Council's exclusive jurisdiction in the matter of the interpretation and application of the convention. The Council alone is thus empowered to determine its proper jurisdiction whenever this matter is raised either before it or in the course of the arbitration procedure provided for in the annex.

The annex, which is explicitly regarded as an integral part of the convention and to which no reservation is allowed, directs the parties to disputes subject to its provisions to attempt first to reach a negotiated settlement. Failing agreement on such a settlement within six months of a party's request to enter into negotiations, the dispute could then be submitted to a voluntary conciliation procedure. If the conciliator fails to submit his report to the contesting parties within the agreed time (not exceeding six months), or if no agreement could be reached on resort to conciliation in the first place, the dispute must be settled by arbitration in accordance with the detailed provisions of the annex. No appeal or review of the arbitral award is permitted, but disputes on its interpretation may be submitted within three months from the date of the award, to the tribunal which issued it or, failing this, to a new arbitral tribunal constituted especially for this purpose. Voluntary conciliation, as an intermediate course between unsuccessful negotiations and compulsory arbitration, is obviously meant to provide the parties, if they so agree, with a more friendly and speedier procedure to settle their differences. But, for a delinquent party, it may just serve the opposite purpose causing unnecessary prolongation of the settlement procedure.

(iii) Disputes arising under contracts of guaranty between the Corporation and contracting investors are to be settled in accordance with the procedure adopted in the contract itself. This procedure may be uniformly established in the standard terms of contracts to be later prepared by the Corporation. Since the convention is silent on the nature of such a procedure, it may include reference of the dispute to an *ad hoc*, or even a permanent, arbitral tribunal, or may simply require recourse to a designated domestic jurisdiction.

(iv) Disputes not included in the above-mentioned categories, i.e., disputes between the Corporation and third persons (other than the parties to the convention, the Corporation's members and the contracting investors) are to be settled by competent courts in the contracting states. In other words, the Corporation does not enjoy immunity from jurisdiction in the territories of its members (nor, naturally, in other countries). National courts may thus exercise jurisdiction over all disputes with the Corporation which are not reserved by the convention for another method of settlement.

CONCLUSION

The convention establishing the Arab Corporation for Investment Guarantee has probably covered all the basic issues involved in the creation of a multi-national investment guarantee programme. Since it will be the first experience of its kind on the international scene, unexpected legal questions may nevertheless arise in practice. Two considerations should be borne in mind in this respect. The Corporation will not be selling insurance in the technical sense. Analogy with that system should therefore be drawn only with the greatest caution. More relevant precedents will ordinarily be found in the work of different national investment guarantee programmes. The convention has attempted, on the other hand, to establish a special legal system for the Corporation. In the absence of an applicable provision in the convention and the regulations issued by the Corporation's Council, "common principles in the laws of contracting parties and recognized principles of international law" will be applied to the case at hand. In case of arbitration, the arbitral tribunal may also decide the case *ex aequo et bono*, if the parties so agree. The value of such a formula should not be exaggerated, however. It certainly helps in insulating the Corporation's activities from the sphere of the domestic law of any particular member. But this negative aspect is hardly balanced by the suggested alternative of applying common domestic principles and recognized international rules in a field where precedents are less than scarce.

CHAPTER 14

THE FUTURE OF ARAB AID

Published in Arabic in The Arab Future, *No. 16, June 1980 and republished by the OPEC Fund for International Development (in Arabic). This English version is a translation by the Publisher of the original Arabic text.*

Arab aid to Third World nations is no longer the modest enterprise initiated by Kuwait immediately after its independence in the early sixties to assist other Arab nations, within an institutional framework, to finance their development projects. In its size, diversity, geographical dimensions and political effects, that enterprise has surpassed all the expectations which attended its beginnings. Arab aid has now become an important factor in international economic relations, and an influential feature of the financial and indeed political role which the Arab region plays in the world today.

It is about two decades since its inception, and no further time should pass without an examination of a development of such importance, within a conceptual framework that seeks to secure the maximum economic and political return for the countries which provide this aid, while ultimately ensuring that it becomes an effective instrument in serving the interests of all the developing countries. The importance of this approach is that it pursues the most far-reaching and general aims (the interests of the Third World) through safeguarding the interests of the donor countries, not only in terms of a reasonable return for the sacrifices made by those countries, but also as an essential guarantee that the development itself will continue.

CHARACTERISTICS OF ARAB AID

Arab aid is characterized by certain basic features which should be clarified at the outset:

(a) Arab aid accounts nowadays for enormous sums, particularly when compared with the Gross National Product (GNP) or even the national wealth of the Arab donor countries. Whereas the official aid given by the United States, the richest country in the world, is approximately 0.22 per cent per annum of its GNP, this proportion exceeds ten per cent in the case of some Arab countries in the Gulf. Whereas the Western countries as a whole have been unable to meet the target stipulated by the United Nations a little over ten years ago for financial flows from the developed countries to the developing countries (one per cent per annum of the GNP, seventy per cent of that to be given in the form of what is called "Official Development Assistance", i.e., official financial transfers which include a grant element of not less than 25 per cent), all of the aid-giving Arab countries have exceeded that level in recent years, and four of them have given many times that, as appears from Fig. 10, page 256.

As a result, the aid-giving Arab countries have since 1974 occupied a position high on the list of aid-giving nations in the world as a whole, in terms of proportion of aid to GNP (Fig. 11, page 258). Some of them occupy a very high place, if we consider the sums given in absolute terms and not only on a proportional basis (Fig. 12, page 259). In the years 1976 and 1977 the Kingdom of Saudi Arabia gave sums exceeded only by the United States, and in 1977 Kuwait gave more than Japan or Germany, and so on. This is in spite of the enormous differences between the volume and nature of the national incomes of those countries. In order to make a comparison we need only note that the GNP of Japan alone (642 billion dollars in the year 1977) is equal to six times the GNP of Saudi Arabia, Kuwait, the United Arab Emirates, Qatar, Libya and Iraq combined (106 billion dollars in the same year). The GNP of the United States exceeded by seventeen times the GNP of all the Arab countries mentioned. (See Figs. 11 and 12).

(b) Arab aid differs in many respects from the aid given by the industrial countries. The former is given by countries which are still underdeveloped. Their power to give is derived from a temporary situation and not from true wealth resulting from a great and renewable productive capacity. For that reason Arab aid represents a greater sacrifice than the aid given by the industrial countries. On the one hand, aid is deducted from income which is in reality a cash exchange for a depletable natural resource. On the other hand, when the donor countries themselves seek foreign financing on a commercial basis, they pay a higher cost for that financing than that paid by the industrial countries. Furthermore, Arab aid is not given, except rarely, to encourage the donors' exports, but is used chiefly to finance purchases from third countries, which are usually the developed countries, i.e., this aid represents a transfer of wealth to the industrial countries in exchange for goods and services exported to the recipient developing countries. Thus it can be said that Arab aid definitely benefits the developed countries, by virtue of the employment and export opportunities it creates for them while it is intended to benefit the developing countries which ultimately receive those goods and services. The Arab countries do not have any great choice in the matter as long as they continue to lack productive capacity and are unable to provide aid in kind to the other developing countries in the form of goods and services produced by themselves.

For that reason as well Arab aid represents a sacrifice greater than that borne by the developed countries when they give aid to finance their own exports.

(c) Despite the great variety of forms of Arab aid extended since 1974, it has mostly been for general or balance of payments support. This form of aid made up two-thirds of the amounts disbursed in 1975, and approximately forty per cent in the following year, compared to about eleven per cent disbursed by the Western countries during that period. This did not necessarily reflect a preference on the part of the donor Arab countries for this form of assistance. Rather, it was a response to urgent and repeated requests from the beneficiary nations for swift and uninterrupted support which was not related to projects whose implementation inevitably requires long periods of time. Thus an important aim of Arab aid was, and still is, to give the beneficiary countries a large measure of freedom of choice in the uses to which the money is put, as well as freedom of choice to import from the most appropriate source.

(d) Likewise Arab aid has been characterized over recent years by the geographical diversity of the beneficiary nations, for it now covers approximately seventy-five countries, having been confined before 1974 to Arab countries. Moreover, this aid has directly reached countries which have no direct economic or political relations with the donor countries, such as the scattered island states of the Pacific and Caribbean. Here again Arab aid differs from that of the other donor countries, which usually confine it to countries that are of obvious economic or political interest to the donor. It is then used to achieve such typical objectives as securing markets for their products or sources of raw materials, preserving former influence, attempting to acquire new influence, or at least ensuring the neutrality of the aid recipient.

(e) Arab aid is also characterized by the fact that a large part of it reaches the beneficiary countries by way of institutions in the running of which the Arab countries do not have any great role, such as the World Bank Group or the International Monetary Fund. The sums paid by the Arab countries in the form of loans to these institutions are regarded as being the property of the borrowing institutions as soon as the loans are made, and those sums are disposed of thereafter according to the decisions made by the individuals administering the institutions, without the Arab countries having an effective say on the boards of management, or a prominent role in the administrative organs. Not infrequently those sums have been greater than sums given by the same Arab countries to institutions which they wholly own, or effectively control. It is nevertheless to be noted that with regard to the resources obtained by the beneficiary institutions, the sums paid by the Arab Countries still account, despite their large size, for a small proportion of the total resources of these institutions, and of the total loans obtained by them each year, with the exception of the International Monetary Fund, where Arab loans made up 44.3 per cent of the resources of its Oil Facility and approximately 32 per cent of the resources of its Supplementary Facility.

If this situation is somewhat justified with regard to the sums which are paid in the form of loans to the World Bank and the International Monetary Fund, which can be regarded as secure investments for liquid assets, the justification becomes more difficult in respect of sums on which there is no financial return, such as shares in the resources of the International Development Association (IDA), or the African Development Fund, etc., except that some indirect influence in the institution is gained as a result. There is in any event some progress in this direction as donor Arab countries are becoming major participants in international and regional institutions. They have a major, if not the major, role in institutions such as the Arab Bank for Economic Development in Africa (1975), the OPEC Fund (1976) and the International Fund for Agricultural

Development (1976).

(f) However, the most important distinguishing characteristic of Arab aid, and that which is the prime reason for the publication of this chapter, is that its philosophy and impact have undergone a fundamental change since 1974. This change has been so rapid that its dimensions and results have yet to be analyzed. It began in response to a change in world circumstances, and to numerous pressures from outside the Arab World, i.e., it was not the result of a natural evolution or of a plan as to the direction the aid should take. It is almost as if the change was discovered because of its magnitude, after the fact.

Just as the institutional framework of Arab aid was initiated with the establishment of the Kuwait Fund in 1961, its expansion began when the function of that Fund changed in 1974 from an institution for the financing of projects in Arab countries, to an institution for financing development in the developing world as a whole, with a five-fold increase in its capital. In the same year the Abu Dhabi Fund underwent a similar widening of its geographical scope, as well as an increase in its capital. Then the Saudi Development Fund and the Iraqi Fund for External Assistance were set up, their mandates being from the outset the financing of projects in all developing countries. The Arab countries were not slow thereafter to direct their funding to institutions the beneficiaries of which were not limited to the Arab countries, and indeed some of them stipulated that Arab countries were not eligible to benefit (as in the case of the Arab Bank for Economic Development in Africa). That development was accompanied by a great expansion in bilateral aid, much of which was given without prior analysis of the relative needs of each country, the objectives of the aid and the most appropriate means of achieving those aims. There was not merely an expansion in the number of countries benefiting from the aid; but a basic change in the philosophy of aid. From being a purely inter-Arab phenomenon, an attempt by some Arab countries with liquid funds to assist other Arab countries to achieve faster development without regard to other considerations, and based on a common cultural heritage between the aid donors and beneficiaries, Arab aid became an integral part of financial co-operation between developing countries. It was also connected, in the minds of many, with the increase in the price of oil and interpreted as an amelioration of its effects. Among the Arab financing institutions, only the Arab Fund for Economic and Social

Development continued to confine its activities to the Arab world.

It is not relevant here to determine whether the path taken by Arab aid was the most appropriate one at the time, or whether it would have been better if the Arab funds had maintained their purely Arab character and left the task of assisting non-Arab countries to other institutions founded for that purpose. The important thing is to demonstrate that when the Arab Funds operated within a purely Arab framework, they did not distinguish greatly between the interests of the country giving the aid and the interests of the country receiving it, or they assumed a correspondence between those respective interests and consequently did not regard the securing of the interests of the donor nations as a problem requiring a search for the best solution. This situation changed after the huge expansion in the geographical scope of the Arab Funds and the extension of Arab aid to countries the aiding of which could not be justified except in altruistic terms in the absence of obvious benefits to the donor countries. Gradually, the concept which characterized Arab aid at its inception, namely that it was an expression of Arab solidarity based on moral and political considerations and governed by inter-Arab relations, underwent a substantial change.

The rapid increase in the number of aid institutions, and the processes through which Arab funds were transferred, sometimes without prior co-ordination, as well as Arab participation in institutions not subject to the control of the Arab countries, led to a certain loss of effectiveness of Arab aid, particularly as it was no longer possible to consider the aid as useful no matter how it was used or to accept that the interests of the recipient were necessarily the same as the donor. Such a situation led to the extreme view that the mere giving of funds to other developing countries benefited the Arab donor country whatever the circumstances, or that the aid was no more than a compensation to the developing countries for the increased prices of oil imported by them from the Arab countries.

ARAB AID AND THE QUESTION OF OIL PRICES

Because the expansion of Arab aid began after the increased income from oil derived by the Arab oil-exporting countries following the events of 1973, there was a prevailing view among many that the aid was a compensation to the oil-consuming developing nations for the increased price of oil, rather than simply enabled by the increased oil revenues. This view was intensified by the fact that new forms and increased amounts of aid were announced concurrently with oil price increases.

It is however, easy to prove the falsity of that argument:

Historically, Arab aid appeared, as we have seen, at the beginning of the sixties, i.e., long before the increase in oil prices, and indeed at a time when the price of oil was falling. Also, Arab aid was, and still is, given to countries which do not import any oil at all. For example, until recently a substantial proportion of Arab aid was allocated to Egypt and Syria, neither of which is an oil-importing country. Furthermore, aid is still given out of Arab or semi-Arab funds to countries such as Tunisia, Oman, Bahrain, Malaysia, Indonesia and Bolivia, all of which are oil-exporting countries.

Likewise, Arab aid has concentrated mainly on African and Asian countries, and only rarely reached Latin America (chiefly through the OPEC Fund) in spite of the fact that the Latin American countries represent more than 35 per cent of the total oil imports of the developing countries. This is because Arab aid gave priority to the poorest and least developed countries, which use less fuel than the semi-industrialized countries, many of which are in Latin America. A recent study has shown that more than 70 per cent of all the oil imported by the developing countries is imported by only eight countries. Those countries are, in order, Brazil, South Korea, Turkey, India, Taiwan, The Philippines, Thailand and Singapore. (See Fig. 13, page 260).

Only some of the eight countries in category (a) have received limited aid from the Arab countries, because most of them have a relatively high income, and are considered to be less deserving than the poorer countries in Africa and Asia. For example, imports of oil by Brazil alone amount to approximately one quarter of the total oil imports of developing countries, three times the amount imported by the thirty countries designated by the United Nations as Least Developed, and more than is used by the continent of Africa as a whole. If Arab aid were given as compensation for the increases in oil prices, a large part of that aid would have been given to Brazil, which has not been the case. An analysis published by the Organization of Arab Petroleum Exporting Countries has shown that the aid given by the OPEC countries as a whole, much of which is Arab aid, is equivalent to a large part of the value of the oil imports of the beneficiary countries and in some years has exceeded that value (that is, if we disregard the oil imports of Brazil, South Korea, Taiwan, Argentina and India, which represent more than 50 per cent of the total. It should be noted that that study was based upon assumptions which may not be universally accepted)(Fig. 14). An analysis undertaken by the United Nations Conference on Trade and Development (UNCTAD) shows that there is no correlation between the aid received by each country from OPEC sources, and the increased oil import bill of the beneficiary, whereas the aid given to the poorer countries has exceeded their increased oil import bill. It has been insufficient, in the case of the relatively richer countries, to cover even a small part of it (Fig. 15, page 262).

If Arab aid were given as a compensation, it would have ceased in years when there were no increases in oil prices, and would decrease to those countries which managed to buy at prices lower than other countries. Nothing like that has happened. On the contrary, aid has increased at times when there has been no increase in oil prices. Aid reached its maximum level in 1975, a year which saw no increase in prices. Furthermore, it is known that there was no increase in oil prices in real terms in the period 1974 to 1978, and indeed the real price decreased during that period, as a result of the increased inflation rate and decrease in the value of the dollar (as can be seen from Fig. 16, page 263). The large relative increase in oil prices in June 1979 is itself regarded as compensation for the reduction in the real price of oil exported in the preceding period. If aid were given as a compensation for the additional burden upon the oil consumers, there would be no satisfactory explanation for increasing it, or even for its being there at all in those years.

Finally, the giving of aid only to those who import oil, and in proportion to their imports, would be very difficult to explain on rational grounds, because a country which imports oil may export many other things and may not need assistance at all. Likewise a country which does not import oil may be in a position where it must import many other goods, which could put it in a difficult financial position, particularly if the prices of the goods it imports are also increasing at a high rate. The need for assistance is not dependent on the complications caused by importing one commodity, but on the whole financial and economic situation of a country. Linking the price of oil to the level of aid could lead to a disruption in international trade relations, by introducing an element difficult to justify if applied to one commodity such as oil.

It is evident that Arab aid was not given in the past, and is not given now, in order to compensate for the increase in the price of oil imports. It is indeed fortunate. Otherwise, the bulk of the aid would go to the most industrialized and advanced developing countries, and the most needy countries, which import the least oil, would be deprived of it. Also, the oil-importing countries would have had an incentive to squander oil, as long as they continued to import it at what was in effect less than the market price.

It is nevertheless clear that the increase in oil revenues has led to an increased ability to give aid, thus to an expansion of the circle of non-Arab recipient countries. In selecting which countries should benefit, consideration has sometimes been given to the relative needs of these countries, and their general financial and economic position, including the burden created by the importation of oil, without that burden being the sole criterion. There are of course cases in which Arab countries have sold oil to other developing countries by inst-alment, or by way of barter, and there are also cases where the Arab financing institutions have shown a preference for projects which reduce reliance on the importation of oil, such as hydro-electrical power projects and the like. Indeed it is evident that the increase in oil prices has created a new climate and has allowed Arab aid to help alleviate the balance of payments deficits suffered by many developing countries in recent years. In the final analysis there is a connection between the rise in the price of oil, and the volume of Arab aid, but it is not a relationship of compensation, which incidentally has not been alleged in respect of any other commodity, including commodities exported by really rich countries, the prices of which are continually rising.

THE CONTINUATION OF ARAB AID

Although Arab aid was not given as compensation for the increase in the prices of oil, the increase in prices was undoubtedly the most important factor promoting the rapid increase in volume of that aid, until it reached its present proportions. The majority of the oil-exporting Arab countries were not in a position to use all of the revenues for their immediate requirements, which resulted in an accumulation of liquid assets commonly called, without a proper examination of their nature, a cash "surplus". This "surplus" does not, by its very nature, last, for it necessarily decreases with the increasing capacity of the country to absorb it into its local economy, particularly if there have not been other increases in the price of oil permitting the accumulation of liquid assets to continue at the same rate. According to the Annual Report of the Arab Monetary Fund (1978), the surplus trade balance of the oil-producing Arab countries fell to its lowest level in 1978, reaching 22.1 billion dollars after it had stood at 40.8 billion dollars in the preceding year.

This fact arouses fears in the oil-producing countries, which view this surplus as merely another form of their depletable oil, and it has also aroused fears in the countries and institutions which have come to rely heavily on Arab aid, and which see that this aid may gradually diminish with the disappearance of the "surplus".

A recent report by UNCTAD echoes these fears, and calls upon the industrial nations to prepare themselves to fill the gap left by decreased aid from the OPEC countries:

"If the OPEC countries ceased to perform this great task of accumulation, with a continuing increase in their import requirements, the resulting gap would have to be filled by the traditional donors, i.e., the industrial nations, or at least by those among them who will continue to have a large balance of payments surplus and it will be necessary to make a sufficiently great adjustment in the financial and aid policies of those countries to fulfil that role, to prevent serious disruptions in the development process of a number of countries which have come to rely in recent years on OPEC sources for financing."

(United Nations Conference on Trade and Development, *Financial Solidarity for Development Efforts and Institutions of the Members of OPEC 1973-1976 Review*. Arabic translation p. 17.)

However, the matter cannot be left with such a simple generalization. Part of Arab aid is provided through existing institutions, endowed with their own capital and resources. Those institutions will not disappear. Rather, they have been founded as ongoing concerns, and they will continue to carry out their operations, even if they do not obtain new resources in the future, relying on their existing assets and perhaps on loans from the money markets. Likewise, the sudden termination of other forms of aid will be no easy matter from the practical point of view, having regard to the numerous interests which have sprung up from the existing situation, and the enormous complications that could occur in developing countries in the event that Arab aid were suddenly cut off. That is why it is important to postulate a framework which would make it in the interests of the donor countries to go on giving, since that is the real guarantee of the continuation of this phenomenon which has grown without any previously conceived plan. Also the current balance of payments went down to 14.4 billion dollars in 1978, having stood at approximately 27 billion dollars in 1977. The report added: "The developments of 1978 have proved that the prophecies circulated by many in the mid-seventies that the surplus would become an unceasing flow, are wrong." Arab Monetary Fund, *Annual Report, 1978,* (Abu Dhabi, 1978) p. 7.

FUTURE PROSPECTS

If we take the last remark as a starting point for conceiving a future approach, there appear to us three areas where Arab aid can play a role, to ensure the maximum economic return for the donor countries while at the same time allowing the recipient countries to benefit:

1. Aid as a stimulus to commercial investments by the donor countries.

There is no doubt that the natural mode of economic co-operation between the oil states and the other developing countries is that which provides mutual benefits to both parties, particularly if we remember that the oil rich countries are usually poor in other resources, indeed poorer in some instances than the countries which seek their assistance. Consequently, the investing of the resources of the oil countries in other developing countries for profit provides the obvious form of co-operation which can further the interests of both sides, as opposed to the giving of grants or concessional loans, which represent a financial loss to the aid-giving countries, and a net gain to the recipients. Likewise, the investing of this wealth in a number of developing countries allows the oil states to diversify their investments and so spread their risks.

In spite of the many arguments in defence of investment in developing countries, it is known that only a small proportion of the wealth of the Arab oil states has been invested in other developing countries, and that most of their external investments are still made in the industrialized countries of the West. That is attributable to two clear factors. The first is the general feeling that the political risks are greater in the developing countries than they are in the advanced countries (a feeling which is not always justified) and the second is the weak capacity of the developing countries to absorb investment because of the lack of the necessary infrastructure, whether of material facilities, or the appropriate institutions and legislation.

An important role can be played in this area by national Arab aid institutions, such as the Kuwaiti, Saudi, Iraqi and Abu Dhabi Funds, namely by financing infrastructure development in those countries in which the donor countries are interested in making investments. In that event it would become one of the basic tasks of the national aid institutions to assist the recipient countries which are likely to host investments of the donor countries, to carry out infrastructure projects such as ports, roads, electrical transmission and communication systems, and to develop their institutions. This approach will have obvious effects on the choice of beneficiary countries and sectors which would receive finance. It will also require continuous co-ordination between the aid agencies and the investment institutions in the donor countries, since the latter will acquire a direct interest in the continuation of aid and will become a source of support for the former.

It is to be noticed that the Arab aid agencies have concentrated on financing infrastructure projects. However, this was not based on a policy of linking aid with future investments, and is not the result of co-ordination with local investment institutions, but is rather a direct result of the soft terms of the financing provided, which by its very nature is appropriate for infrastructure projects which are difficult to finance through commercial channels. For that reason the change required is mostly to concentrate the aid on countries to which it is expected that investment will flow, and to co-ordinate that aid with investment agencies. There will undoubtedly result from that the emergence of projects which receive easy-term financing from the Arab Funds, and commercial financing from the Arab investment agencies, to the gain of all parties concerned.

From another side, aid can help reduce alleged political risks by giving guarantees to serious investors against such risks. It is known that the "Arab Investment Guarantee Corporation" was set up for that purpose in 1974, but it is also known that that institution has never had adequate resources to enable it to play a major role despite the fact that it is regarded as a successful operation, even when judged by the criterion of profit and loss. This institution requires a major increase in its resources (which need not be in the form of paid-up capital), and a widening of the geographical scope of its operations.

Bilateral Arab aid should also be directed towards serving Arab investments in the developing countries, which are predominantly from the public sector, by helping to create the most favourable investment climate in those countries. This will help bring about increased investment by the Arab oil states in other developing countries, and this form of co-operation will predominate as the most balanced example of economic co-operation between Third World countries.

2. Aid as a tool for promoting Arab exports and economic co-operation among developing countries

As mentioned above, Arab aid has not played a significant role in promoting the exports of the Arab donor countries. However, as some of these countries move towards industrialization, there will arise the need to support the export efforts of the national industries, particularly those which are in competition with the industries of the developed countries, which for the most part receive financial backing from their governments.

Each oil-producing Arab country is capable of establishing its own agency to support its exports, through long and medium-term guarantees. The efforts of the Arab nations could be co-ordinated through the creation of an Arab Exports Guarantee Agency, which would provide guarantees for Arab exports to other developing countries. This would be a major step in the opening of new markets for Arab exports. There is no need to set up a new Arab agency for the purpose; the "Arab Investment Guarantee Corporation" could provide export credit, in addition to its function of insuring against non-commercial risks, as is the case with many similar organizations operating on a bilateral basis in the developed, industrialized countries.

On the other hand, with increased Arab industrialization, in particular in hydrocarbon-based industries, the national Arab aid funds will be able to institute procurement policies which give priority to tenders submitted from donor countries, Arab countries, or other developing countries. New markets will be opened for Arab exports, at the expense of industries in the developed countries, which on the whole enjoy unfair advantages, thus expanding economic co-operation among developing countries. If such an approach appears at first sight to offend the liberal demands for untied aid it is justified in the interest of the developing countries, particularly those which make sacrifices by giving aid. It is also consistent with the trend in new international financial institutions such as the International Agricultural Development Fund, the constituent agreement of which gives clear preference to goods and services originating from developing countries so that the aid will benefit more than one developing country in each instance.

Such steps are likely to lead to an expansion of markets for Arab products, and a consequent promotion of industrialization in Arab countries on a competitive basis, which will in turn encourage Arab economic integration.

The support of the Arab Fund for Economic and Social Development, in particular by enabling it to participate in the equity capital of joint enterprises, and to go beyond the role of financing to actual assistance in Arab development planning, and in the identification and preparation of projects, is important for the regional consolidation of Arab aid in support of Arab economic integration.

3. Aid as a factor in continued oil revenues in the future

Finally, one of the functions of the giving of aid is that it should perpetuate the capacity of the donor country to go on giving. Because that capacity in the Arab oil countries is wholly or almost wholly dependent upon their oil revenues, some recipient states in the Third World have an interest in the increase of oil prices, at least to the extent to which it is estimated that they will receive aid in excess of the cost that they might bear as a result of the increased oil prices. This brings us back to a point we have dealt with previously, namely that the group of least developed countries have received Arab aid in excess of the total costs of their oil imports and some other countries have received annual aid in excess of their incremental oil import bills.

The exception to this was 1979, which witnessed a large relative increase in oil prices which was not accompanied by a similar increase in the total amount of aid given by the Arab or oil-exporting countries.

It seems that in these instances the Arab countries are playing a role of redistributing income on a world-wide level, by demanding sums from the industrialized or semi-industrialized nations, part of which is then distributed to the non-industrialized and poor countries. The aid can be used in a positive manner, not by considering it as compensation for an increase in oil prices, but as an instrument to evolve the international economy on more equal bases, in which oil, partially and indirectly, imposes a tax upon the rich countries which is distributed among the poor countries.

However, the fact that Arab aid plays this role presupposes sufficient awareness in the beneficiary countries that what they receive from the oil-producing countries is as a result of their continuing ability to obtain a certain income from their oil exports. This role loses a good deal of its effectiveness when the aid reaches the recipient country by way of sources which do not bear the name of the donor countries, but bear the stamp of other groups of countries. Perhaps it is most effective to give the aid through organizations connected in people's minds with an increase in the income of the oil states as a result of oil price rises, organizations such as the national Funds and the OPEC Fund. The last mentioned Fund has been able to project its identity as an instrument of solidarity among developing countries having the greatest need, and not as an instrument for compensating oil-importers.

Most of the loans made by the OPEC Fund have been extended to the least developed countries, and those most affected by economic crises. These countries have received approximately seventy-five per cent of all loans extended by the Fund, whereas they do not import more than about twenty per cent of the total oil imports of the developing countries. The semi-industrialized countries, which enjoy a relatively high income, did not benefit by more than a small extent from this Fund, even though they import large quantities of oil.

This does not of course mean that the OPEC Fund ignores the burden borne by the developing countries as a result of the increased prices of the oil they import. Although the Fund concentrates its operations on the relatively poorer countries, it has extended loans to the richer developing countries which are troubled by major balance of payments deficits, partly because of their oil imports, such as Turkey and Jamaica. In determining the amount which each country will receive, the Fund also considers the extent of its reliance on energy imports and gives priority to the financing of projects which will reduce the reliance of the borrowing country on imported oil.

The OPEC Fund has consequently been somewhat successful in creating a broad front of developing countries which look upon the oil price rises as the main factor contributing to the resources of the Fund. Therefore the assistance given by the oil states becomes a contributory factor in enabling these countries to gain support for adjusting oil prices, since they can then extend aid to a large number of other developing countries.

On the other hand, the fact that Arab and partly Arab financing organizations give priority to projects which will lessen the reliance of developing countries on imported oil, as does the OPEC Fund, will help take some of these countries out of the circle of countries which are harmed by oil price increases and place them among the countries which derive a net benefit from the increased capacity of the oil countries to give, which will ease the acceptance by the developing countries generally of decisions to raise oil prices.

CONCLUSION

In summary, Arab aid has reached a volume and scope which demand a fresh and comprehensive outlook so that it may be guided and perpetuated into the eighties, to the benefit of the donors and recipients.

Perhaps the most appropriate means to realize this aim is to regard this aid in its present considerable volume as a means for the redistribution of income on a world-wide scale for the benefit of the poorer countries, carried out by the oil states through the income they derive from their exports to oil-consuming countries, which are basically the industrialized and semi-industrialized countries. Conceived in this way, Arab aid plays a historical role in bringing about solidarity among the countries of the Third World, which can give them greater importance in the framework of international politics.

In affirmation of that role, collective aid should be given through a limited number of organizations which are identified with the donor oil states and which extend aid directly to the beneficiary countries, or else through organizations in which the role of those countries is clearly recognized such as when the OPEC countries participated in the International Fund for Agricultural Development through the OPEC Fund.

Bilateral aid, on the other hand, may be directed in such a way that it serves the mutual interests of the donor and recipient countries. It should concentrate on the financing of infrastructure projects in those countries which are particularly suitable for investment by the oil states. Part of the aid could be used to finance an export Arab credit scheme, and to improve the investment climate in the recipient countries. In this way the Arab countries could diversify their external investments, and a more balanced form of co-operation could arise between developing countries.

It is important that the donor Arab countries define their conception of foreign aid, and the aims they seek to achieve by giving it, whether within the framework suggested, or within any other framework, to the greatest extent that they estimate they are capable of in the coming years. If they leave the initiative to others Arab aid will appear to be, however great its size, no more than a response to outside pressures. The Arab countries will then find themselves victims of pressure, despite the fact that it is they who began to give aid and go on giving it, in a manner the like of which has not been seen before.

(Annex of Tables and Graphs to Chapter 14 may be found on p. 256.)

PART III

ON WORLD HUNGER

FOOD PRODUCTION IN DEVELOPING COUNTRIES: MAJOR CONSTRAINTS AND POSSIBLE SOLUTIONS

First published in OPEC Review, *Vol. III, No. 3, Vienna, Austria, Autumn 1979.*

INTRODUCTION

Despite the shocks of past droughts and famines and an increasing recognition of the precarious world food situation, the goal of eliminating hunger and malnutrition remains elusive. An estimated 1.3 billion people or one-third of the world population have incomes of less than US $200 per year. In this group, at least 750 million live in a state of absolute poverty, without the means to acquire minimum requirements of food, clothing and shelter. According to the Food and Agriculture Organization (FAO), more than 450 million people, half of them children, suffer from malnutrition. The World Health Organization estimates that 30 million die each year from illness connected with malnutrition. These predicaments of hunger do not occur only during periods of economic downturn or natural calamities. They are an integral part of the daily existence of the malnourished whose number is, in fact, swelling at an even higher rate than that of population growth[1].

The magnitude of the problem should not be masked by the often-quoted aggregate figures of world food production and consumption. According to these figures, world production has more than doubled over the past 25 years and has been sufficient, at world level, to exceed average per capita requirements. But on the more significant country level, production has fallen short of requirements in a large number of developing countries.

From a global perspective, the persistence of hunger, even when global food production is in line with world requirements, is one of the most challenging problems facing governments and the international community. This complex problem encompasses not only the bottlenecks to increased food production and improved distribution, but also a host of other considerations embedded in the socio-economic fabric of nations.

In June of 1978, the fourth Ministerial session of the United Nations World Food Council adopted the Mexico Declaration which called for consultations within the international community to identify urgent steps to be taken in order to meet the challenge of solving the hunger problem. The Governing Committee of the OPEC Fund welcomed the invitation extended by the Council to participate in the implementation of the Mexico Declaration. It also expressed the wish that the Fund's report on this matter take into account the views and experience of the national aid agencies of OPEC member countries as well as those of other OPEC-assisted institutions.

This report is, therefore, written from the general perspective of several aid agencies of OPEC member countries[2]. As such, it takes into account the special characteristics which help shape their role and policies. It may, therefore, be useful to highlight, at the outset, some of these characteristics which may have a bearing on the issues under discussion.

RELEVANT CHARACTERISTICS OF OPEC AID

Financial assistance from OPEC countries and OPEC-supported aid institutions to other developing countries differs in many aspects from aid extended by other sources – be they bilateral or multilateral. Firstly, OPEC financial co-operation in the Third World represents a transfer of resources from a group of developing countries to other developing countries. Secondly, this co-operation is not influenced by motives characterizing the activities of other aid-givers, such as promoting donors' exports, maintaining a post-colonial relationship or inducing structural economic or political changes within individual aid recipient countries.

The solidarity of OPEC countries with other Third World nations is rooted in the history of underdevelopment which OPEC members have experienced and share with other developing countries.

Their aid, made possible through the export of a depletable natural resource, is yet another expression of this solidarity, whose ultimate objective is the fostering of the New International Economic Order.

OPEC aid is also a relatively recent phenomenon dating back to 1961 when the Kuwait Fund for Arab Economic Development was founded. OPEC aid, however, was not channelled uniquely through the Kuwait Fund. During the ensuing years, bilateral aid on a grant basis was also extended by Saudi Arabia and Libya, as well. At the turn of the last decade, new institutions concerned mainly with granting project loans had come into being. The Abu Dhabi Fund for Arab Economic Development was created in 1971 as a national institution of an OPEC member country like the Kuwait Fund. The Arab Fund for Economic and Social Development, which was established in 1968 as a regional institution by Arab countries including OPEC and non-OPEC members, became operational in 1972. During that year, OPEC aid, on a disbursement basis, was estimated at US $700 million, which then represented a relatively high percentage of the GNP of the main Arab aid donors.

The oil events of 1973 enabled OPEC countries to inaugurate a new chapter in their aid record, which culminated in a total commitment figure of some $15 billion in 1975, representing, at that time, 7.5 per cent of the combined GNP of OPEC donors or the equivalent of net oil imports of other developing countries as a whole. OPEC annual aid commitments have remained above the $10 billion mark ever since, with actual disbursements ranging between 2 and 2.7 per cent of their combined GNP.

These facts have important implications on the operational philosophy of OPEC aid institutions. Firstly, since the aid is to further the common interests of developing countries, of which OPEC members are part, it is extended to support sound development priorities established by individual recipients. In practice, this means that "project issues" proper are the main areas of concern, with economic and other policies, sectoral priorities and "country issues" in general being the strict prerogative of individual recipient Governments. The OPEC Fund may represent a major exception in this respect as it gives a clear priority to two sectors: energy and food production, without restricting, however, its financing of projects to these two areas. Secondly, the relatively recent experience of most OPEC agencies in the field of project lending in general has meant a gradual build-up of their technical capabilities, a process which obviously could not be accompanied by the development of ambitious lending strategies for each recipient country. In practice, this has also meant that project identification initiatives remained primarily the responsibility of recipient Governments.

These characteristics, in turn, have implications on the means and level of contribution which OPEC agencies could bring to the solution of the world food problem. This, in no way, however, diminishes OPEC member countries' concern for the elimination of hunger in the world, as indicated by their support and financial assistance to new agencies established specifically to tackle the problem. Nor does this mean that agencies for OPEC aid do not engage in consultations with individual recipient countries which submit various competing demands for the resources available for project financing.

On the contrary, it is towards projects that directly or indirectly help spread the benefits of economic development by reducing poverty and socio-economic imbalances that the aid activities of OPEC agencies are directed. However, what the above characteristics of OPEC aid do mean is that the level of financing for food production by these agencies has, in absolute and relative terms, been determined, and is likely to continue to be determined, by the priority accorded to this area by the recipient countries themselves.

OPEC countries, all of which are food deficit countries, recognize that, although the economies of developed and developing countries are and will remain interrelated, supply shortfalls in developing countries cannot be met adequately or indefinitely through increased output in the developed parts of the world. The deficits in developing countries can be eliminated only by increasing the emphasis on food production in these countries. This aim obviously cannot be achieved if the developing countries themselves are not prepared to evolve and implement a development strategy geared to this objective. Because of constraints other than capital, such as limitations in technology and physical resources, however, the benefits of any such strategy are likely to be downstream and reaped only in the longer term.

FOOD SECURITY

A system of appropriate storage and distribution of grain reserves of a size adequate to ensure a high degree of world food security and trade stability seems to present the viable short-term palliative to the problem of wide-spread hunger and malnutrition. This solution is justified by two vital needs: the need for a stop-gap mechanism until the long-term solutions of the food problem are implemented, and the need for a buffer against conjunctural food shortages caused by bad weather and other disruptive natural conditions.

Unfortunately, a consensus has yet to be reached on a mechanism based on mandatory contributions. A United Nations Conference was held in February/March 1978 for the purpose of establishing a new international agreement, but failed to do so. Yet, world grain stocks in relation to consumption are today no larger than they were before the 1972-74 food crisis. Moreover, the expected increases in North American grain exports to the Soviet Union and other food deficit countries able to meet the cost of their food import bill, and the resulting pressure on prices, will directly affect the low-income food deficit countries. In fact, adverse weather conditions in North America, where the emphasis is on rain-fed agriculture, especially if coupled with a fall in the production of major food deficit countries, could lead to famine in the low-income countries on the same scale as that of the last food crisis. It is, therefore, imperative to mobilize the international community for action. The lead in such mobilization should continue to come from advisory food and agricultural organizations, with the strong support of major grain-exporting countries, principally the United States.

To ensure adequate participation of developing countries, a mechanism for grain reserves must include special provisions for preferential access, and special assistance to acquire grain, develop storage capacity and meet maintenance costs at national levels. The scheme itself could be financed mostly by existing financial institutions, as well as bilateral donors, including OPEC members or their agencies. The absence of a scheme of grain reserves would not only increase the risks of famine but also perpetuate the plight of the hungry throughout the world.

FOOD PRODUCTION AND INCOME GROWTH

It is now widely recognized that the food problem is, in most regions, one of poverty rather than of limitations in physical resources. This is particularly the case in rural areas where large segments of the population do not have the means of obtaining the agricultural inputs, or the purchasing power for access to the food available in the market.

Increased food production is a necessary condition for overcoming shortages and solving the nutrition problem. However, it is by no means a sufficient condition. Increased production may indeed by-pass the neediest segments of the population if it does not also help to raise their incomes. Thus, there are two aspects of the solution of the food problem: increased production of food in developing countries and widespread increases in family incomes particularly among the poor in rural areas. The increased incomes may come from off-farm or on-farm employment; from the development of primarily labour-intensive industry in rural areas, from employment creation in construction and public works schemes, from the increases in productivity and profitability of agriculture and, finally, from the generation of the services that will become in demand as income and employment in rural areas increase.

Only a development strategy which seeks to distribute gains from development to the poor sections of the population via increased income can meet the problems of inadequate food consumption. Development policies must, therefore, focus on increasing the purchasing power of the neediest consumers and reducing imbalances, while simultaneously raising the productivity of agriculture.

PRODUCTIVITY INCREASES IN AGRICULTURE

Disparate incomes, difficult access to resources, and the associated problem of unemployment pose critical constraints on agricultural productivity in many developing countries. Appropriately developed technologies which are suitable for adoption on small farms and which increase the use of local resources, particularly labour, would no doubt alleviate these constraints. In fact, there is now ample evidence indicating that the gains in productivity of small farms are higher than those of large holdings utilizing traditional technology. The shift to modern, mechanized agriculture to increase yields may be necessary in areas such as East Asia, where land available for intensive farming at reasonable cost is becoming scarce. Mechanization and other means of modern agricultural production should, nevertheless, be appropriate to the specific tasks involved and should be designed and constructed, whenever possible, by utilizing local skills.

At the same time, policies must be developed to ensure that the rise in productivity is not confined to large holdings which could threaten the security of tenure on small farms. Security of tenure, regardless of the type of tenure, is important, if all long-term potential gains in productivity are to be realized.

Complex and often contradictory price policies also pose constraints on productivity. The positive and negative features associated either with input subsidies or higher output prices are well-known. In most developing countries, pricing and subsidy policies have hitherto proved to provide disincentives to agricultural production. Without underestimating the complexities of these issues and the difficulty of finding an overall solution for them, it is becoming increasingly evident that minimum output price guarantees may offer a more effective policy tool than low pricing of outputs coupled with input subsidies. Raising food prices (towards the level prevailing in international trade) should not, however, result in diminishing the level of consumption of the poor, who should be protected through other mechanisms. It is also advisable to protect farmers against the effects of short-term fluctuations in world prices. The optimal policy to be followed by governments in this area would have to depend, however, on the conditions prevailing in each country and is often influenced by considerations which may have little connection with agriculture as such.

TRAINING AND EXTENSION

Training is a prerequisite, if not an integral part, of improvements in technology and institutional reforms. Because of the low prestige associated with agriculture-related professions in many developing countries, and the general enthusiasm for industrialization, inadequate attention has been paid to formal training in modern agriculture. Too few successful programmes are available for the training of public sector personnel and the reorientation of farmers using antiquated techniques. Western nations and international agencies would provide a valuable service to lower income countries by promoting and increasing opportunities for the training of their personnel involved in the planning and implementation of the accelerated efforts required in agriculture.

OPEC countries support international fora that promote co-operation in agricultural training, research and extension services. The Arab Fund and BADEA are members of the Consultative Group on International Agricultural Research (CGIAR) and support it for its emphasis on promoting research at the regional level. The OPEC Fund has also recently joined the membership of CGIAR and has approved financial assistance to four of its research centres, including the newly established International Service for National Agricultural Research. It is particularly hoped that OPEC funds would be available to strengthen the capabilities of developing countries in research and extension services, both through their support of CGIAR and its centres and their direct efforts in project assistance.

PROJECT AID FOR FOOD PRODUCTION

The need for financial institutions to reconsider the criteria and thresholds of what constitute "bankable" projects is generally recognized. This need is particularly justified in the case of agricultural projects. Strict adherence to economic criteria will not help increase food production and reduce rural poverty, particularly in countries where limited agricultural potential, infrastructure base and absorptive capacity dictate some measure of flexibility without necessarily sacrificing reasonable standards of economic viability. The countries of the Sahel which have become among the most unfortunate nations in terms of food requirements and agricultural development potential, are valid cases in point. There may well be a need, in fact, for developing new criteria and analytical techniques that explicitly take into account the objectives of food production increases and nutrition improvements, as the current attempts to include social objectives in cost-benefit criteria are clearly not sufficient. OPEC institutions have, in the past, been flexible in their evaluation of projects which promote food self-sufficiency or demonstrate potential social benefits beyond what is captured by traditional cost-benefit analysis.

It is also the view among OPEC-supported agencies that despite appreciable efforts in recent years, aid organizations in general can do much to contribute to the solution of the food problem at the project level by shortening the relatively long period of time between initial project consideration and actual financial commitment and disbursement. OPEC agencies have been concerned to shorten the project cycle. Their impact in this respect may have been diminished, however, by their participation with other co-lenders in financing most of their projects.

Partly to offset this trend, OPEC-supported agencies are building up their project pipelines. While the responsibility for project identification will, in the foreseeable future, continue to fall on recipient governments, OPEC agencies are beginning to assist in the preparation stage through the financing of feasibility studies in association with such agencies as the FAO's Investment Centre. The Kuwait Fund for Arab Economic Development has, for instance, introduced this financing facility since the late 1960s as an integral part of its operations.

Co-financing is itself an area where one finds an urgent need for improvement. There is at present much duplication of effort on the part of aid institutions. This duplication, mainly in the pre-commitment stage, takes the form of multi-appraisals of the same project and extensive independent reviews of the same issues by each institution. This, in turn, complicates the process of reaching a consensus when meetings are called and thus, unnecessarily, creates the need for more meetings. The end result is often a delay in project start-up and an increase in costs. Promoting the joint appraisal of projects and reducing the number of meetings to a minimum by settling preliminary issues at the outset, would substantially speed up project processing.

Joint appraisal missions by OPEC-supported institutions are being mounted increasingly, resulting in improved co-ordination and project preparation and, above all, shorter project cycles to the benefit of aid donors and recipients. Such joint appraisal with other non-OPEC affiliated institutions is being considered.

It is the view within OPEC-supported aid institutions that greater flexibility and selective judgement could also be introduced in the nature and number of covenants that accompany project financing proposals. While there will always be a need for covenants to ensure that a project is properly executed and that its objectives are achieved, it is generally believed that covenants which are likely to defy these very objectives by unduly delaying the entry into force of agreements or delaying disbursements and thus project implementation, may be better not formalized. The difficulties experienced by borrowers in fulfilling some of the conditions placed on them are real, and there is no evidence that the very existence of these conditions would, by themselves, cause borrowers to speed up their procedures. OPEC aid agencies have shown their concern by continuously attempting to streamline their lending procedures and keep to a minimum the number of conditions precedent to loan effectiveness or disbursements. In projects where OPEC aid agencies have been involved as co-financiers with other institutions, they have endeavoured to play a role in discouraging unnecessary conditions.

Some of the conditions relating to institutional reforms are imposed on borrowers through the "leverage" that project assistance is perceived to afford. The objectives of some of these reforms may be more swiftly achieved through additional technical assistance built into the projects themselves. In any event, when implementation of the reforms is likely to delay or conflict with the immediate achievement of the project's objectives, the latter should, in principle, take priority. In such a case, reforms can still be pursued through the continuing dialogue with the recipient countries. The efforts of OPEC aid agencies in this respect, and in respect of simplified lending procedures in general, will continue. Institutional building activities, both within projects and in general, will continue to be emphasized, with particular attention being given to technical assistance that serves to build and strengthen local capabilities and skills.

Technical assistance channelled on an *ad hoc* basis through scattered projects is, however, of limited merit when it is found that government efforts are not themselves concerted. Whenever possible, the project planning and implementation functions which are often fragmented among departments within Ministries, or even among Ministries, should be consolidated or properly co-ordinated. This would improve the capability for project preparation, accelerate project implementation and perhaps reduce the need for expatriate technical assistance.

Another bottleneck to increased agricultural project assistance is the budgetary constraints of governments in meeting the local costs of food production projects financed by external aid agencies. Unfortunately, these constraints often reflect government priorities in areas other than food production and in such cases there may be little that external aid agencies can do. However, in those cases where the government's maximum allocations of budgetary and human resources for agricultural and rural development are simply insufficient in relation to any reasonable measure of sectoral needs, external

aid agencies may be called upon to finance the local costs of projects –
especially those targeted primarily to the poorer small farmers and
which, by their nature, have relatively large local cost components.

Increases in food production through intensive agriculture require
the use of such manufactured inputs as fertilizers, pesticides and
herbicides. Difficulties in farmers' access to production inputs can be
improved in many countries through economic incentives that
establish a more favourable relationship between prices of inputs and
products. The OPEC Fund has, on occasion, provided financing for
such inputs as fertilizers under its balance of payments aid programme. However, it should be noted that few countries among those
eligible for programme aid from the OPEC Fund have requested
financing for agricultural production inputs.

Unfortunately, sufficient food supplies in future will not be met
simply by the application of more fertilizer. In fact, experience in
some countries has shown that optimal utilization of fertilizers may
necessitate a reduction in the amount used by farmers. In addition to
efficient extension services, much research is needed on fertilizer
application and controlled release systems to improve fertilizer efficiency and nitrogen recovery while maintaining or reducing the
amount of fertilizers used. As such research may not be forthcoming
from multi-national corporations, it should be an area of concern to
development finance and advisory institutions. Proper marketing
and distribution, coupled with appropriate extension and credit
services, are also essential ingredients of an efficient fertilizer use.

It is recognized that smallholder needs for credit – essential to rural
development – are not efficiently met by current systems of agricultural finance in developing countries. The attempts of many local
credit institutions to help the small farmer have been frustrated by
the unprofitability and high risk of smallholder credits. Such institutions have thus been forced, in many cases, to allocate the bulk of
their resources to borrowers in commercial and industrial activities
or to a select group of large farmers. Unfortunately, the experience
of agencies for OPEC aid in lending to local development finance
institutions specializing in agricultural development credit is limited.
It is expected, however, that more of their aid resources will be
channelled through these institutions. Agencies for OPEC aid
would welcome the establishment of a forum where experience can
be shared, and ways and means to improve access to credit in rural
areas, explored. As the institutional aspects of providing local credit

to farmers are of as much importance as the financial aspects, much can be learned from the sharing of experiences among aid agencies.

The question of recurrent cost financing – another bottleneck to increased food production – is more complex. Some international aid institutions regard the obligation of governments or project beneficiaries to meet recurrent costs as a reasonable commitment to the project. A similar line of reasoning, as well as other considerations, makes it difficult for local agricultural finance institutions to meet, when feasible, these costs through their credit schemes. Nevertheless, local finance institutions may still be the best vehicle for meeting the recurrent cost needs of farmers and farm cooperatives. To the extent that the local finance institutions providing agricultural credit are clients of international lending agencies, it may be useful to explore possibilities of assisting them in this particular field[3].

Some governments of low-income countries are showing a new determination to increase the production of basic food commodities, with more emphasis on the extension of input supplies and marketing channels into areas where none had existed before. Efforts to improve local marketing facilities and thus food storage and distribution, long neglected aspects, is a particularly welcome development. Part of the blame for the past neglect can be attributed to institutional structures of developing countries inherited from colonial times when marketing was largely focused on export crops. Some governments continue to give disproportionate attention to such crops, often because of the limited options open to them for acquiring foreign exchange.

But the blame for inadequate efforts to improve local marketing channels should also be directed to external financing institutions, which have made little investment in marketing facilities as the emphasis has been more on tangible project components. The superficial treatment of marketing issues in the past may, therefore, be indicative of a bias in the selection, design and appraisal of projects. There is a need for developing guidelines that focus as much on the integration of basic foods into the market economy as on the food production aspects themselves. The experience to be gained from the increasing number of food production projects coming on-stream will help OPEC aid agencies address this issue.

The primary concerns of any government are, or should be, the fundamental requirements of its citizenry. Essential among these are an adequate food supply and the means for an improved standard of living. Improvement in the standard of living and productivity in rural areas, particularly of the poorest agrarian countries, may best be achieved through an integrated approach which covers all the elements required for a balanced rural development. These should provide the preconditions of successful implementation covering, in particular, the institutional aspects, the development of secondary infrastructure and the social components. Institutional aspects include such broad areas as the role of government, especially in the water-soil relationship (irrigation, drainage and flood control), the taxation system, pricing of inputs and outputs, credit, extension services, etc. Social components should focus on health care, shelter, education and other essential services required for a rural community. Without direct assistance to these services, all other efforts to increase food production could fail or may by-pass the landless, whose condition as tenants or labourers is the root cause of poor land yields and low labour productivity.

This integrated approach no doubt has a complex nature which could lead to delays in implementation. However, such delays may be avoided through appropriate planning and execution in stages. This approach should also pave the way for greater recourse by lending agencies to sector lending and the financing of development programmes, or of a certain time slice of the large programmes, without necessarily limiting their support to well-defined projects.

THE POPULATION FACTOR

Successful efforts to accelerate the pace of agricultural development must simultaneously involve efforts to curb population growth in certain countries where such increases still largely offset gains in farm output.

The time taken for the world population to double is now only 35 years (it was 1400 years until 1350 AD). The population of developing countries doubles at an even more rapid rate. The poorer the country, the greater its population growth rate is likely to be. Although population growth is only one determinant on the demand side, in the long-term it is the crucial variable if the objective is not simply increased food production, but increased consumption by the rural poor. With rapid population growth it will require a high rate of investment merely to maintain the present output per person. It is likely to depress wages and accelerate migration to urban areas, thus aggravating the already precarious situation in many developing countries. Agencies for OPEC aid have so far not been involved in population projects, partly because they have not been requested to finance such projects and partly because of their concentration on economic projects in the more narrow sense. It is hoped, however, that both recipients and donors will give greater attention to the practical steps that need to be taken to tackle this problem in the countries where its solution is a prerequisite for sustained growth.

CONCLUSION

The solution of the world food problem will require capital, technology, institutional reforms and, above all, a shared commitment by developed and developing countries to the long-term development of land resources. OPEC countries have, individually and collectively, demonstrated their commitment to increased food production and the elimination of world hunger. Almost half of the one billion dollar initial capital of the International Fund for Agricultural Development was subscribed to by OPEC donors in 1977. In the previous year, the Arab donors established the Arab Authority for Agricultural Investment and Development, with an initial capitalization of $525 million and a six-year plan for investing $2.8 billion in rural development and food production in the Arab countries, with particular attention to developing the resources of the Sudan.

It is important to recognize that the world food problem is not due to physical limitations on production, or only to financial resource constraints. The limitations exist also in the social fabric and political structure of nations and the economic relations among them. OPEC donors have and will continue to assist other developing nations in achieving food self-sufficiency. This commitment is naturally shared by specialized agencies for OPEC aid, which constitute the major instrument of this assistance effort. A similar commitment to the food problem by aid recipient countries, as should be reflected in their assistance requests, policies and institutional improvements, should ensure further resource flows for increased food production and improved human nutrition.

CHAPTER 16

ON WORLD HUNGER

The substantial text of a statement made before the Committee on Development and Co-operation, of the European Parliament on 2 April 1980. Subsequently published in OPEC Review *Vol. III/4 and IV/1 Winter 1979/Spring 1980, Vienna, Austria. The Author presents some of his personal views.*

My work in the OPEC Fund, and my previous responsibilities in the Kuwait Fund have closely associated me with the efforts toward development of most of the countries which have come to be known in Western terminology as the "Third World". From my experience in this field certain general considerations emerge which may be summarized as follows:

(i) There are immense opportunities in developing nations for high priority, economically sound investments which at present lack the required capital.

(ii) The complexities of development are so enormous that additional capital alone cannot resolve them; there is at least as great a need for a more efficient use of funds, more responsible and effective management, a better trained and more disciplined work-force, more suitable technologies and a more equitable distribution of development gains.

(iii) A politically stable system run by dedicated and serious individuals is at least as important in the development process as the availability of abundant funds and natural resources. Foreign assistance cannot provide this requirement, although it may help in maintaining stability.

(iv) The development process, as experienced in the now developed countries, with its oil-based technologies does not befit present conditions in developing countries and must give way to development patterns based on greater energy efficiency.

(v) Development problems and issues are so interrelated that objectives and priorities may be ill-defined and confusing when formulated outside a clear and rational framework. Such a framework may ideally be formulated in terms of a comprehensive strategy that will form, on a national level, the basis of an overall realistic plan into which particular policies and individual programmes and projects can be fitted as integral parts.

More generally, development efforts should pay greater attention to indigenous cultural values and should attempt to reconcile the positive aspects of modernization with the preservation of the cultural identity and dignity of the developing society.

It is within the above general context that the problem of hunger and the urgency of its solution should be discussed. The statistics of hunger are, of course, well-known and I will not dwell on them here in detail. Suffice it to say that one-third to one-half of the population of developing countries, at least 800 million people, continue to live in absolute poverty; 450 million, half of them children, continue to suffer from severe malnutrition, and an estimated 30 million die each year from illness connected with malnutrition. The ravages of hunger do not only occur during periods of economic downturn or natural calamities. They are an integral part of the daily existence of the malnourished whose number is swelling at an even higher rate than that of population growth.

The magnitude of the problem should not be masked by the often-quoted aggregate figures of world food production and consumption. According to these figures, world production has more than doubled over the past twenty-five years, rising by over 2.5 per cent annually and has been sufficient, at world level, to exceed average per capita food requirements. On the more significant national and regional level, however, production has fallen short of requirements in a large number of developing countries, turning many of them from self-sufficient or even food-exporting countries into food-deficit countries. Cereal imports of these countries have already reached the unprecedented figure of nearly 80 million tons in 1978/1979 (compared to 30 million in 1970-1972) and are estimated to reach 145 million tons by 1990, if current trends are not reversed. In fact, developments in world trade in grains since World War II have been consistently moving against all the developing regions of the world. This could be clearly surmised from the following comparisons, (+) signifying exports and (–) signifying imports in millions of tons:

	1934/38 average	1975/77 average
North America	+ 5	+110 (1977)
South America	+ 9	– 13
Asia	+ 2	– 40
Africa	+ 1	– 8
Western Europe	–24	–20/25

From a global perspective, the persistence of hunger, even when world food production is in line with world requirements, is one of the most challenging problems facing governments and the international community. This complex problem encompasses not only the bottlenecks in increasing production and improving distribution of food, but also a host of other considerations embedded in the socio-economic fabric of nations. It is particularly aggravated by the inequitable income distribution and irrational consumption patterns to be found on both the international and domestic levels. The problem of hunger, therefore, cannot be treated separately from its general causes. Isolating it from its obvious cause, the general problem of poverty will only result in temporary solutions which may at best simply postpone its devastating effects. Short of a direct attack on poverty itself, which is necessarily a long-term process, hunger may well remain a permanent scar on our society, with the already intolerable situation breaching new moral limits during times of adverse weather conditions or natural calamities. The relative absence of such disasters since the early seventies should not lull the international community into a false sense of comfort.

In a rich country, the poverty of some segments of society is due to inequitable income distribution. It could thus be regarded as an internal problem, pure and simple. In generally poor countries, bad income distribution accentuates the poverty of the majority, but cannot be the reason for this phenomenon. The abject poverty of many countries speaks for the failure of the present international economic system and is, therefore, a problem for the whole international community to face. Just as it befits a modern nation to solve the problem of inequality among its citizens, it is, I believe, incumbent on the community of nations to solve the poverty problem of the majority of its members. Hence, the special responsibility of countries in a position to help, such as the advanced European nations.

To quote the recent report of the Independent Commission on International Development Issues chaired by former West German Chancellor Willy Brandt: "The idea of a community of nations has little meaning if that situation is allowed to continue, if hunger is regarded as a marginal problem which humanity can live with."

The sad truth is that the world community has yet to progress significantly in establishing an appropriate collective mechanism to stem current hunger and mitigate the adverse impact of unforeseen contingencies, let alone progress in permanently eradicating hunger through a direct assault on poverty.

The first problem confronting the world in this context is essentially that of food security, and it is by definition the most pressing. A system of appropriate storage, coupled with efficient and equitable distribution of grain reserves of a size adequate to ensure a high degree of world food security and trade stability presents the viable short-term palliative, although not the cure, to the hunger problem. Such a scheme is justified by two vital needs: the need for a stop-gap mechanism until the longer-term solutions are implemented, and the need for a buffer against conjunctural food shortages caused by bad weather and other disruptive natural conditions.

Unfortunately, a consensus has yet to be reached on a mechanism based on mandatory contributions to a global grain reserve. A United Nations Conference was held in 1978-1979 for the purpose of establishing a new International Grains Arrangement, but failed to do so. No agreement was reached on the levels of the so-called "trigger prices"[1], on the size of stocks[2], or on the assistance to be provided to developing countries to build up their own reserves. The proposal to create a fund to finance the construction of storage facilities, the purchase of grain and the costs of running the reserves has yet to gain momentum. As a result, world grain stocks in relation to consumption are today no larger than they were before the 1972-74 food crisis.

More recently, because of a decline in the 1979 cereal harvest, the United Nations Food and Agriculture Organization has forecast a drop of 11 million tons or 4 per cent of the total stocks of wheat, rice and coarse grains. The estimated 260 million tons of stock expected at the end of the 1979-1980 season will amount to 18 per cent of total world consumption, a critically low level for world food security[3]. About 40 per cent of these stocks are held by the United States and Canada. With the expected increase in demand for American grain, despite the current US embargo against the Soviet Union, as well as the resulting upward pressure on prices, the prospects facing the low-income food-deficit countries, are, to say the least, precarious. In fact, adverse weather conditions in North America, where the emphasis is on rain-fed agriculture, especially if coupled with a further fall in the production of the major food-deficit countries, could lead again to the threat of famine in the low-income countries.

Importing developing countries do not have a common agriculture policy, like that of the EEC, to protect them against fluctuation of grain prices. Nor do they have the financial ability to conclude long-term grain purchase agreements, as some developed importing countries do. Their precarious position can hardly be improved through their own action alone. It is, therefore, imperative to mobilize the international community to take a collective initiative. While the impetus for action is coming from advisory food and agricultural organizations, the strong support of the major grain-exporting countries is essential to achieve any appreciable measure of success.

But a mechanism of internationally controlled security reserves, or even the less desirable "internationally co-ordinated system of national reserves", must also ensure the adequate participation of developing countries, if it is to succeed at all. For this, it must include special provisions for preferential access, and special assistance for the acquisition of grain, the development of storage capacity and the meeting of maintenance costs at national levels. Developing countries would need to hold some 5-7 million tons of reserves, the acquisition and storage construction costs of which have been put at roughly $1.75 billion[4] (the equivalent, I am told, of the cost of construction of one nuclear-fuelled submarine). In addition, the UN target for an international emergency food reserve, which has never been met in full, will soon be revised upward. In 1975, the target was set at 500,000 tons of cereals stock, of which 350,000 tons were attained in 1979. The need is now estimated by FAO as 2 to 3 million tons a year due to crop failures alone.

The implementation of such schemes remains possible and attainable within a relatively short period of time. I hold this view in full awareness of the continuing failure of the world, despite long years of negotiations, to agree on a meaningful international wheat agreement or to reach the targets set for food aid and for grain reserves.

In a renewed attempt to break the deadlock, the United Nations World Food Council will submit to its next Ministerial Meeting in Arusha in June of this year (1980), a proposal for the strengthening of international mechanisms for world food security. The proposal calls for a dual plan consisting of:

(i) the establishment of a nucleus international food grain reserve, in advance of the conclusion of a new international wheat agreement. The volume envisaged is 12 million tons, including at least 5 million tons to be located in developing regions for which additional storage capacity is required;

(ii) the establishment of an international food crisis pledge, embodying precise commitments to action on various measures related to food crisis management when a global crisis occurs.

The exact contingency provisions and commitments under both plans, as well as the modalities for their administration, are to be negotiated among interested countries under the UN auspices.

It is hoped that the negotiations will be tackled by all concerned with a sense of urgency and with a focus on global, rather than nationalistic, considerations. Both plans would go a long way towards averting the famines of the scale experienced in the early seventies and deserve, I believe, the full support of the international community. They are not, however, a substitute for increased food aid, for which the 1976 target level of 10 million tons of cereals a year is hardly attained. Protracted negotiations of the new Food Aid Convention have just resulted in an agreement on a "minimum food aid level" of 7.6 million tons. Nor does this mean that food aid should only be limited to grains. The EEC dairy surpluses, for instance, are badly needed in many developing countries: greater parts of such surpluses could be used to feed the labour force engaged in agricultural projects, as is successfully being done by the World Food Programme.

It has been previously argued that aid in the form of food supply is at best a temporary solution to the hunger problem. The permanent eradication of hunger calls for a more equitable international economic system, and for greater collective efforts inspired by a more determined political will, on the part of developed and developing countries alike. Alleviation of poverty is no doubt a longer-term objective. But it is a difficult task that cannot be avoided if a solution to the hunger problem is to be seriously sought.

If the people of the poor countries are to be fed, the food will have to be produced primarily on their soil, from their resources and by their farmers. The surplus production of a few exporting countries can serve on occasion to buffer the impact of bad weather or other disasters, natural or man-made, as the above-cited World Food Council proposals are intended to achieve. But there should be no illusion that the world's food security can be permanently ensured by abundant harvests from the fields of the American mid-west or Canada which, together, still account for 80 per cent of the world's traded wheat.

Unfortunately, not all developing countries show evidence of having understood that food independence should largely be a domestic objective, and that if agricultural development is given priority, it can lay the foundation for the modernization of the entire economy.

This observation is all the more disconcerting when it is realized that most developing countries are better endowed for agricultural progress than for any other kind of economic advance. The myth of "industrialization for its own sake" without the foundation that agricultural and rural development provides, remains deeply entrenched in the psychology of the Third World. Yet, the drive for modernization which feeds this myth, is taking place under conditions quite different from those which existed a century ago for the now industrial nations. Technological and scientific modernization is becoming more complicated and more risky and if this modernization by-passes the aspiring poor of the rural world, it could be counter-productive. As Sir Arthur Lewis, the recipient of the 1979 Nobel Prize award in Economics has ably demonstrated in his recent work entitled *The Evolution of the International Economic Order*, the industrial revolution began and succeeded in countries that had the highest agricultural productivity. Industrial development, he argued convincingly, ought to be based on prior or simultaneous agricultural development. A developed agricultural sector produces the surplus food and raw materials directly or indirectly consumed in the industrial sector and at the same time enables farmers, through their rising incomes, to become a market for the industrial products. The interrelationship between agricultural development and industrial growth should not be underestimated.

The reasons for which food production has failed to keep pace with the demand for food in the developing world are well-known. Along with the relative neglect of investment in this sector, especially in rural infrastructure, governments have also tended to respond less favourably to the politically weaker demands of the rural populations for higher farm revenues. And when the rural landlords were powerful enough to command government attention, land reform policies were lacking and wealth remained in a few hands. Due to the high rate of population growth, the increase in demand for food went well beyond the growth of agricultural output. Research in tropical food production received little attention from both colonial powers and successive independent governments as a result of their concern for exportable cash crops. Farmers continued to receive poor extension services, little help in the acquisition of modern inputs and little credit at reasonable terms.

A reverse of these trends would require much greater attention to the agricultural sector in developing countries. This in turn requires, *inter alia*, massive new investments which would need external assistance at least three times the $3-5 billion or so given at present to this sector in low income countries[5].

In addition to such financial requirements, the agricultural sector would require a whole range of supplementary measures covering a number of diverse areas of activity. These include in particular the strengthening of research facilities, the improvement of extension services, the introduction of small farmers' credit, the application of appropriate land reform packages, the rationalization of consumption patterns and habits, favourable pricing policies and, more generally, measures which ensure a rise in the income that could be earned in producing food.

Thus there seem to be two aspects of the solution to the food problem: increased production of food in the developing countries *and* widespread increases in family incomes, particularly among the rural poor. The increased incomes could come from off-farm employment, from the development of labour-intensive industries, in rural areas, from development in construction and public works schemes, from the increase of productivity and profitability in agriculture and, finally, from the generation of the services that will come to be required as income and employment in rural areas increase.

In summary, only a development strategy which seeks to distribute the gains from development to the poor sections of the population via increased income can meet the problems of inadequate food consumption. Development policies must, therefore, focus on increasing the purchasing power of the most needy consumers and reducing imbalances, while simultaneously raising the productivity of agriculture.

To turn to the rich industrial countries, it may be fairly said, and indeed the record speaks for itself, that these nations have not fully recognized that a massive transfer of technology and capital from rich to poor countries is essential for any strategy on which the world's food supply, and even mankind's survival, depends.

What are the long run alternatives to such a massive transfer, particularly considering current demographic trends? Several of these have been advanced. One, called euphemistically by some writers "the lifeboat analogy", holds that the earth can support only a finite number of people and those who are safely aboard must not jeopardize their ability to survive by extending a helping hand to the millions of others who would swamp the vessel. A modified version of this ethic is called "triage", after the battlefield practice of categorizing the wounded in three groups: those likely to survive without immediate attention, those likely to die in any case, and those likely to survive if they get immediate attention. Under this scenario, some countries would receive help and the less hopeful ones would be abandoned. Both of these approaches seem as impractical as they are inhumane. Fortunately, poor countries are not as easy to dispose of as a desperate drowning person.

Another suggestion, infinitely more humane, finds its basis on the fact that rich populations consume five times as much grain as poor ones because most of it is processed into meat – not always an efficient conversion. If the rich in all countries reduce their fat diets, and that of their pets, as the argument goes, they could make available enough food to feed those millions at the margin of society. In a complicated world, such as ours is, this simple argument may, however, lose its weight, especially if applied over a significant period of time. Eventually, distributive economics, given the increase in population growth, would again result in a distribution of poverty and a return to the previous diet imbalance. In any event, merely saving food on one side does not automatically give anyone on the other side the means to acquire it. There is definitely room for distributive justice in the world, but this should take the form of economic and technical assistance, commodity-pricing agreements and trade reforms that give the poor nations a better chance at development.

The problem is seriously aggravated by the unchecked population growth in Third World countries. With only 58 per cent of the total harvested area in the world, developing countries have 72 per cent of the world population. In about 40 of these countries, the average availability of arable land per rural inhabitant is now no more than half a hectare. As a result, about 750 million of the rural population of developing countries are landless and mostly malnourished. This situation is not likely to improve under the present population growth rates.

The time it will take for the world population to double is now estimated at 36 years (it took about 1400 years five centuries ago). The population of developing countries doubles at an even more rapid rate. The poorer the country, the greater its population growth rate is likely to be. This is not by coincidence. There is, in the long run, a definite link between slow population growth rates and such factors as better health care, adequate diets, better education, especially for women, rising incomes and improved human welfare in general. Unabated, rapid population growth requires a high rate of investment merely to maintain the current level of food output per person. It also leads to depressed wages and accelerated migration to urban areas, thus aggravating the already precarious situation in many developing countries. In fact, it is becoming obvious in a number of nations that limitation on population growth must now be induced directly, regardless of the development efforts that may help contain it in the long run. The need for control draws its rationale from one fact: without an immediate defusing of the population explosion, the life awaiting millions upon millions of the earth's future inhabitants could be wretched and tragic. This is happening now, and this undeniable fact takes us far beyond the population problem to a larger one, pinning rich against poor for survival in a climate of increasing social and political unrest.

Aside from the action to be taken by advanced Western countries, questions naturally arise concerning the role to be played by OPEC member countries. This question becomes all the more relevant at a time when the Western mass media are harshly accusing such countries of accumulating excessive wealth and causing great hardship to other developing countries.

In this context I would like to submit very briefly, and in all modesty, the following facts:

The OPEC countries are themselves developing countries in need of tremendous efforts to attain a balanced development which is not dependent forever on the exportation of a single commodity. They are fully aware that their oil revenues are nothing but another form of their depleting wealth. They equally realize that exchanging oil in the ground with depreciating paper claims, which cannot be fully translated into useful goods and services, is hardly a profitable proposition. Despite all of this, the OPEC countries have been providing concessional assistance to other developing countries, at a much higher ratio to their GNP, than that of the assistance provided by the really developed countries. Suffice it to mention that according to OECD statistics, countries like Kuwait, UAE, Qatar and Saudi Arabia are giving non-tied Official Development Assistance (ODA) funds, which, relative to their GNP, is five to ten times higher than that given by any Western country. Even in absolute terms, Saudi Arabia has been for years the second largest donor in the world. Kuwait alone was in 1977 giving more than Germany, while the latter's GNP is four times higher than that of all Arab oil-producers combined. The same comparison applies, for stronger reasons, to other EEC donors whose record is less impressive than that of Germany.

The OPEC countries, all of which, incidentally, are food-deficit countries, have given great support to the creation of the International Fund for Agricultural Development, by contributing 43 per cent of its initial capital resources, a percentage far out of proportion to their relative wealth or expected benefits (most of the OPEC donors do not expect to receive assistance from IFAD and none of them expects to be a source of procurement for the goods and services financed through IFAD). They stand for co-operation with OECD countries in the replenishment of the resources of IFAD, which, I strongly hope, will receive the full support of EEC countries. Meanwhile, the agricultural sector is gaining greater importance in the activities of the exclusively OPEC-financed agencies, be they national funds or collective facilities. It is also hoped that EEC aid will give this sector the greater attention it deserves.

The OPEC Fund in particular is giving priority to the development of indigenous energy sources, especially in rural areas, and to food production projects with the objective of assisting developing countries in achieving self-sufficiency in these two vital sectors. Instead of waiting for the establishment of the projected IMF "Financial Food Facility", the OPEC Fund's balance of payments support loans have also been specifically used to finance imports of foodstuffs. In addition, the OPEC Fund is now extending grants to the CGIAR agricultural research centres and for the financing of fisheries' surveys, in realization of the importance of strengthening applied research in these areas. It is a fact, however, that advanced biological and chemical research, especially in the field of protein reproduction, will have to depend for a long time on the facilities of the most advanced countries.

Realizing the importance to developing countries of the stabilization and increase of the export revenues of raw materials, including foodstuffs, the

OPEC countries have played a positive role in the on-going negotiations for the creation of the Common Fund. They have announced their readiness to meet, through the OPEC Fund, the cost of the equal shares of all the Least Developed Countries in the Fund's capital. In addition, the OPEC Fund will make a sizeable voluntary contribution to the "Second Window" of the Common Fund. OPEC members will also have their mandatory contributions to the capital of the Common Fund and some of them will contribute to that Fund's guarantee-capital through the associated International Commodity organizations of which they are members.

Far from building barriers against food imports from other developing countries, OPEC members have their growing markets wide open to the exports of other developing countries. Some OPEC countries are even studying the possibility of giving preference to imports from other developing countries in order to increase further the volume of these imports which have substantially increased in the last few years.

At the close of this statement, I feel that it is important to stress that the related problems of food and poverty do not arise from insurmountable physical limitations on potential output, nor do they create a danger of unduly stretching environmental limits. The global food potential is far from being fully exploited and the successful development of the available resources depends on the will and the actions of concerned individuals and institutions. As I said at the outset, investment opportunities abound. And, as I have tried to demonstrate, the returns – moral, political and economic – on these investments are self-evident.

The relevant question for mankind, however, may not be one about return on investment. It may rather be: What is the long-term cost of not initiating now a programme of investing in man's future food supply? This question is left to those who may be better qualified to formulate its answer.

APPENDIX OF TABLES
AND GRAPHS

ANNEX TO CHAPTER 1

Fig. 1 Some Economic and Financial Indicators of OPEC Member Countries

	Algeria	Ecuador	Gabon	Indonesia	Iran
Population mid-1979 (million)[1]	18.23	8.07	0.64	138.89	36.87
GNP 1979 (US$ billion)[1]	28.94	8.46	2.11	52.20	75.70[2]
Per Capita GNP 1979 (US$)[1]	1580	1050	3280	380	2160[2]
Oil Revenues 1980 (US$ million)[3]	10787	1200	1600	10500	11600
Concessional Assistance 1980 (US$ million)[4]	83	–	–	–	3
Concessional Assistance as Percentage of GNP 1980[4]	0.21	–	–	–	–
Adult Literacy Rate 1976 (%)[5]	35	77	12	62	50
Life Expectancy at Birth 1979 (years)[5]	56	61	45	53	54
Distribution of GDP 1979 (%)[5]					
Agriculture	7	15	6	30	9
Industry	58	37	65	33	54
(of which: Manufacturing)	(11)	(19)	(NA)	(9)	(12)
Services	35	48	29	37	37
Average Annual Growth Rate (%)[5] 1970-1979					
Public Consumption	9.4	12.1	12	11.4	20.4[6]
Private Consumption	11.1	8.9	36	7.9	10.0[6]
Gross Domestic Investment	11.4	10.3	30	14.8	22.0[6]
Per Capita Energy Consumption[5] 1979 (Kgs. of coal equivalent)	671	654	NA	237	1214
Percentage shares of merchandise Exports 1978[5]					
Fuels, minerals & metals	97	41	12	72	95
Other primary commodities	2	57	–	26	2
Textiles and Clothing	–	1	2	–	2
Machinery & other Transport Equipment	–	–	39	1	–
Other Manufactures	1	1	46	1	1

NA = Not Available
[1]World Bank Atlas 1980
[2]1977 (1978 and 1979 not available)
[3]Annual Statistical Bulletin 1980, OPEC Secretariat
[4]Official development assistance net disbursements, OECD Statistics
[5]World Development Report 1981, The World Bank
[6]Average annual growth rate 1970-1977
[7]Separate figures are not available for public consumption, which is therefore included in private consumption.

Iraq	Kuwait	Libya	Nigeria	Qatar	Saudi Arabia	U.A.E	Venezuela
12.64	1.27	2.85	82.50	0.23	8.49	0.83	14.40
30.43	21.87	23.39	55.31	3.75	62.64	12.99	45.15
2410	17270	8210	670	16590	7370	15590	3130
25981	18016	22527	20000	5377	102212	19344	14881
829	1188	281	42	319	3040	1062	130
2.12	3.88	0.92	0.05	4.80	2.60	3.96	0.23
NA	60	50	NA	NA	NA	NA	82
56	70	56	49	58	54	62	67
8	–	2	22	NA	1	NA	6
73	81	73	45	NA	74	NA	47
(6)	(5)	(3)	(5)	(NA)	(5)	(NA)	(16)
19	19	25	33	NA	25	NA	47
–[7]	NA	21.6	12.4	NA	–[7]	NA	8.2
17.0	NA	18.7	6.3	NA	18.8	NA	11.0
27.2	22.4	10.6	17.8	NA	46.7	NA	7.0
692	6348	2360	83	NA	1554	NA	3055
99	90	100	91	NA	100	NA	97
1	1	–	8	NA	–	NA	1
–	1	–	–	NA	–	NA	–
–	3	–	–	NA	–	NA	–
–	5	–	1	NA	–	NA	2

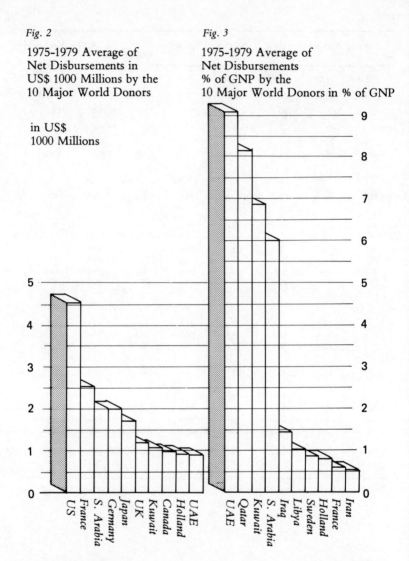

Fig. 2

1975-1979 Average of
Net Disbursements in
US$ 1000 Millions by the
10 Major World Donors

in US$
1000 Millions

Fig. 3

1975-1979 Average of
Net Disbursements
% of GNP by the
10 Major World Donors in % of GNP

Source: Organization for Economic Co-operation and Development (OECD)/
Development Assistance Committee (DAC) – November 1980

Fig. 4

Non-OPEC Oil –Importing Developing Countries:
Value of Net Oil Imports vs the Value of Total Merchandise Imports
(in billion US$)

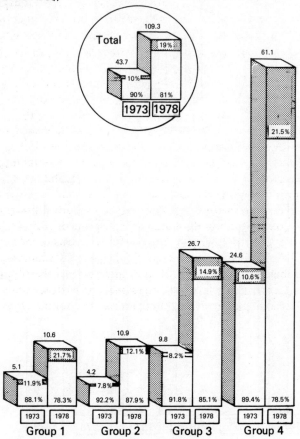

N.B. Reference is to oil imports from OPEC countries only.

Net oil imports

Source: OPEC–Secretariat

Fig. 5

Non-OPEC Developing Countries: Oil Price Impact vs Inflation Impact of Exports from Industrialized Countries in Terms of Constant 1973 Volumes (in billion US$)

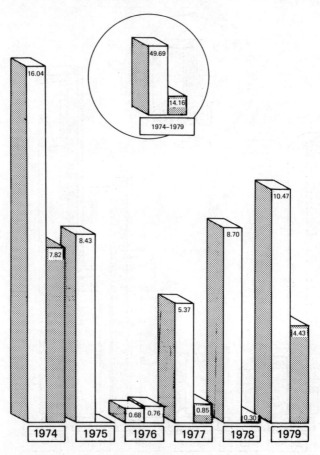

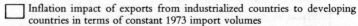

☐ Inflation impact of exports from industrialized countries to developing countries in terms of constant 1973 import volumes

▨ Oil price impact in terms of constant 1973 oil import volume in developing countries from OPEC members

Source: OPEC-Secretariat

Fig. 6

Non-OPEC Developing Countries: Increase in Value of Imports from Industrial Countries vs Increase in Oil Import Bill 1974–1979 (in billion US$)

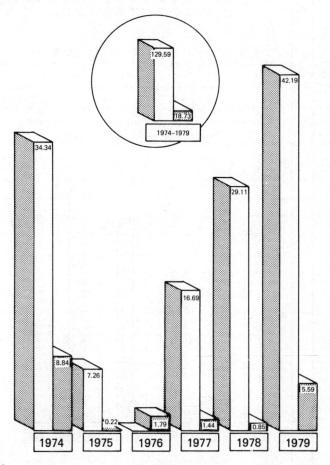

Increase in value of imports of developing countries from industrial countries

Increase in oil import bill in terms of actual volumes of oil imported into developing countries from OPEC members

Source: OPEC-Secretariat

Fig. 7 Total net flows from OPEC members to Developing Countries OECD and UNCTAD Statistics dated November 1978 and 4 November 1977, respectively

Donor Country		$ million				As per cent of GNP			
		1973	1974	1975	1976	1973	1974	1975	1976
Algeria	OECD	29.8	51.4	42.2	66.6	0.36	0.43	0.31	0.43
	UNCTAD	30	52	42	75	0.36	0.43	0.30	0.48
Iran	OECD	4.9	739.4	936.1	807.3	0.02	1.59	1.74	1.22
	UNCTAD	5	1182	1595	820	0.02	2.54	2.97	1.24
Iraq	OECD	11.1	440.2	254.4	116.5	0.21	4.16	1.91	1.60
	UNCTAD	11	436	288	91	0.21	4.12	2.18	0.57
Kuwait	OECD	555.7	1186.1	1711.2	1874.7	9.27	10.88	11.44	13.24
	UNCTAD	581	1369	2112	1807	9.69	12.56	14.12	11.08
Libya	OECD	403.8	263.2	362.8	363.2	6.25	2.21	2.96	2.38
	UNCTAD	414	218	367	262	6.41	1.83	2.99	1.71
Nigeria	OECD	5.7	134.8	347.5	176.8	0.04	0.60	1.37	0.57
	UNCTAD	7	135	545	337	0.05	0.60	2.15	1.15
Qatar	OECD	93.7	217.9	366.7	240.3	15.62	10.90	16.90	9.82
	UNCTAD	94	253	366	445	15.64	12.67	16.88	18.81
Saudi Arabia	OECD	334.9	1622.1	2466.7	2817.3	4.12	7.19	7.42	6.85
	UNCTAD	342	2372	3870	3625	4.21	10.51	11.65	9.03
UAE	OECD	288.6	749.4	1206.6	1144.5	12.03	9.78	13.59	11.81
	UNCTAD	90	765	1375	1221	3.76	9.99	15.49	12.22
Venezuela	OECD	17.7	483.4	473.8	385.3	0.11	1.93	1.80	1.24
	UNCTAD	18	779	899	296	0.11	3.10	3.43	0.94
TOTAL	OECD	1745.9	5887.9	8168.0	8130.7	1.89	3.43	4.01	3.33
	UNCTAD	1591	7561	11457	8978	1.72	4.40	5.62	3.70

Fig. 8 Concessional Assistance by OPEC members, 1973-1976

Donor Country	Commitments $ million				Net disbursements $ million				As per cent of GNP			
	1973	1974	1975	1976	1973	1974	1975	1976	1973	1974	1975	1976
Algeria	23.0	63.7	59.6	77.9	25.3	46.9	40.7	53.6	0.31	0.39	0.30	0.33
Iran	8.8	805.5	1448.5	429.3	1.9	408.3	593.1	752.5	0.01	0.88	1.10	1.13
Iraq	115.7	497.7	370.8	297.3	11.1	422.9	(215.4)	231.7	0.21	3.99	(1.63)	1.46
Kuwait	378.8	838.9	1190.0	1456.1	345.3	621.5	975.3	614.3	5.76	5.70	6.52	4.34
Libya	238.4	266.9	291.6	217.2	214.4	147.0	261.1	93.6	3.32	1.23	2.13	0.61
Nigeria	4.6	15.7	35.8	136.5	4.7	15.3	13.9	82.9	0.04	0.07	0.05	0.27
Qatar	93.1	227.7	369.1	335.9	93.7	185.2	338.9	195.0	15.62	9.26	15.62	7.95
Saudi A.	568.2	1287.6	2790.1	3570.0	304.9	1029.1	1997.4	2407.1	3.75	4.56	6.01	5.84
UAE	318.1	676.6	1123.6	1480.9	288.6	510.6	1046.1	1060.2	12.03	6.66	11.79	10.94
Venezuela	18.1	112.4	11.6	161.3	17.7	58.8	30.0	95.9	0.11	0.23	0.11	0.31
Total	1766.8	4792.7	7690.7	8162.4	1307.6	3445.6	5511.9	5586.8	1.41	2.01	2.70	2.29

Fig. 9 Total Net Flows from OPEC Members to Developing Countries, 1973-1976

Donor Country	$ million				As per cent of GNP			
	1973	1974	1975	1976	1973	1974	1975	1976
Algeria	29.7	51.4	42.2	66.6	0.36	0.43	0.31	0.43
Iran	4.9	739.4	936.1	807.3	0.02	1.59	1.74	1.22
Iraq	11.1	440.2	254.1	116.1	0.21	4.16	1.91	1.60
Kuwait	555.7	1186.1	1711.2	1874.7	9.26	10.88	11.44	13.24
Libya	403.8	263.2	362.8	363.2	6.25	2.21	2.96	2.38
Nigeria	5.7	134.8	347.5	176.8	0.04	0.60	1.37	0.57
Qatar	93.7	217.9	366.7	240.3	15.62	10.90	16.90	9.82
Saudi A.	334.9	1622.1	2466.7	2817.3	4.12	7.19	7.42	6.85
UAE	288.6	749.4	1206.6	1144.5	12.03	9.78	13.59	11.81
Venezuela	17.7	483.4	473.8	385.3	0.11	1.93	1.80	1.24
Total	1745.8	5887.9	8168.0	8130.7	1.89	3.43	4.01	3.33

ANNEX TO CHAPTER 14

Fig. 10 Aid given by Arab Countries, 1973-1980 (as percentage of Gross National Product)

(a) Commitments

Country	1973			1974			1975			1976		
	C	N	T	C	N	T	C	N	T	C	N	T
UAE	5.19	4.52	9.71	9.61	4.31	14.07	13.72	2.91	16.63	11.36	4.92	16.28
Algeria	0.43	0.05	0.49	0.65	0.07	0.72	0.53	0.16	0.69	0.54	0.02	0.56
Libya	12.39	4.48	16.87	2.40	1.53	3.93	3.16	2.91	6.08	0.86	0.60	1.46
Iraq	2.63	–	2.63	5.17	0.75	5.91	3.07	0.26	3.33	0.53	0.03	0.56
Saudi A.	7.09	1.43	8.52	6.04	10.62	16.66	8.90	6.53	15.43	6.69	3.15	9.85
Qatar	16.05	3.38	19.43	12.70	2.21	14.91	17.14	5.77	22.91	8.07	14.55	22.62
Kuwait	7.81	7.26	15.08	9.52	10.22	19.73	7.81	12.90	20.72	4.13	12.69	16.82

Country	1977			1978			1979			1980		
	C	N	T	C	N	T	C	N	T	C	N	T
UAE	8.57			6.02			6.07			4.59		
Algeria	0.32			1.03			0.25			0.25		
Libya	0.77	not available		3.68	not available		0.49	not available		2.44	not available	
Iraq	0.72			2.63			3.59			2.88		
Saudi A.	5.27			6.22			2.15			2.18		
Qatar	6.11			8.55			1.56			4.93		
Kuwait	8.28			7.05			2.89			4.15		

(b) Actual Disbursements

Country	1973			1974			1975			1976		
	C	N	T	C	N	T	C	N	T	C	N	T
UAE	3.66	0.10	3.76	6.83	3.16	9.99	12.01	3.48	15.49	10.20	2.01	12.22
Algeria	0.31	0.05	0.36	0.43	0.01	0.43	0.30	0.01	0.30	0.41	0.07	0.48
Libya	3.38	3.03	6.41	1.23	0.59	1.83	1.73	1.26	2.99	0.88	0.82	1.71
Iraq	0.21	–	0.21	3.95	0.17	4.12	1.78	0.40	2.18	0.53	0.04	0.57
Saudi A.	3.84	0.31	4.21	4.65	5.86	10.51	6.22	5.42	11.65	5.72	3.31	9.04
Qatar	15.64	–	15.64	11.02	1.65	12.67	13.70	3.18	16.88	10.30	8.52	18.81
Kuwait	6.14	3.49	9.62	5.74	6.80	12.52	6.10	8.05	14.15	3.83	8.02	11.85

Country	1977			1978			1979			1980		
	C	N	T	C	N	T	C	N	T	C	N	T
UAE	8.49			5.05			5.87			3.96		
Algeria	0.24			0.18			0.87			0.21		
Libya	0.65	not available		0.93	not available		0.45	not available		0.92	not available	
Iraq	0.33			0.76			2.53			2.12		
Saudi A.	4.10			2.66			3.01			2.60		
Qatar	7.91			3.57			5.89			4.80		
Kuwait	10.02			7.37			4.09			3.88		

C = Concessionary payments (grant element in excess of 25 per cent)
N = Non-concessionary payments.
T = Total (C+N).

Source: United Nations Conference on Trade and Development, Financial Solidarity for Development, Efforts and Institutions of OPEC, 1973-1976 Review, TD/B/C.7/13 (New York: UN, 1979); and, Organization for Economic Co-operation and Development/Development Assistance Committee.

It is to be noted that this source differs from the source of Fig. 11, where the Development Assistance Committee of the Organization for Economic Co-operation and Development, quoted for the comparison contained in Fig. 11, includes industrial countries.

Fig. 11 A List of the 10 Countries with the Highest Level of net dispersed Concessional Flows Relative to their Gross National Product, 1974-1980

1974		1975		1976		1977	
Country	% ratio	Country	% ratio	Country	% ratio	Country	% ratio
1. Qatar	9.25	1. Qatar	15.62	1. UAE	9.21	1. Kuwait	10.02
2. UAE	7.05	2. UAE	11.68	2. Qatar	7.95	2. UAE	8.49
3. Kuwait	5.81	3. Kuwait	8.11	3. Saudi A.	5.15	3. Qatar	7.91
4. Saudi A.	4.45	4. Saudi A.	5.62	4. Kuwait	4.56	4. Saudi A.	4.10
5. Iraq	3.98	5. Libyan		5. Iraq	1.45	5. Sweden	0.99
6. Libyan		A.J.	2.31	6. Iran	1.16	6. Holland	0.86
A.J.	1.26	6. Iraq	1.65	7. Holland	0.83	7. Norway	0.83
7. Iran	0.88	7. Iran	1.12	8. Sweden	0.82	8. Libyan	
8. Sweden	0.72	8. Sweden	0.82	9. Norway	0.70	A.J.	0.65
9. Holland	0.63	9. Holland	0.75	10. Libyan		9. Denmark/	
10. France	0.59	10. Norway	0.66	A.J.	0.63	France	0.60
						10. Canada	0.50

1978*		1979		1980	
Country	% ratio	Country	% ratio	Country	% ratio
1. Kuwait	7.37	1. Qatar	5.89	1. Qatar	4.80
2. UAE	5.05	2. UAE	5.87	2. UAE	3.96
3. Qatar	3.57	3. Kuwait	4.09	3. Kuwait	3.88
4. Saudi A.	2.66	4. Saudi Arabia	3.01	4. Saudi A.	2.60
5. Libyan A.J.	0.93	5. Iraq	2.53	5. Iraq	2.12
6. Norway	0.90	6. Sweden	0.94	6. Libyan A.J.	0.92
7. Sweden	0.90	7. Holland	0.93	7. Holland	0.99
8. Holland	0.82	8. Norway	0.93	8. Norway	0.82
9. Iraq	0.76	9. Algeria	0.87	9. Sweden	0.76
10. Denmark	0.75	10. Denmark	0.75	10. Denmark	0.72

*Data for the year 1978 is an estimate.

Source: Organization for Economic Co-operation and Development, Development Co-operation, 1980 and 1981 Reviews, Paris.

Fig. 12 The 10 Countries Giving the Greatest Amount of Aid to the Developing Countries (Net Disbursement in Millions of US Dollars) 1974-1980

1974		1975		1976		1977	
Country	Amount	Country	Amount	Country	Amount	Country	Amount
1. U.S.	3674	1. U.S.	4161	1. U.S.	4360	1. U.S.	4682
2. France	1616	2. France	2093	2. Saudi A.	2415	2. Saudi A.	2410
3. Germany	1433	3. Saudi A.	1997	3. France	2146	3. France	2267
4. Japan	1126	4. Germany	1689	4. Germany	1593	4. Germany	1717
5. Saudi A.	1029	5. Japan	1148	5. Japan	1105	5. Kuwait	1517
6. U.K.	783	6. UAE	1046	6. UAE	1059	6. Japan	1424
7. Canada	716	7. Kuwait	976	7. Canada	887	7. UAE	1238
8. Kuwait	632	8. U.K.	904	8. U.K.	885	8. U.K.	1014
9. U.S.S.R.	600	9. Canada	880	9. Iran	753	9. Canada	991
10. UAE	511	10. Holland	608	10. Holland	728	10. Holland	908

1978		1979		1980	
Country	Amount	Country	Amount	Country	Amount
1. U.S.	5663	1. U.S.	4684	1. U.S.	7138
2. France	2705	2. France	3370	2. France	4053
3. Germany	2347	3. Germany	3350	3. Germany	3517
4. Japan	2215	4. Japan	2637	4. Japan	3304
5. Saudi A.	1719	5. Saudi A.	2298	5. Saudi A.	3040
6. U.K.	1465	6. U.K.	2105	6. U.K.	1781
7. Kuwait	1270	7. Holland	1404	7. U.S.S.R.	1580
8. Holland	1074	8. U.S.S.R.	1403	8. Holland	1577
9. Canada	1060	9. UAE	1115	9. Kuwait	1188
10. U.S.S.R.	954	10. Kuwait	1055	10. UAE	1062

Source: Organization for Economic Co-operation and Development, Development Co-operation 1978, 1979, 1980 and 1981 Reviews, Paris.

Fig. 13

Net imports of Crude Oil and Refined products of Non—OPEC
Developing Countries, * 1978

Total: 4.38 million barrels per day

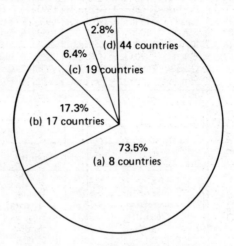

(a) Countries with net imports of more than 100,000 barrels
per day or 73.5 per cent of the total

(b) Countries with net imports between 20,000 and 100,000
barrels per day or 17.3 per cent of the total

(c) Countries with net imports between 10,000 and 20,000
barrels per day or 6.4 per cent of the total

(d) Countries with net imports of less than 10,000 barrels
per day or 2.8 per cent of the total

*Excludes Non-OPEC Developing Countries which are net exporters of crude oil
and refined products

Source: OPEC-Secretariat

Fig. 14 Proportion of Financial Aid given by OPEC Countries to the Developing Countries (with the exception of the OPEC Countries) in respect of the Financial Burdens* borne by the Developing Countries after the Revision of Oil Prices in 1973 (millions of dollars)

YEAR	Financial Aid				Developing Countries					Developing Countries (excluding five of them)**				
	OPEC Countries		Arab OPEC Countries		Financial Burdens	OPEC Countries %		Arab OPEC Countries %		Financial Burdens	OPEC Countries %		Arab OPEC Countries %	
	C	D	C	D		C	D	C	D		C	D	C	D
1974	4792.7	3445.6	3859.1	2963.2	8391.6	57.1	41.1	47.0	35.3	4532.7	105.7	62.0	85.1	65.4
1975	7690.4	5515.9	6194.5	4877.9	8738.7	88.0	63.1	70.9	55.8	4192.3	183.4	131.6	147.8	116.4
1976	6038.0	5586.8	5354.3	4655.5	10788.1	56.0	56.0	49.6	43.2	5053.0	119.5	110.6	106.0	92.1
TOTAL	18521.1	14548.3	15407.8	12496.6	27918.4	66.3	52.1	55.2	44.8	13778.0	134.4		111.8	90.7

C=Commitments
D=Disbursements

*The financial burden of the developing countries in this table is the difference between the price of oil at the prices prevailing in the years after 1973, and the price in the year 1973.

**The countries omitted are: Argentina, Brazil, India, South Korea and Taiwan.

Source: The Relationship Between Financial Aid from OPEC Countries and the Financial Burden borne by Developing Countries as a result of the Adjustment of Oil Prices since 1973, prepared by the Economic Office of the Organization of Arab Petroleum Exporting Countries, *OAPEC Bulletin*, No. 10, p.25 (October 1979).

Fig. 15 Net imports of oil by selected developing countries, and total imports from OPEC countries

REGION	Net imports of oil			Increase since 1973		Total rec'd from OPEC sources		Total amount rec'd as a share in the increase of net oil imports	
	In Millions of Dollars							Per cent	
	1973	1974	1975	1974	1975	1974	1975	1974	1975
North Africa (a)	55	227	221	172	166	17	113	10.0	78.2
Other African Countries (b)	364	882	996	518	632	552	702	100.7	111.0
	(340)	(797)	(900)	(457)	(561)	(406)	(159)	(34.9)	(72.5)
Middle East Asia (c)	6	16	17	10	11	89	148	893.0	1347.3
Asia (d)	2228	5563	6572	3335	4344	1168	1532	35.0	35.3
Latin America (e)	1281	4612	4569	3331	3282	231	606	6.9	18.5
TOTAL (f)	3934	11300	12376	7366	8441	2027	3101	27.5	36.7
Of which land-locked countries (g)	53	115	139	62	87	10	48	16.9	55.2
least developed countries (h)	127	334	372	207	245	574	617	227.3	251.9
most seriously affected countries (i)	1298	2480	2827	1182	1529	1685	2023	142.5	132.3
Members of the Arab League (j)	86	328	334	243	248	468	557	193.0	224.0

(a) Morocco.
(b) 16 countries: The Central African Republic, Burundi, Togo, the United Republic of Tanzania, the United Republic of Cameroon, Zaire, Zambia, the Ivory Coast, Senegal, Sudan, Sierra Leone, Ghana, Kenya, Liberia, Malawi, Mauritius.
(c) The Yemen Arab Republic.
(d) 12 countries including: Pakistan, Bangladesh, Trinidad, The Republic of Korea, Sri Lanka, Singapore, the Philippines, Malaysia, Nepal, India, and Thailand.
(e) 13 countries: Argentina, Uruguay, Paraguay, Brazil, Panama, Peru, Jamaica, El Salvador, Chile, Guatamala, Nicaragua, Honduras, and Costa Rica.
(f) 42 countries.
(g) 5 countries.
(h) 8 countries.
(i) 19 countries.
(j) 3 countries.

Source: United Nations Conference On Trade and Development: Intergovernmental Group of Experts, 2nd Session, Geneva, 5-16 December 1977. Report of the Intergovernmental Group of Experts on the External Indebtedness of Developing Countries, TD/B/685/add. 1 (New York: UN, 1977). *Ibid*, Financial Solidarity for Development Efforts and Institutions of the Members of OPEC 1973-1976 Review, p.25.

Fig. 16

Development of Oil Prices 1972–1979 (In US Dollars per Barrel)

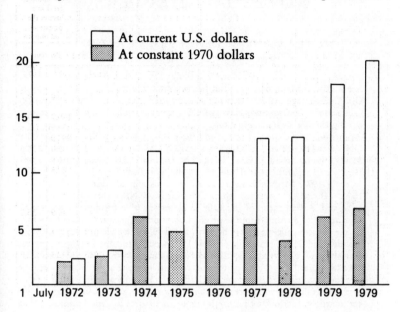

Source: International Bank for Reconstruction and Development, World Development Report 1979 (Washington DC: 1979) p.11.

NOTES TO CHAPTERS

NOTES AND REFERENCES TO CHAPTER 1:
OPEC AS A DONOR GROUP

1   See Figure 1 where data on adult literacy rates, the pattern of distribution of GNP, percentage shares of merchandise exports and even, in some cases, the per capita energy consumption classify OPEC countries individually and as a group among the less developed nations.

2   According to the most recent *World Bank Atlas* (1980), in 1978 the collective GNP of the thirteen OPEC members was $379 billion, a mere 7.4 per cent of the $5100 billion combined GNP of the US, Canada, EEC, Japan, Australia and New Zealand, and barely 4 per cent of the world's GNP.

3   In early 1974, Mr McNamara explained in his annual address to the World Bank's Board of Governors that, "The OPEC GNP figures are not strictly comparable with those of the OECD countries. The former include a high proportion of income from the production of non-replaceable assets for which no depreciation allowance has been provided. Were this factor to be taken into account, the OPEC per capita GNP in 1973 would probably be 30 per cent less than shown". 1974 Address, p.21, footnote (a). In his 1975 address Mr McNamara added that "(the OPEC countries') capacity to make aid available is not the size and strength of their combined GNP – which is only a small fraction of that of the OECD – nor even of their GNP per capita, which on average is also substantially less, but rather the levels of their surplus trade balances". 1975 Address p.7. The special nature of these surplus balances was not discussed, however, in Mr McNamara's analysis.

4   ODA, or Official Development Assistance, is defined in OECD publications as "grants or loans undertaken by the official sector, at concessional financial terms (if a loan, at least 25 per cent grant element, using the conventional discount rate of 10 per cent), with the promotion of economic development and welfare as main objectives". It has been argued that this definition may not be suitable for assistance from OPEC countries where a higher discount rate should apply. See "The OPEC Aid Record" (Shihata and Mabro), Chapter 3 of this publication, p.40.

5   For an elaboration of this and the following point, see M. Khouja, "Some Observations on the Flow of Financial Resources to Developing Countries", *OAPEC Bulletin*, Vol. 6, pp. 9-15. (March 1980).

6   More generally, lending by private banks in OECD countries to developing countries represents to a great extent an intermediation process in the use of OPEC surpluses. This point is not emphasized here, however, as the amounts are lent in the name of the lending banks and at their risk. However, as OECD publications caution, in respect of bank lending in an OECD member country to developing countries of amounts originating in another OECD member country, "care is required when interpreting the relationship of the total shown for a given country, or any sub-total thereof, which includes bank sector flows, to the GNP of that country". OECD, *Review on Development Co-operation*, p.212, footnote to Table A12. (1979).

7   The Brandt Commission has recently estimated that if this target were to be met by all donor countries by 1985, an additional $30 billion would be available for concessional assistance to the Third World. See "North South: A Programme for Survival", *The Report of the Independent Commission on International Development Issues*, p.242. (1980).

8   The countries and their respective ODA to GNP ratios are as follows: Qatar 15.62 per cent; UAE 14.12 per cent; Kuwait 8.12 per cent; Saudi Arabia 5.40 per cent; Libya 2.31 per cent; Iraq 1.65 per cent; Iran 1.13 per cent. (OECD Statistics).

9   Capital Surplus Countries as defined by the IMF are those countries "that had a current account surplus each year in the 1970's. IMF, *World Economic Outlook*, May 1980. The surplus countries according to this source are: Iraq, Kuwait, Libya, Qatar, Saudi Arabia and the UAE.

10   *Financial Solidarity for Development — Efforts and Institutions of the Members of OPEC: 1973-1976*, Report by the UNCTAD Secretariat. (TD/B/C/7/31, New York 1979), p.13.

11   For a detailed list, see the UNCTAD document referred to in note 10 above, and Chapter 8 of this book.

12   It may be worth noting in this respect that the oil imports of the thirty Least Developed Countries were, in 1979, less than one-third of the oil imports of Brazil alone, which also exceeded those of the whole African continent. Burma and Bolivia, countries with the lowest per capita incomes in their respective regions, are not oil importers. They have repeatedly received assistance from the OPEC Fund. In fact, only eight developing countries accounted for more than 70 per cent of the oil imports of the Third World in 1979. These were mostly the semi-industrialized developing countries, which also accounted for more than 70 per cent of the total manufactured goods exported by developing countries.

13   For an elaboration of this proposal, see e.g., "Interview with Mr Abdullatif Al Hamad, Director General of the Kuwait Fund for Arab Economic Development", *OAPEC Bulletin*, Vol. 6, No. 3, March 1980, p.31.

14   GATT, *International Trade 1978/1979*, Appendix Table H, (1979).

15   World Bank, *Interim Report on Labour Migration and Manpower in the Middle East and North Africa*, p.19. (1979).

16   See Figs. 4, 5 and 6, pp.251-253. These charts were prepared by the OPEC Secretariat on the basis of statistics published by the IMF and the UN. They are quoted from an unpublished lecture by Dr Fadhil Al-Chalaby entitled "OPEC and the other Developing Countries", delivered at the *8th Round Table on Energy and Developing Countries* held in Zagreb, Yugoslavia, 20-22 October 1980.

17   To illustrate this point, Arab banks are reported to have lent or co-managed $31.7 billion in commercial loan syndications for developing countries between 1977-1979. According to recent data, two Arab banks, Gulf International and UBAF, figured among the fifty most active lead managers of syndicated Euroloans during the first half of 1980 with the value of loans lead-managed by them exceeding $1.6 billion. An equivalent amount has recently been reported as the volume of issues managed in the Euromarket by one Arab investment company, Kuwait International Investment Co., in the period January-September 1980.

18   This point is best elaborated in the writings of Dr Hazem Biblawi. See e.g., "Petro-Surpluses and the Structure of the World Economy", *Oil and Arab Co-operation, Vol. IV, No. 4 (1978)*. (in Arabic): Biblawi and Shaley "Strategic Options of Development for Kuwait", *The Industrial Bank of Kuwait, Series No. 1, pp.26-35, (1980)*.

NOTES AND REFERENCES TO CHAPTER 2:
SOME PREREQUISITES FOR THE NORTH-SOUTH DIALOGUE

1   World Bank, *World Development Report*, p.11.
2   World Bank, op. cit., p.45.
3   (The Brandt Commission), *North South: A Program for Survival*, p.117.
4   Frank Andre Cunder, "Arms Economy and Warfare in the Third World", *Third World Quarterly*, Vol. 2, No. 2, April 1980, p.231.
5   See *Agriculture: Toward 2000*, FAO, Rome, November 1979.
6   *Investment and Input Requirements for Accelerating Food Production in Low Income Countries by 1990*, IFPRI, Sept. 1979, Washington, D.C.
7   World Bank, *Energy in Developing Countries*, p.49 (1980). It is to be noted, however, that the World Bank includes in the figures the energy requirements of several countries which are not usually included under the term "developing countries".
8   World Bank, op. cit., p.7.
9   IMF, *Annual Report 1980*, p.3.
10 World Bank, *World Development Report, 1980*, p.7.
11 Triffin, R., *Annex of Final Act*, Second World Scientific Banking Meeting, Dubrovnik, 26-31 May 1980. *Bulletin No. 3*.
12 Morgan Guaranty & Trust, *World Financial Markets*, Sept. 1980, p.1. In fact, according to an analysis carried out by the OPEC Secretariat and based on IMF figures, the increase in value of the oil imported by non-OPEC developing countries from OPEC sources represented only 18.7 per cent of the increase in value of their imports from industrialized countries in the period 1974-1979.
13 IMF, *Annual Report 1980*, p.5.
14 GATT, *Report on Prospects for International Trade*, 1979.
15 OPEC Secretariat, *The Impact of Oil Price Adjustments on the Economies of the Major Industrialized Countries*, DEF 35/80/51 CEB/123, May 1980 (unpublished). This conclusion is supported by GATT's Annual Report, *International Trade 1978/79*, (Sept. 1979), p.10, which categorically described the view that the oil price increase was a major causative factor behind the resurgence of inflation as "dangerously wrong".
16 IMF, *Annual Report, 1980*, p.5.
17 Ibid, p.25.
18 A recent study has confirmed that in 1978 South Korea, Taiwan and Hong Kong accounted for some 50 per cent of the total imports of manufactured goods by the industrialized West from non-oil producing LDCs, and seven countries (the above three plus Mexico, Brazil, Singapore and India accounted for 75 per cent of such imports). See *Financial Times*, 17 November 1980, p.4.
19 IMF, *World Economic Outlook — Situation of the Non-Oil Developing Countries*, ID/80/4, 31 March 1980, p.60.
20 World Bank, *World Development Report 1980*, p.29.
21 Morgan Guaranty & Trust, op. cit., p.1. In fact, according to the *World Development Report, 1980*, of the World Bank, the middle income countries of East Asia, the Pacific, achieved a growth rate in GNP of 8 per cent in 1970-80 (as against 7.7 per cent in 1960-70) and the Latin American and Caribbean countries achieved 3.8 per cent in 1970-80 (as against 5.7 per cent in 1960-70). Op. cit., p.99.
22 IMF/World Bank Development Committee, *International Capital Markets — Recent Development and Near-Term Prospects and Developing Country Access to Capital Markets*, DC/80-16, 15 August 1980, p.3, (mimeo).

23   It has been estimated that Arab banks alone have lent or co-managed some \$40 billion worth of commercial loan syndications between 1977-79, of which \$32 billion went to developing countries. See Rehman Sobhan, Institutional Mechanisms for Channelling OPEC Surpluses within the Third World, *Third World Quarterly, Vol. 2, No. 4*, October 1980, p.735.

24   The lecture now appears as Chapter 4 of this publication.

25   Cf. Hazem Biblawi, *Petro-Surpluses and the Structure of the World Economy*, Oil and Arab Co-operation, Vol. IV, No. 4, 1978 (in Arabic), and Biblawi and Shafey, "Strategic Options of Development for Kuwait", *The Industrial Bank of Kuwait Papers, Series No. 1*, 1980, pp.26-35.

26   GATT, *International Trade 1978/1979*, Appendix Table H (1979).

27   World Bank, *Interim Report on Labour Migration and Manpower in the Middle East and North Africa*, p.19, (1979).

28   For further details see Chapter 6 of this publication.

NOTES AND REFERENCES TO CHAPTER 3:
THE OPEC AID RECORD

1   Small differences between the two sources in other years seem to be due to differences of judgment on the timing of some transactions. The differences would disappear if the figures were aggregated or averaged over a period of two or three years.

2   In fact, if the contributions to the IMF oil facility were added to the OECD figures for non-concessional multilateral disbursements, the discrepancies with UNCTAD become insignificant.

3   According to UNCTAD estimates, receipts between 1975 and 1976 decreased by some \$1.5 billion, of which \$1 billion is attributed to the IMF oil facility.

4   "OPEC" in this paper always means ten members (Ecuador, Gabon and Indonesia are excluded). For a fairer comparison with DAC one should also exclude Algeria and Nigeria which are themselves capital-importing countries with a relatively modest per capita income.

5   Of this average the percentages for each country are: 16.9 per cent for Qatar, 13.59 per cent for the UAE, 11.44 per cent for Kuwait, 7.2 per cent for Saudi Arabia, 2.96 per cent for Libya, 1.9 per cent for Iraq, 1.8 per cent for Venezuela, 1.74 per cent for Iran, 1.37 per cent for Nigeria and 0.31 per cent for Algeria.

6   According to UNCTAD estimates the disbursement/GNP ratio for Saudi Arabia amounts in 1975 to 11.65 per cent, which, with the addition of the depletion factor, would become 16.6 per cent. The corresponding figures for Kuwait would be 14.1 and 20 per cent respectively.

7   UNCTAD estimates are somewhat higher: 81.3 per cent for 1974, 73.6 per cent for 1975 and 78.87 per cent for 1976.

8   P. D. Henderson, "The Distribution of Official Development Assistance Commitments by Recipient Countries and by Sources", *Bulletin of the Oxford Institute of Economics and Statistics*, 33(1), 1971, p.2.

9   On a disbursement basis, general support assistance accounted for two-thirds of OPEC bilateral concessional aid in 1975; on a commitment basis it only accounted for 32 per cent of the comparable category. In this respect OPEC aid differs again from DAC flows. In the latter case, gross official flows by \$4.6 billion, the latter amount representing amortization of existing debt of aid recipients.

NOTES AND REFERENCES TO CHAPTER 4:
OPEC AID, THE OPEC FUND, AND CO-OPERATION WITH
COMMERCIAL DEVELOPMENT FINANCE SOURCES

1   United Nations, Conference on Trade and Development, *Financial Solidarity for Development: Efforts and Institutions of the Members of OPEC — 1977 Review* (draft of 31 October 1977, mimeographed, scheduled for publication).
2   Disbursement of concessional flows (on ODA terms) from OPEC members to other developing countries reached $1.1 billion in 1973, $3.5 billion in 1974, $5.2 billion in 1975, $5.2 billion in 1976, and $5.5 billion in 1977, corresponding roughly to a percentage of the GNP of the donors ranging from 1.5 to 2.7 per cent.
3   Net official disbursements (on ODA terms) from DAC countries reached in the same year $13.5 billion, rose to slightly above $13.6 billion in 1976, and reached $14.8 billion in 1977, corresponding to about 0.3 per cent of their GNP, according to OECD sources.
4   United Nations, Conference on Trade and Development, op. cit.
5   Co-financing is now a general phenomenon in OPEC assistance. According to OECD sources, by the end of March 1978 up to 106 projects, including projects in an advanced stage of negotiation, had been financed jointly by OPEC and non-OPEC sources. The total amount involved was roughly $7.3 billion of which some $3 billion were from OPEC sources. Chapter 5 of this publication offers details on supported projects and procedures.
6   The economist Hazem El Biblawi has established this point succinctly in his recent article, *Oil Financial Surpluses and the World Economic Structure*, Oil and Arab Co-operation, Vol. 4, No. 3, 1978 (in Arabic).

NOTES AND REFERENCES TO CHAPTER 6:
THE OPEC FUND AND THE NORTH-SOUTH DIALOGUE

1   The urgent need to create a "New International Economic Order" (NIEO) was expressed by the UN at an earlier date. On 1 May 1974, a day to which we can trace back the formalization, on a global basis, of the North-South Dialogue, the UN General Assembly, at its Sixth Special Session, adopted resolutions on the "Declaration of the Establishment of a NIEO", and the "Programme of Action" for its establishment in order to "correct inequalities and redress existing injustices, and make it possible to eliminate the widening gap between the developed and the developing countries".
2   The Tokyo Round trade package signed in Geneva on 12 April 1979 has so far been accepted by only one of the developing country participants in the MTNs, the rest finding it short in meeting their minimum demands.
3   The specific demands put forward by the developing countries were related in particular to the following: adoption of UNCTAD's Integrated Programme for Commodities; energy conservation, development and finance; protection of the purchasing power of export earnings and assets; debt relief and debt reorganization; adoption by the developed countries of the 0.7 per cent ODA target; access to capital markets of the developed world; infrastructural development; full implementation of the "Lima Declaration and Plan of Action" calling for an increase in the percentage share of developing countries to at least 25 per cent of

the total world industrial production by the year 2000; increased food production in developing countries, food security and food aid; transfer of technology through private foreign investment; and international financial and monetary reforms, that is, in IMF and IBRD resources, new allocation of Special Drawing Rights (SDRs), and greater access by developing countries to these resources.

4   Disbursement figures, though naturally lower, indicate a transfer of more than $7 billion a year, or some 2.5 per cent of the GNP of the OPEC donors.

5   This ratio would be even lower if we excluded countries such as Spain, Portugal, Yugoslavia, Greece, Israel (a recipient of large DAC assistance) and others, which are included in the group of recipient developing countries according to the DAC classification.

6   The Common Fund, as proposed by the developing countries, is to be established as an independent international agency with substantial powers of intervention in international commodity markets through the financing of buffer stocks and other measures, in order to meet the requirements for price support, a condition to any improvement of the terms of trade. It should have sufficient resources at its disposal for prompt use, as the need for market intervention arises, to protect the interests of all developing countries. The capacity to intervene in favour of these countries' export markets calls also for an internal structure of the Common Fund that will enable the developing countries to participate effectively in the decision-making process.

NOTES AND REFERENCES TO CHAPTER 10:
ARAB OIL POLICIES AND THE NEW INTERNATIONAL
ECONOMIC ORDER

1   *Programme of Action on the Establishment of a New International Economic Order*, G.A. Res. 3202, 6th Special Sess., UN GAOR, Supp. 1, UN G.A., UN Doc. No. A/9559, para. vii, 1(a) (1974). Hereinafter cited as *Programme of Action*.

2   For the general contention that the Western origins of contemporary international law constitute a hindrance to its universal acceptability, see B. Roling, *International Law in an Expanded World*, 66-86 (1960); Abi-Saab, *The Newly Independent States and the Rules of International Law*, 8 How, L. J. 95 (1962). Compare Shihata, *The Attitude of New States Toward the International Court of Justice*, 19 *Int'l Org.* 203, 216-19 (1965). See generally Rozental, *The Charter of Economic Rights and Duties of States and the New International Economic Order*, 16 *Va. J. Int'l L.* 309 (1976).

3   For discussion of these latter differences and their possible effects on oil production policies, see Chenery, "Restructuring the World Economy", 53 *Foreign Affairs* 242, 249-53 (1975). See also F. McFadzean, "Economic Implications of the Energy Crisis", in *In Search of a New World Economic Order*, 120, 126-27, (H. Corbet and R. Jackson, eds., 1974).

4   See e.g., Professor R. Mabro's lecture summarized under the title "Can OPEC hold the Line?" (hereinafter cited as R. Mabro) in 18 *Middle East Economic Survey* 1,5 (No. 19, 1975) (hereinafter cited as *MEES*).

5   The members of OPEC include Algeria, Ecuador, Gabon, Indonesia, Iran, Iraq, Kuwait, Libya, Nigeria, Qatar, Saudi Arabia, the United Arab Emirates and Venezuela. The only non-Arab members are Ecuador, Gabon, Indonesia, Iran, Nigeria and Venezuela. See Council on International Economic Policy, *International Economic Report of the President*, 59 (1974). See also Note, "Operation of the Foreign Tax Credit in the Petroleum Industry: A Dry Hole", 15 *Va. J. Int'l L.*

421 and n.1 (1975); *IMF Survey* 13 Oct. 1975, at 304. For a general discussion of the formation of OPEC, see M. Al-Otaiba, *OPEC and the Petroleum Industry* (1975).

6   Reprinted in 18 *MEES* (No. 20, 1975) (hereinafter cited as *The Algiers Solemn Declaration*).

7   For a description of Saudi Arabian policy, see 18 *MEES* 2,3 (No. 23, 1975). Oil production in Saudi Arabia is currently running at approximately 7-8 million barrels per day, while the volume necessary to meet its financial needs would not exceed 3-4 million barrels daily.

8   R. Mabro, *supra* note 4, at 2.

9   See text at notes 30-34 *infra*.

10 R. Mabro, *supra* note 4, at 1.

11 An account of the deliberations of the Algiers Conference on this point is contained in Ian Seymour's report in 18 *MEES* 2 (no. 20, 1975).

12 See Oppenheim, *International Law* 321-24 (8th ed. 1955). Cf. H. Kronstein, *The Law of International Cartels* 4, 18-21, 29-30 (1973), the Havana Charter of International Trade Organization, U.N. Doc. E/Conf 2/78 (1947), and the General Agreement on Tariffs and Trade (GATT), 30 Oct. 1947, 61 Stat. pts. 5-6, T.I.A.S. No. 1700. 55 U.N.T.S. 194, *as amended*, Mar. 2 1970. 1970 2 U.S.T. 1090, T.I.A.S. No. 6864 attempted to change the status of international in this respect and to establish the principle that parties in their legislation ought to ensure that enterprises shall, in the sphere of international trade, refrain from practices which foster monopolistic control. These objectives, however, were not achieved since the Havana Charter never entered into force and GATT allowed for many exceptions and was restricted in its application to parties which had entered into tariff negotiations with each other. Among all Arab oil-exporting countries, only Kuwait is a contracting party to the GATT. See K. Kock, *International Trade Policy and the GATT, 1947-1967*, at 304 (1969).

13 For the substantial role played by private cartels and restrictive international commodity agreements concluded between exporting countries see E. Hexner, *International Cartels* (1945); Radetzki, *International Commodity Market Arrangements* 38-59 (1970); Walker, "The International Law of Commodity Agreements", 28 *Law & Contemp. Prob.* 392 (1963). See also H. Kronstein, *supra* note 12, at 82-96; Fawcett, "The Function of Law in International Commodity Agreements", 44 *Brit. Y.B. Int'l L.* 157 (1970). Even proposals *de lege ferenda* for the adoption of a code of impermissible practices in international trade tend to except producers' associations in developing countries. See e.g., *Report of UNCTAD Committee of Experts on Restrictive Business Practices in Relation to the Trade and Development of Developing Countries*, U.N. Doc. TD/B/C.2/119 (1973); Schachter, "Just Prices in World Markets: Proposals *de lege ferenda*", 69 *Am. J. Int'l L.* 101, 107 (1975).

14 See *Declaration on the Establishment of a New International Economic Order*, G.A. Res. 3201, 6th Special Sess., U.N. GAOR, Supp. 1, U.N. Doc. No. A/9559, item 4(t), (1974) hereinafter cited as *Declaration; Programme of Action, supra* note 1, items 1(c) and 3(a) (iii). See also "Co-operation and Co-ordination Among the Group of Raw Material Producer-Exporter Developing Countries", Resolution No. 6, Conference of Developing Countries on Raw Materials, Dakar Feb. 3-8, 1975, reprinted in 14 *Int'l Legal Materials* 534 (1975), hereinafter cited as Dakar Conference.

15 G.A. Res. 3281, 29 U.N. GAOR, Supp. 31, at 50, U.N. Doc. A/9631, art. 5 (1974), hereinafter cited as *Charter of Economic Rights and Duties*. The Resolution was adopted by a margin of 120 votes to 6, with 10 abstentions.

16 The *Algiers Solemn Declaration, supra* note 6.

17 See *id.* para. 10.

18 See e.g., the policy statement delivered by King Khalid of Saudi Arabia on 1 April 1975, as reported in *MEES* (No. 24, 1975); the statement of Prince Fahd of Saudi Arabia, as reported in 18 *id.* 2 (No. 20, 1975). See also Al-Hamad, *International Finance: An Arab Point of View*, 5-6 (1974); Sayigh, "The Reconciliation of Self-Interest and International Responsibility", 4 *J. Palestine Studies* 70 (1975).

19 See *id.*

20 This question is raised, but not answered, in Kubbah, *OPEC: Past and Present* 97 (1974).

21 Testimony of the US Treasury Under-Secretary for Monetary Affairs before the house Banking and Currency Committee, reported in *The Financial Times*, 10 July 1974. A responsible US official has even cited military action against oil-producers as one possible option in extreme cases. See the oft-quoted statement of Henry Kissinger, first reported in *Bus. Week*, 13 Jan. 1975, at 69.

22 For the unconvincing general contention that "exporting countries are better off producing than keeping their oil in the ground", see Chenery, *supra* note 3, at 253.

23 See 13 *MEES* 1-3 (No. 33, 1970); 12 *id.* 2-4 (1969).

24 See *id.* 1 (No. 25, 1972).

25 For a comparison of September 1973 production levels with those of July-December 1974, see R. Mabro, *supra* note 4, at 3-4.

26 See *The Algiers Solemn Declaration*, *supra* note 6, para 6.

27 See General Agreement on Tariffs and Trade, Oct. 30, 1947, 61 Stat. pts. 5-6, T.I.A.S. No. 55 U.N.T.S. 194, as amended, Mar. 2, 1970 (1970) 2 U.S.T. 1090, T.I.A.S. No. 6864, art. 20.

28 Declaration, *supra* note 14, para. 4(g).

29 Speech of Henry A. Kissinger at the National Press Club in Washington D.C., 3 Feb. 1975, reprinted in 72 *Dep't State Bull.* 237, 240 (1975). See also an analysis of the need for oil conservation in Foley and Nielson, "Energy Conservation in Perspective of International Energy Requirements", in *Energy: Demand, Conservation and Institutional Problems*, 516, (M. Macrakis, ed., 1974).

30 For a detailed and documented treatment of this subject, see Shihata, "Destination Embargo of Arab Oil: Its Legality Under International Law", 68 *Am. J. Int'l L.* 591 (1974).

31 *Id.* at 608-16.

32 *Id.* at 621-25.

33 *Id.* at 616-19.

34 *Id.* at 619-21.

35 Cf. Bowett, "Economic Coercion and Reprisals by States", 13 *Va. J. Int'l L.* 1, 5 (1972). Bowett, "International Law and Economic Coercion", 16 *Va. J. Int'l L.* 245, 246 (1976).

36 See e.g., UNCTAD, Resolution on Permanent Sovereignty over Natural Resources, 19 Oct., 1972, UN Doc. TD/B/421 (1972), where reference is made to earlier UN General Assembly resolutions on this matter. See also Charter of Economic Rights and Duties, *supra* note 15; Dakar Conference, *supra* note 14, item 7 (41). For a discussion of the rationales of one Western State, the United States, for oil price regulation, see Note, "National Security and Oil Import Regulation: The License Fee Approach", 15 *Va. J. Int'l L.* 399, 412-20 (1975).

37 The membership of UNCTAD includes those states which are members of the United Nations, of its specialized agencies, or of the International Atomic Energy Agency. As a permanent organ of the General Assembly, it seeks to promote international trade with a view toward alleviating the trade gap of the

less developed countries through an increase in the volume and prices of their exports.

38 Charter of Economic Rights and Duties, *supra* note 15, at art. 6.

39 See text of the 1971 Tehran Agreement in 14 *MEES* (No. 17, Supp. 1971).

40 Schurr, "Minerals Trade and International Relations", in *The Future of the International Economic Order: An Agenda for Research*, 181, 191 (C. Bergsten ed. 1973).

41 See Schachter, *supra* note 13, at 101–09.

42 Kubbah, *supra* note 20, at 64.

43 While consumers paid $17-18 per barrel on the open market, and on one occasion $20, the Arab producers set the price at $11.651 per barrel. It has been reported that the latter figure reflected a compromise between the much higher price desired by Iran and the lower price suggested by Saudi Arabia and others, such that the Shah of Iran in announcing the new price described it as set "on the basis of generosity and kindness". 17 *MEES* 1 (No. 10, 1973).

44 See Schachter, *supra* note 13, at 103–04.

45 to quote a striking example in this respect: Kuwait was receiving no more than 75-80 cents per barrel of oil up until 1970, and $1.80 per barrel immediately before the rise of October 1973, but was paying at the same time $32 for every imported barrel of mineral water. See Amin, "The Oil Crisis – An Arab Point of View", 65 *L'Egypte Contemporaine*, 291, 293 (1974).

46 The principle of unjust enrichment has been frequently discussed in recent Western literature on the matter of nationalization. See Friedmann, "The Uses of General Principles in the Development of International Law", 57 *Am. J. Int'l L.* 279 (1963).

47 US oil imports in 1972 were 4740 million barrels per day, but in 1973 they jumped to 6705 million barrels per day. See *British Petroleum Statistical Review of the World Oil Industry*, 1973 (1974). Oil imports of Western Europe and Japan also increased in 1973, though not as drastically (about 10 per cent and 17.5 per cent respectively). *Id.*

48 Kubbah, *supra* note 20, at 94.

49 For a calculation of this inflation rate for the period of November 1973-November 1974, see *IMF Survey*, 3 Feb. 1975, at 41.

50 The Organization for Economic Co-operation and Development (OECD) was set up pursuant to a convention signed in Paris on 14 Dec. 1960. It seeks to co-ordinate the policies of its members with respect to world trade, economic growth, and aid to less-developed countries. The current membership is composed of Austria, Belgium, Canada, Denmark, Finland, France, the Federal Republic of Germany, Greece, Iceland, Ireland, Italy, Japan, Luxembourg, the Netherlands, Norway, Portugal, Spain, Sweden, Switzerland, Turkey, the United Kingdom and the United States. See generally *IMF Survey*, 5 Aug. 1974, at 243; *Activities of the OECD in 1970, Report by the Secretary General* 4 (1970).

51 Before the price increase of 16 Oct. 1973, the revenue accruing to the producing countries as a percentage of the final cost to the European consumer represented only 7.8 per cent, as against the 62 per cent collected by the consuming nations in the form of taxes and duties. The remainder, minus the one per cent production cost, reverted to the oil companies. 3 *Arab Oil and Gas* 4 (No. 56. 1974). "This means that even after the fourfold increase from 1 January of the exporter's fiscal revenues, the price at the consumption end could remain unchanged provided the consuming state cuts taxes from $12.72 to about $8 per barrel". *Id.* Instead, most consuming countries have imposed tax increases on the consumption of oil products. On the other hand, the producing countries' share of the price of a barrel of crude in the first quarter of 1974 was 36.5 per cent, while the companies retained 38.5 per cent. 6 *Id.* 3-4 (No. 123, 1974).

52   E. Monroe and R. Mabro, *Oil Producers and Consumers: Conflict or Co-operation* 39, (1975).
53   *Id.* at 17.
54   *Programme of Action, supra* note 1, para. vii (1)(a).
55   *The Algiers Solemn Declaration, supra* note 6, at iv.
56   See generally R. Haan, *Special Drawing Rights and Development,* (1971).
57   *Declaration, supra* note 14, para. 4 (j).
58   *Programme of Action, supra* note 1, para. 1(1)(d).
59   *Id.* para. 1(3)(a)(viii).
60   See Dakar Conference, *supra* note 14.
61   *The Algiers Solemn Declaration, supra* note 6, para. 7.
62   Address of President Boumediene of Algeria to the Algiers Conference 4 Mar. 1975, quoted in 18 *MEES,* 1 (No. 20, supp., 1975).
63   See Amin, *supra* note 45, at 296.
64   The Development Assistance Committee (DAC) of the OECD was formed for the purpose of expanding the aggregate volume of resources made available to less-developed countries. See Organization for Economic Co-operation and Development, *OECD, History, Aims, Structure* 16, 24-25 (1971). The members of DAC include Australia, Austria, Belgium, Canada, Denmark, France, Germany, Italy, Japan, the Netherlands, Norway, Portugal, Sweden, Switzerland, the United Kingdom, and the United States. See generally *IMF Survey,* 23 July 1973, at 220.
65   See *IMF Survey,* 12 May 1975, at 141.
66   *Organization for Economic Co-operation and Development 1974 Review,* 115, 118 (1975). In 1973, the most recent year for which statistical information is available, the flow of resources from DAC countries to developing countries reached 0.79 per cent of the former nations' GNP, and their official development assistance only 0.30 per cent of their GNP. *Id.*
67   See text at notes 22-23 *supra.*
68   See e.g., the $110 million agreement between Iraq and India signed on 28 March 1974, reported in 17 *MEES* 6 (No. 24, 1974); the agreement between Libya and India signed on 12 Oct. 1974, reported in 17 *Id.* 6 (No. 52, 1974); the agreement between the United Arab Emirates and India signed on 4 Jan. 1975, reported in 18 *Id.* 5 (No. 12, 1975). See also Dawson, "The Role of the Private Banker in the New International Economic Order", 16 *Va. J. Int'l L.* 297 (1976).
69   *The Algiers Solemn Declaration, supra* note 6, para. 9.
70   *Id.*
71   *Organization for Economic Co-operation and Development, 1974 Review,* 36 (1975). See also Dawson, *supra* note 68.
72   *Id.* at 39.
73   Chenery, *supra* note 3, at 242, 262.
74   UNCTAD, Report, 29 Oct., 1975, UN Doc. TD/B/AC. 19/R.8 (1975).
75   The Kuwait Fund for Arab Economic Development, established in 1961 to finance development in other Arab countries, is now endowed with a $3.45 billion capital and its activities have been extended to cover all developing countries. The Saudi Development Fund, the Abu Dhabi Fund for Economic and Social Development, and the Iraqi Development Fund, with respective capitals of $2.8 billion, and $500 million and $170 million, have also been set up to provide development assistance to all developing countries. See generally "OPEC Members Lift Aid Overflows to New Peak of Nearly $9 Billion", *IMF Survey,* 18 Nov. 1974, at 357.
76   The Arab Fund for Economic and Social Development, with capital that has recently been increased to about $1.4 billion, provides assistance to Arab countries, while the Arab Bank for Economic Development in Africa (with capital of

$231 million) and the Arab Solidarity Fund for African Countries (with capital of $200 million) donate aid to non-Arab African countries. Saudi Arabia was instrumental in setting up the Islamic Bank (with capital of $2 billion SDRs), and Kuwait is presently playing an important role in establishing the Solidarity Fund for Economic and Social Development in Non-Aligned Countries. Finally, Arab assistance through the traditional multilateral institutions (World Bank Group and IMF) is even more impressive. See generally *id*.

77 See the four-tier pricing proposal which Libya presented to the Islamic Summit Conference held in Lahore, 22-25 Feb. 1974, as reported in 17 *MEES* 1 (No. 19, 1974).

78 See *IMF Survey*, 24 Mar. 1975, at 93; 14 Apr. 1975, at 97, 107.

79 The Financial Support Fund (FSF) was established by the OECD to assist its members in avoiding unilateral measures which would disrupt international trade, and in developing such domestic policies as would maintain an adequate balance of payments and promote increased production and conservation of energy. See *IMF Survey*, 14 Apr. 1975, at 97.

80 The agreement establishing this Fund was open for signature in Paris between 9 April and 31 May 1975. Its provisions are explained in *id*. at 97, 104-06.

81 Provisions on economic aid already abound in the UN General Assembly resolutions relating to the new international economic order and to the economic rights and duties of states. See e.g., *Declaration, supra* note 14, para. 4(k); *Programme of Action, supra* note 1, sec. 11. See also White, "A New International Economic Order?", 16 *Va. J. Int'l L.* 323 (1976).

82 See e.g., T. Gihl, *International Legislation* 25 (1937); N. Politis, *The New Aspects of International Law* 15-16 (1928). For the pertinent theory that the "formation and existence of a custom depend upon its conformity with the social needs of a legal order", see Kopelmanas, "Custom as a Means of the Creation of International Law", 18 *Brit. Y.B. Int'l L.* 127, 148, (1937).

83 For a lucid explanation of Arab investment strategies which stresses, however, the "should be" rather than the "is", see Al-Hamad, *Arab Capital Markets and the Recycling of Petrofunds* (1974); *International Finance — An Arab Point of View* (1974); *Investing Surplus Oil Revenues* (1974); *Arab Capital and International Finance* (1973); *Arab Funds and International Co-operation* (1973). These lectures, by the Director-General of the Kuwait Fund for Arab Economic Development are all reproduced as Kuwait Fund Publications. See also Statement of Kuwaiti Minister of Finance Before the National Assembly, quoted in 17 *MEES* i-vii (No. 35, 1974) – detailed description of Kuwaiti investment policy.

84 Higher figures were quoted, however, by the IMF in March 1975. According to these figures the current surplus of the major oil-exporting countries was approximately $70 billion, out of which $11 billion was invested in the United States, $7 billion in the United Kingdom, $21 billion in Euro-currency markets, $5 billion in loans to official institutions in developed countries other than the United States and the United Kingdom, $4 billion in grants and loans to developing countries, $16 billion in oil export credits, and $4 billion in other items. (*IMF Survey*, 24 Mar. 1975, at 81.) Of this total amount, the increase in assets of OPEC countries regarded as "official reserves" was only about $35 billion. (*Id*. at 93.) See also *IMF Survey* 26 May 1975, at 151-152.

For a general discussion of the Arab investment in one major western country, the United States, see Niehuss, "Foreign Investment in the United States: A Review of Government Policy", 16 *Va. J. Int'l L.* 65 (1975); note, "US Regulation of Foreign Direct Investment: Current Developments and the Congressional Response", 15 *Va. J. Int'l L.* 611 (1975).

85 See Statement of Gerald L. Parsky, Assistant Secretary of the US Treasury, on

investment of OPEC funds in the United States, delivered before the Sub-committee on Multinational Corporations, of the Senate Committee on Foreign Relations on 18 March 1975, reprinted in 18 *MEES* 1,3 (No. 22, 1975). Compare . *Newsweek*, 10 Feb. 1975, at 62 with *New York Times*, 13 Feb. 1975, at 1, col. 7 (city ed.).

86 See e.g., *International Currency Review*, Sept.-Oct. 1974, at 11. OPEC surpluses are projected to reach more than $1,000 billion by the early 1980s. Quite naturally, this publication concludes that such "unsustainable (funds) will *not* be handed over". (*Id.*).

87 Cf. Al-Hamad, *International Finance — An Arab Point of View, supra* note 83, at 5.

88 Cf. Farmanfarma *et al.*, "How Can the World Afford OPEC Oil?", 53 *Foreign Aff.* 201, 212 (1975). Attempts to secure guarantees from the consuming countries, such as those expressed in the *Algiers Solemn Declaration, supra* note 6, at para. 11, or suggested in E. Monroe and R. Mabro, *supra* note 52, at 64-66, have not so far met with success.

89 Farmanfarma *et al.*, *supra* note 88, at 209.

90 See the statement of Gerald R. Parsky, *supra* note 85, at 2.

91 Cf. Al-Hamad, *International Finance — An Arab Point of View*, *supra* note 83, at 7-8.

92 Al-Hamad, *Arab Funds and International Economic Co-operation, supra* note 83, at 10. The above objective was recently defined by Crown Prince Fahd of Saudi Arabia in the following language: "We must have a three-sided formula which will link Western progress with Arab money and the hidden potential of the developing countries". 18 *MEES* (No. 24, 1975).

93 See *Declaration, supra* note 14, para. 4(p); *Programme of Action, supra* note 1, para IV.

94 See *Declaration, supra* note 14, para. 4(g); *Programme of Action, supra* note 1, para. V. The fear, sometimes expressed in the West, of an Arab takeover of these giant corporations is completely unrealistic, for Arabs simply "have neither the means nor the desire for such a luxury". Al-Hamad, *Investing Surplus Oil Revenues, supra* note 83, at 17; statement of Gerald R. Parsky, *supra* note 85, at 3.

95 See 17 *MEES* 12 (No. 1, 1973); 15 *id.* 3-7 (No. 7, supp. 1971).

96 See generally A. Fatouros, *Government Guarantees to Foreign Investors*, 249-51 (1962); 3 G. Hackworth, *Digest of International Law*, 555, 645 (1942); 8 M. Whiteman, *Digest of International Law*, 376-82 (1967). See also S. Friedman, *Expropriation in International Law*, 189-93 (1953). But cf. Weston " 'Constructive Takings' under International Law: A Modest Foray into the Problem of 'Creeping Expropriation'," 16 *Va. J. Int'l L.* 103 (1975).

97 See *Charter of Economic Rights and Duties, supra* note 15, art. 2(c).

98 See text at notes 36-59 *supra*. See also Niehuss, *supra* note 84, at 600.

99 *The Algiers Solemn Declaration, supra* note 6, para 2.

100 *Id.* para 3.

101 *Id.* para. 4. The grouping together of sixteen consuming countries in the International Energy Agency (IEA) has at times been described by US officials as aimed at "breaking OPEC" or "hastening its demise". See speech of Henry Kissinger, *supra* note 29. Kissinger also described the possible strategy and techniques to be followed by IEA in this respect. *Id.*

102 See Shihata, *supra* note 30, at 592-97.

103 See e.g., "Statement of the Kuwaiti Minister of Finance and Oil", 16 *MEES* 1-3 (No. 37, 1973).

104 3 *Arab Oil and Gas* 3 (No. 55, 1974).

105 *Id.*

106 For a discussion of the interrelationships among these systems and the necessity

for dealing with them collectively when seeking reform, see Curzon, "Crisis in the International Trading System", in *In Search of a New World Economic Order*, 33-34 (H. Corbet and R. Jackson eds. 1974); Malmgren, "Need for a New System of World Trade and Payments", *id.* at 107-10.

107 See *The Algiers Solemn Declaration, supra* note 6, para 5. See also Rozental, *supra* note 2.

108 See *id.* According to Shaikh Yamani, Oil Minister of Saudi Arabia, the idea for such a meeting was first suggested by Saudi Arabia and was later the subject of consultation between the French and Saudi Arabian heads of state. 18 *MEES* 5 (No. 27, supp., 1975).

109 "(The) discussions have not permitted either a precise definition of the points to be dealt with by the Conference or a determination of the relative importance to be accorded to them." 18 *MEES* 4 (No. 26, supp., 1975) – from the communiqué of the Paris meeting.

110 *The Algiers Solemn Declaration, supra* note 6, paras. 8-12.

111 See e.g., the speech of Henry Kissinger, *supra* note 29. It was reported that the United States, toward the end of the Paris Meeting, "emerged somewhat from the shadow to make its own tough line more evident" against the package deal proposed by the OPEC countries. 18 *MEES* 2 (No. 26, supp., 1975). On 27 May 1975, Henry Kissinger proclaimed, in his speech to the first ministerial meeting of the International Energy Agency, what he termed a "new and constructive approach" to energy problems by the United States. The details of this new approach, however, at least as reported by the press, do not appear to meet the minimum requirements of the demands made by the developing countries (including OPEC members). See *International Herald Tribune*, 28 May 1975, at 1, col. 2.

112 See e.g., Dawson, *supra* note 68, at 302.

NOTES AND REFERENCES TO CHAPTER 11: INTER-ARAB EQUITY JOINT VENTURES

1 See e.g., Decree Law No. 348/1969 in Syria; Revolutionary Council Decision No. 899/1970 in Iraq and Law No. 43/1974 in Egypt.

2 Estimated, perhaps with some exaggeration, on the basis of 10-11 per cent of the estimated amount of disbursed annual investment expenditures. Of the figures mentioned above $1-1.2 billion is estimated for engineering consultants and $600-700 million for administration and legal fees, general consulting, financial services and marketing studies. Source: *Citicorp's Relationship with Development Funds and Economic Aid Institutions*, (Mimeo 1975).

3 E.g. the manual drawn up in 1971 by UNIDO on the establishment of Industrial Joint Venture Agreements in Developing Countries (ID/68).

4 E.g. the Model Provisions for Joint Venture Agreements in Fisheries, prepared in 1975 by the Indian Ocean Programme of FAO (IOFC/DEV/75/37).

NOTES AND REFERENCES TO CHAPTER 13: ARAB INVESTMENT GUARANTEE CORPORATION – A REGIONAL INVESTMENT GUARANTEE CORPORATION

1 See e.g., Kidron, "Pearson on Private Foreign Investment", a paper read to the Columbia University Conference on International Economic Development,

(Pearson Conference, Doc. No. 28), New York, February 1970; Streeten, "The Contribution of Private Overseas Investment to Development", *id.*, (Doc. No. 27).

2   For a general study of these treaties, see Preiswerk, *La protection des investissements privés dans les traités bilateraux* (1963).

3   See e.g., *Laws and Regulations Affecting Foreign Investment in Asia and the Far East*, UN Doc. ECAFE/L. 122, 12 March 1957; *Investment Laws and Regulations in Africa*, UN Doc. E/CN. 14/INR/28/Rev. 2 (1965). See also a study of the legal treatment of private foreign investment in forty countries, in Friedman and Bugh (ed.), *Legal Aspects of Foreign Investment* (1959).

4   For appraisal of the practicability and usefulness of the concept, see Snyder, "Foreign Investment Protection: A Reasoned Approach", 16 *Michigan Law Review 1087* (1963); Committee on International Trade and Investment of the American Bar Association, *Protection of Private Property Abroad* 115 (1963).

5   See for the development and details of the US Investment Guarantee Program: Whitman, *The United States Investment Guaranty Program and Private Foreign Investment* (1959); Clubb and Vance, "Incentives to Private US Investment Abroad Under the Foreign Assistance Program", 72 *Yale Law Journal* 475 (1963); Lillich, *The Protection of Foreign Investment* 127-147 (1964); Rubin, "The Investment Guaranty Program of the United States", 56 *Am. Soc. Int'l L. Proc.* (1962).

6   For a general description of major national investment insurance agencies see, Kuwait Fund for Arab Economic Development, *A Study of Investment Guarantee Systems* (1968) – (in Arabic; mimeo); IBRD, *Multinational Investment Insurance, A Staff Report* (1962).

7   For the advantages of a multinational programme over the existing national programmes, see Porter, "Multilateral Protection of Foreign Investment: A Pragmatic Approach", 3 *Int'l Development Rev.* (No. 1) at 23 (1961); Brewer, "The Proposal for Investment Guarantees by an International Agency", 58 *Am. J. Int'l L.* 62 (1964).

8   See text in IBRD, *Draft Articles for International Investment Insurance Agency* (R 68-156, dated 19 August 1968 – Mimeo). For a summary of former proposals, see IBRD, *Multinational Investment Insurance, A Staff Report*, 30-37 (1962). See also a study of the OECD proposal of 1965 in Martin, "Multilateral Investment Insurance: the OECD Proposal", 8 *Harvard Int'l L. J.* 279 (1967).

9   See Fouchard and Mourgeon, "Le Fonds d'Entraide et de Garantie des Emprunts du Conseil de l'Entente", 96 *Journal de Droit Int'l* 22 (1969).

10   For the original Arabic text of the convention, along with a detailed comparative study of former projects and proposals, see Shihata, *The International Guarantee of Foreign Investments*, (Cairo 1971 – in Arabic).

11   Only recently Syria, Iraq and Egypt promulgated legislation categorically directed towards the encouragement of imported Arab investments. See the Syrian Decree-Law No. 348 dated 29 December 1969, the Iraqi Decree (of the Revolution Council) No. 899 dated 12 August 1970, and the Egyptian Law No. 65 dated 3 September 1971.

12   Convention on the Payment of Current Accounts and Capital Transfers signed on 7 September 1963, between Lebanon, Jordan, Egypt, Saudi Arabia, Syria and Iraq. See also: Draft Convention for the Investment and Transfer of Arab Capital between Arab Countries, approved by the Council of Arab Economic Unity in its fourth Session (May 1970). (Not in force by 1972.)

13   Most of these treaties were held between Kuwait and other Arab countries. E.g., Agreement between Kuwait and Iraq dated 25 October 1964 (in force); between Kuwait and the UAE dated 12 February 1966; between Kuwait and Sudan dated

7 May 1969; between Kuwait and Syria dated 10 August 1969 (in force).

14   Kuwait Fund for Arab Economic Development, *Towards a Convention for the Guarantee of Arab Investments* (1967, in English and Arabic, Mimeo).

15   For the different patterns of international public corporations in general, see Fligler, *Multinational Public Enterprises* (IBRD, 1967, in Arabic).

16   See e.g., Article III, Section (iv) of the Draft Articles of Agreement of the International Insurance Agency, referred to in note 8 *supra*; OECD, *Report on the Establishment of a Multinational Investment Guarantee Corporation* (June 1965).

17   The term "taking of property" is used above for the relative certainty it has acquired in standard writings and judicial application.

18   All through, the convention uses the term "country" instead of the legal term "state" in order to allow for the participation of Arab Emirates and Sheikdoms which are not fully sovereign states.

19   For the nationality of public joint business ventures, see Fligler, op. cit., at 92-3; Shihata, op. cit., note 15 at 27-30.

20   See the comparative analysis of the details of different proposals in IBRD, *Staff Report*, op. cit., note 8.

21   Shihata, op. cit., note 10 at 35-53. For a discussion of the legal nature of the relevant "export credit insurance" system, compare Fontaine, *Essai sur la nature juridique de l'assurance-credit*, 83-142 (1966) with Monts, "L'assurance-credit à l'exportation: est-elle une operation d'assurance?", *Melanges Hamel*, p.525 (1961).

22   The practical importance of this requirement is particularly proved by the one arbitration case in the field of foreign investment guarantee. See *Valentine Petroleum and Chemical Corp. v. US Agency for International Development, IX Int'l Legal Materials* 889 (1970), commented upon in Shihata, "The First Arbitration in the Field of Foreign Investment Guarantee", 26 *Egyptian Rev. Int'l L.* (1970, in Arabic).

23   See Article VI, Section 1 of the above-mentioned Article of Agreement where disputes "between members or between the Agency and a member with respect to the interpretation or the application of this Agreement" are to be settled by "arbitration", if negotiations fail and the parties could not agree to another method of settlement.

NOTES AND REFERENCES TO CHAPTER 15:
FOOD PRODUCTION IN DEVELOPING COUNTRIES: MAJOR CONSTRAINTS AND POSSIBLE SOLUTIONS

1   The FAO estimates that the number of malnourished in the world grew from some 400 million in 1969-71 to more than 450 million in 1972-74, or by about 4 per cent per annum.

2   Before preparing this report the OPEC Fund sought the advice of the following agencies: Abu Dhabi Fund for Arab Economic Development, Arab Authority for Agricultural Investment and Development (AAAID), Arab Bank for Economic Development in Africa (BADEA), Arab Fund for Economic and Social Development, Iraqi Fund for External Development, Islamic Development Bank (IsDB), Kuwait Fund for Arab Economic Development, Saudi Fund for Development and Venezuelan Investment Fund. Written statements on the issue were received from BADEA, AAAID and IsDB. The topic was also discussed in the meeting of the Co-ordination Committee of Arab Aid Agencies (also attended by the IsDB and the OPEC Fund) held in Khartoum, Sudan, in

December 1978. It must be noted, however, that the views expressed in this report do not necessarily represent the position of any of the above-mentioned agencies on the issues under discussion.

3   The OPEC Fund is experimenting with one such form, with its loans, generally interest free, to Governments for on-lending to entrepreneurs through development finance institutions. In these cases, the share of the proceeds to be committed in the agricultural sector is agreed upon with the Government and the local institution. Also agreed upon is a ceiling (normally determined by size of asset holdings) for the credit eligibility of the ultimate beneficiaries. Interest revenues from the Government on-lending are deposited in a special account held by the local institution. These revenues may then be used by the institution, after consultation with the Fund, to subsidize interest rates on loans to ultimate beneficiaries, to meet its higher administrative costs because of emphasis on small borrowers in the agricultural sector, as well as to finance some of its technical assistance needs.

NOTES AND REFERENCES TO CHAPTER 16:
ON WORLD HUNGER

1   While the price range for a ton of wheat acceptable to the US and Canada was £140-210, the developing countries argued for a range of £130-160.
2   The US favoured a reserved stock of 25-30 m. tons (with its contribution of 5 m. tons), Japan, a level of 12 m. tons and the EEC, 15 m. tons. (In 1972, the gap reached 58 m. tons. The annual increase in the demand for grain is about 25 m. tons).
3   These stocks are held by: selected exporters (28 m. tons), developing countries (91 m. tons), selected importers (12 m. tons), developed countries (169 m. tons) and others (3 m. tons). With the exclusion of rice, which is widely consumed (250 m. tons) but little traded (4 per cent), consumption of all grains by developing countries is now about 390 m. tons, of which 120-190 m. is consumed by subsistence farmers. Total stocks of grain of these countries do not exceed 30 m. tons.
4   The World Bank estimates that between 1980-1985 an investment programme to improve infrastructure associated with the storage and distribution of good grains in low income countries alone should include £270-540 m. to strengthen infrastructure to support larger volumes of imports and £500-800 m. to improve storage and distribution systems for locally produced grain.
5   The International Food Policy Research Institute calculated the full costs of overcoming the projected food deficits in the 1980s and estimates, on the assumption that 50 per cent of capital cost and 80 per cent of recurrent cost will be met by the developing countries concerned, that annual aid in the order of £12 billion a year (1975 rates) will be needed, calling for additional foreign aid of £8.5 billion (or £13 billion in current terms). The earlier estimates of the World Food Conference were slightly lower.

ABBREVIATIONS

Abbreviations Employed in this Volume

AAAID	Arab Authority for Agricultural Investment and Development.
ABEDA	The Arab Bank for Economic Development in Africa (see BADEA).
ADB	The Asian Development Bank.
AFARCO	African Arab Investment Company.
AID	(The US) Agency for International Development.
AIGC	The Arab Investment Guarantee Corporation.
APC	The Arab Potash Company.
BADEA	Banque Arabe pour le Developpement Economique en Afrique (The Arab Bank for Economic Development in Africa).
CGIAR	The Consultative Group on International Agricultural Research.
CIEC	The Conference on International Economic Co-operation (Paris Dialogue).
DAC	The Development Assistance Committee (of OECD).
EEC	The European Economic Community.
ENA	Executing National Agency (of a member of the OPEC Fund).
FAC	The Food Aid Convention.
FAO	The Food and Agriculture Organization.
FSF	The Financial Support Fund (of OECD).
GATT	General Agreement on Tariffs and Trade.
IBRD	The International Bank for Reconstruction and Development (World Bank).
IDA	The International Development Association.
IDB	The Inter-American Development Bank.
IEA	The International Energy Agency.
IFAD	The International Fund for Agricultural Development.
IFC	The International Finance Corporation.
IFPRI	The International Food Policy Research Institute.
IMC	International Minerals and Chemicals (USA).
IMF	The International Monetary Fund.

IPC	Integrated Programme for Commodities (of UNCTAD).
IsDB	The Islamic Development Bank.
JAP	The Jordan Arab Potash (Company).
KFTCIC	Kuwait Foreign Trading, Contracting and Investment Company.
KIC	Kuwait Investment Company.
LDC	Less Developed Countries.
LLDC	Least Developed Countries.
MSA	Most Seriously Affected (Countries).
MTN	Multilateral Trade Negotiations.
NIEO	The New International Economic Order.
OAPEC	The Organization of Arab Petroleum Exporting Countries.
ODA	Official Development Assistance.
OECD	Organization for Economic Co-operation and Development.
OLADE	Latin American Energy Organization.
OPEC	Organization of Petroleum Exporting Countries.
SDR	Special Drawing Rights.
SEACEN	South-East Asian Central Banks Conference.
UAE	The United Arab Emirates.
UBAF	Union de Banques Arabes et Françaises.
UNCTAD	The United Nations Conference on Trade and Development.
UNDP	The United Nations Development Programme.
UNIDO	The United Nations Industrial Development Organization.
WHO	The World Health Organization.

ABOUT THE AUTHOR

Ibrahim Shihata has been the Director-General of the OPEC Fund for International Development since its establishment in 1976.

His educational background includes three degrees from Cairo University and a doctorate from Harvard University. Dr Shihata was a member of the Conseil d'Etat in Cairo (1957-59), a member of the Technical Bureau of the UAR President in Damascus (1959-60), a lecturer and associate professor of international law in Cairo (1964-66, 1970-72), and a legal adviser and general counsel of the Kuwait Fund for Arab Economic Development in Kuwait (1966-70, 1972-76). Meanwhile, he provided advisory services to several Arab and international organizations.

Dr Shihata is author of many books and essays published in different languages in Europe, the Middle East and the USA on different aspects of international law and finance. Combining academic background with practical experience, Dr Shihata is a leading authority on international economic law. He is also a member of several international associations; an executive director of the International Fund for Agricultural Development (Rome), a member of the Oxford Energy Club (Oxford), a trustee of the Institute on International and Foreign Trade Law (Washington, DC), a member of the Board of the International Fertilizer Development Center (Muscle Shoals, Alabama) and a trustee of the Center of Research on the New International Economic Order (Oxford).